ACCESS YOUR ONLINE RESOURCES

Neurodiversity-Affirming Practices in Early Childhood is accompanied by a number of printable online materials, designed to ensure this resource best supports your professional needs

Go to: https://resourcecentre.routledge.com/speechmark and click on the cover of this book

Answer the question prompt using your copy of the book to gain access to the online content.

NEURODIVERSITY-
AFFIRMING PRACTICES
in Early Childhood

It is not uncommon to hear the myths that young children develop in the same way, or that play does not come naturally to disabled or neurodivergent children. This essential guide challenges these myths and empowers early years educators to adopt neurodiversity-affirming practices which support all children, emphasising the joy, wonder, and possibilities of inclusive practice.

The book explores diverse development and learning through a variety of different lenses, including early years provision, specialist support, and speech and language therapy. The reader is introduced to a range of theoretical perspectives, alongside practical examples, audits, case studies, and strategies which explore the environment and the features and benefits of self-directed play. Topics include:

- An introduction to neurodiversity-informed practice
- Unpacking ableism and disablism in early childhood
- Approaching practice through a neurodiversity-informed lens
- Developing a curriculum that promotes equality and embraces diversity
- Advice for working effectively with parents and carers
- Creating inclusive learning environments that are accessible and enjoyable for all children.

Neurodiversity-Affirming Practices in Early Childhood challenges outdated assumptions and expands our understanding of child development and play, with inclusive practice at its heart. This is a key read for anyone working with young children, enabling them to actively move towards neurodiversity-affirming practices.

Kerry Murphy is an autistic and ADHD early years specialist in neurodiversity, SEN, and disability. She adopts a neurodiversity-affirming framework and is currently a lecturer in early education and SEN. She has worked for a range of local authorities, early years settings, and schools offering training, consultancy, and support. She has also written and worked with several early years organisations including Anna Freud, Nursery World, Early Education, and Thrive.

NEURODIVERSITY-AFFIRMING

Practices in Early Childhood

An Empowering Guide to Diverse
Development and Play

Kerry Murphy

Routledge
Taylor & Francis Group

LONDON AND NEW YORK

Designed cover image: © Getty Images. Design: Jo Steer.

First published 2025
by Routledge
4 Park Square, Milton Park, Abingdon, Oxon OX14 4RN

and by Routledge
605 Third Avenue, New York, NY 10158

Routledge is an imprint of the Taylor & Francis Group, an informa business

© 2025 Kerry Murphy

Figures in this book have been created by the authors using Canva

The right of Kerry Murphy to be identified as author of this work has been asserted in accordance with sections 77 and 78 of the Copyright, Designs and Patents Act 1988.

British Library Cataloguing-in-Publication Data
A catalogue record for this book is available from the British Library

ISBN: 978-1-032-34653-3 (hbk)
ISBN: 978-1-032-34652-6 (pbk)
ISBN: 978-1-003-32321-1 (ebk)

DOI: 10.4324/9781003323211

Typeset in Interstate
by Apex CoVantage, LLC

Access the Support Material: https://resourcecentre.routledge.com/speechmark

The words of James Baldwin are important when we think about this book's time of writing. He said: "the children are always ours, every single one of them, all over the globe, and I am beginning to suspect that whoever is incapable of recognising this may be incapable of morality" (*Essays: The Nation*, 1980, n.p.). At the time of writing, the world is witnessing genocide, including in Palestine and Sudan. Children and their caregivers are victim to unimaginable acts of violence. Children must have a right to childhood(s) that are free from violence, harm, and trauma.

This book is dedicated to children of Palestine, Sudan, and globally who have had their right to play, joy, and safety taken yet who still seek these fundamental rights.

CONTENTS

PUT IT INTO PRACTICE: NEURODIVERSITY-AFFIRMING DOCUMENTATION

INTRODUCTION

IT IS TIME TO CAUSE SOME TROUBLE
IN THE EARLY YEARS . . .

Before exploring the joy, wonder, and possibilities of neurodiversity-affirming practice, it is useful to consider why such a book is needed in the first place, which requires some difficult but necessary reflections. As early educators and caregivers, you will have been involved in the systems and processes that aim to identify, intervene, and support children with disabilities and developmental differences (henceforth neurodivergence). You might also be an early educator or caregiver who has grappled with some of the contradictions that arise within inclusion systems and processes. Research consistently suggests that educators across educational phases have positive attitudes and desires to cultivate meaningful inclusion (Muccio et al., 2014; Mitchell and Hegde, 2007) but often encounter barriers in its implementation. Part of the reason is that educational inclusion in its current format is paradoxical and often results in things other than inclusion. For example, despite children usually being educated in the same space, they are frequently segregated, expected to change to fit in, also known as integration, or excluded if their needs fall outside what is considered "normal".

Similarly, while inclusion is often about embracing and accepting differences, it sits within an educational framework that rejects differences by expecting all children to conform to the same learning and development standards, including standardised outcomes, such as defining progress against a Good Level of Development (GLD). (DfE, 2024) If children do not conform, our policies and procedures advise that we label them as having *special educational needs* (SEN), the definition of which will be unpicked later in the book. For now, it is enough to say that SEN is counterintuitive to inclusion or an acceptance of human differences.

To write candidly, the current aims of educational inclusion have set children, educators, and families up to fail. Why? First, place-based inclusion does not provide you with the skills, tools, and knowledge to develop a dynamic and rich pedagogy that meets children's inevitable differences and needs. Second, not all children demonstrate their learning and development in the same way, meaning that standardised outcomes are both anti-diversity and anti-inclusion. They ultimately make neurodivergent and disabled children stand out for failing to fit in.

Educational inclusion issues are not necessarily down to individuals but speak to a broader systemic failing. Despite this failure, early educators consistently show up with out-of-the-box thinking or navigate difficult processes to find their way to meaningful inclusion for children. It is great that early educators show this commitment, but imagine what we could do if we existed within an inclusion framework compatible with human differences? I wrote my first book, *A Guide to SEND in the Early Years* (2022), a few years ago. This was a guide to navigating unnecessarily difficult systems for children to get support for their differences and needs. In a few short years, however, I have realised I am no longer prepared to navigate this system and neither should you be not worry! *A Guide to SEND* still has lots of useful information). Instead, through collective actions, our early years' workforce, children, and families, we can build anew. A theme that often comes up when I am with early educators is that the only way to do this is to begin to engage in some necessary trouble to resist and challenge the current systems and processes.

And so, if you are an educator who wishes to cause some necessary trouble, do read on!

A NEW NORMAL?

KEY TERMS

Neuronormativity   Neuronormativity, a set of norms, standards, and expectations reinforced throughout society, significantly impacts education. These norms centre a particular way of functioning, including thinking, feeling, communicating, playing and behaving. This way of functioning is often seen as the superior and right way (Wise, 2023, n.p.).

This book challenges the idea that to be considered successful, valuable, productive, or well-developed, one must meet societal expectations of "normalcy" – especially since "normal" is a meaningless concept when applied to humans. Yet, children face pressure to fit into this mould early on, often labelled as typical, average, or meeting age-related expectations. Discussions frequently revolve around how a child fits in or stands out based on their learning, development, and behaviour.

Neurodiversity-affirming advocates refer to the term neuronormativity to describe this process, highlighting how it impacts children with lifelong developmental differences and disabilities. Measures of "normal" often privilege those with typical minds and non-disabled bodies, creating barriers for neurodivergent and disabled individuals. In contrast, neurodiversity-affirming practice resists neuronormativity and embraces human differences as valid and integral to society. This approach values and celebrates the unique ways each child experiences and interacts with the world as outlined in the table below:

Opportunities to pursue their own **play patterns** and **interests**	All children are born with an innate desire to play, interact, and process the world around them. Within this, they will develop intrinsically motivating interests connected to their unique worldview and developmental pathway.
Connections with play protagonists who presume their **competence** and who **care** for them unconditionally	To experience play-filled lives, children need to experience *felt safety* within their circles of care and connection. For example, with primary caregivers and key people. They need to be in the presence of humans who presume their competence and have high expectations of their capacity.
Freedom to be who they are in the moment without constant pressure to become ready for something else	When children feel safe and secure, they are more likely to explore and discover the world around them. By having the freedom to play in ways that are meaningful to them, children can learn what is important and motivating to them, enabling them to understand themselves and others better.
Time to develop in ways that are meaningful to their unique pathway	Early childhood should not be a race to *school readiness* but a space in which they can take time to have developmentally meaningful experiences that shape their unique developmental pathway. Focusing too much on the destination, or outcome can detract from what is important in the moment.

Additionally, human differences cannot be understood without considering the other personal and social aspects of our identity, so I will also draw upon the theory of intersectionality (Crenshaw, 2013) and also be guided by the principles of disability justice (Berne et al., 2018) (see Figure 0.1), all of which will be covered in greater detail across these chapters but have been briefly defined in the key terms box below.

KEY TERMS

Neurodiversity

Neurodiversity refers to everyone and is the recognition and acceptance of the variation in the human mind and body including different

ways of thinking, learning, and experiencing the world.

Intersectionality (Crenshaw, 2013)   Intersectionality refers to the interconnected nature of personal and social identity (racialised identity, gender, social class) which create overlapping and interdependent systems of privilege, and marginalisation.

Disability Justice (Berne et al., 2018)   Disability justice encompasses the understanding of disability within the broader context of social justice, acknowledging the diverse experiences of disabled individuals and advocating for their rights while addressing intersecting forms of oppression such as ableism, racism, sexism, and classism.

Disability Justice Principes

Intersectionality
Leadership of those most impacted
Anti-capitalist politic
Cross-movement solidarity
Recognising wholeness
Sustainability
Committment to cross-disability solidarity
Interdependence
Collective Access
Collective Liberation

Berne, P., Morales, A.L., Langstaff, D., & Invalid, S. (2018). Ten Principles of Disability Justice. WSQ: Women's Studies Quarterly 46(1), 227-230. https://doi.org/10.1353/wsq.2018.0003.

FIGURE 0.1 DISABILITY JUSTICE PRINCIPLES

This book will hopefully provide a springboard for some of that change and the chapters will address key experiences of early childhood.

COMPANION RESOURCES

You can find out more about disability justice on the companion resources website: https://sinsinvalid.org/resources/

CHAPTER FEATURES

As you progress through this book, I have included key features across each chapter so that you can organise your own thinking about neurodiversity, child development, and play but you might also find that not everything is figured out or has a straightforward answer. Neurodiversity provides some of the ingredients for meaningful inclusion, but the way this translates will look and feel different for every educator, child, family and setting.

✦ **Starting Points**

Neurodiversity as a paradigm encourages us to reflect on our current beliefs and practices and to consider how they might be reframed to be more affirming of difference. Each chapter begins with a starting point provocation to get you thinking about the topic covered in that particular chapter. You may choose to do this independently or collectively with others.

✦ **Key Terms**

The reality is that neurodiversity and other associated social justice movements do focus on reframing language to be more inclusive. This means that we will be grappling with some complex or less familiar terms. Throughout, I have included key terms boxes with definitions and explanations.

✦ **Neuroinsights from Early Childhood Practice**

I have drawn upon various insights from educators, childminders, parents, and specialists, all of which have been included here. As some of these insights contain sensitive reflections, I have made these anonymous (unless the person who contributed wanted to be cited). I thank those who offered their ideas and thoughts and challenged my thinking.

✦ **Neuromyths[1] and Neurofacts**

---

1 Neuromyths is also a term used to describe misconceptions in neuroscience, for example, learning styles. In this book neuromyths refers to educational misconceptions rather than purely neuroscientific ones.

Many myths, misconceptions, and misunderstandings surround neurodiversity and educational inclusion. This book will attempt to dismantle some myths while focusing on some facts or more accurate ways of understanding human differences.

✦ Companion Resources ☎

Through the chapters, you will find signposts to companion resources should you wish to explore a topic or concept further. A complete list of these is available on the companion website.

✦ Press Pause

Throughout the book, taking moments to pause and think more deeply about a topic or concept is useful. Feel free to pause at your own pace, but I have also added some moments where I feel further reflection might be helpful.

✦ Planting Seeds for Neurodiversity

These pages cover some complex ideas, and in some situations you may not be sure how to translate what is being said into practice. I have offered end-of-chapter sections where you can think about how you might put your learning into practice, and these are also available within chapters where you will gain practical ideas.

✦ Parent x Carer Solidarity

Rather than having a separate chapter on parent x carer solidarity, each chapter contains a parent solidarity section that outlines how we can stand in solidarity with parents and families to develop neurodiversity-affirming practices.

✦ Chapter Keepsakes

You will also notice the additional keepsake across the chapters where you might want to consider how a particular idea applies or may be differentiated based on individual preferences.

✦ Put it into Practice (PiiPs)

You will also find within this book some tools for you to begin developing neurodiversity-affirming practices. The PiiPs are designed to support more targeted work in becoming neurodiversity-affirming.

DISCLAIMER

I have made every attempt throughout this book to be sensitive to the preferences of intersectional disabled and neurodivergent communities and to represent neurodiversity accurately. With this in mind:

- ✦ I have defaulted to identity-first language (disabled person) as opposed to person-first language (person with a disability) to reflect that disability and neurodivergence is a part of a person's identity, not an add-on.
- ✦ Any book is shaped by the person writing it, their unique lived experience and their bias. I write from the perspective of being autistic, ADHD, and experiencing mental and chronic illness. However, disability, neurodivergence, and neurodiversity spans much further than my own lived experience. While I have expertise in certain areas, there is a broader scope of neurodivergence and disability, and this book is just one perspective. It should be seen as a contribution rather than a comprehensive guide.
- ✦ The neurodiversity paradigm is rapidly growing, and our growing understanding may supersede some of the information in this book.
- ✦ You might notice that this book flits between more informal and more academic writing. This is intentional. I do not believe one-size-fits-all in any facet of life, and so for some practitioners, they may wish to jump to the practical, less wordy bits and others may want to delve a little deeper into ideas or mix and match.

BIBLIOGRAPHY

Berne, P., Morales, A.L., Langstaff, D., and Invalid, S. 2018. Ten principles of disability justice. *WSQ: Women's Studies Quarterly*, 46(1), 227–230.

Crenshaw, K.W. 2013. Mapping the margins: Intersectionality, identity politics, and violence against women of color. In M.A. Fineman (ed.) *The Public Nature of Private Violence*. Routledge, pp. 93–118.

Department for Education (2024) *Early years foundation stage profile handbook*. Available at: https://www.gov.uk/government/publications/early-years-foundation-stage-profile-handbook

Mitchell, L.C. and Hegde, A.V. 2007. Beliefs and practices of in-service preschool teachers in inclusive settings: Implications for personnel preparation. *Journal of Early Childhood Teacher Education*, 28(4), 353–366.

Muccio, L.S., Kidd, J.K., White, C.S. and Burns, M.S. 2014. Head Start instructional professionals' inclusion perceptions and practices. *Topics in Early Childhood Special Education*, 34(1), 40–48.

Murphy, K. 2022. *A Guide to SEND in the Early Years: Supporting Children with Special Educational Needs and Disabilities*. Bloomsbury Publishing.

Wise, S.J. 2023. *We're All Neurodiverse: How to Build a Neurodiversity-Affirming Future and Challenge Neuronormativity*. Jessica Kingsley Publishers.

PUT IT INTO PRACTICE

THE PRINCIPLES OF NEURODIVERSITY-AFFIRMING PRACTICE IN EARLY CHILDHOOD

INTRODUCTION

KEY TERM

Neurodiversity-affirming practice is a framework for advocating and empowering human differences in early education, in particular for those whose development diverges from what is typically expected, for example, being autistic.

THE PRINCIPLES OF NEURODIVERSITY-AFFIRMING PRACTICE

This book has been written as a provocation. It challenges your current understanding of inclusion practices in early childhood education. It encourages you to critically examine and question the current systems and processes that often fall short of being truly inclusive for children with lifelong developmental differences and disabilities. Before exploring each chapter, reflecting on several guiding principles is beneficial. These principles, known as the **Neurodiversity-affirming Principles of Practice in Early Childhood**, provide a general overview of how we can be actively neurodiversity-affirming.

Neurodiversity-affirming practice is a journey, not a destination. Through collective action early educators have an opportunity to adapt their pedagogy and practices to recognise that human differences are an inevitable biological fact and, thus, it makes little sense to have an education system that promotes a one-size-fits-all model. However, it is important to recognise that people are at different points in their journey and solidarity is needed to cultivate neurodiversity-affirming practice. They are outlined below:

DOI: 10.4324/9781003323211-1

1

The Principles of **Neurodiversity-Affirming Practice in Early Childhood**

Right's **Respecting**

Underpinned **by intersectionality**

Led by lived **experience and advoacy**

Honours holistic learning, **development and wellbeing**

Resists ableism **and neuronormativity**

Embraces diverse pathways **of development**

Provides children with **play-full and rest-full lives**

Prioritises an **ethics of care**

Chooses C**onnection over compliance**

Values belonging **over fitting-in**

FIGURE 0.2 THE PRINCIPLES OF NEURODIVERSITY-AFFIRMING PRACTICE IN EARLY CHILDHOOD

Principle One: Rights Respecting

The principles of neurodiversity-affirming practice are underpinned by protecting children's rights in education, as outlined by the United Convention on the Rights of the Child (1989). To be neurodiversity-affirming, education should help all children to develop their personalities, talents, and unique abilities. It should teach them to understand their own rights and to respect other people's rights, cultures, and differences. It should help them to live peacefully and protect the environment (Right 29). Across this book, you will have the opportunity to consider whether rights are afforded to all children, and you will consider which children are most vulnerable to having their rights denied.

Principle Two: Underpinned by Intersectionality

Intersectionality is a term coined by Black feminist scholar Kimberlé Crenshaw to describe how multiple forms of discrimination can occur based on intersecting identity characteristics (1989). Crenshaw, for example, explored how experiences of racism and sexism intersected to marginalise Black women. The purpose of applying intersectionality to neurodiversity-affirming practice is to ensure that early educators have a broader awareness of the factors that might contribute to a neurodivergent or disabled child experiencing discrimination. For example, whether gender disparities are impacting access to diagnosis for a potentially autistic female child or a child's speech differences being blamed on their social class.

Unfortunately, bias and discrimination are baked into our societies, and this can also show up in educational spaces. By understanding intersectionality, educators can be sensitive to the multiple ways a child or family may be discriminated against and take this into context when planning meaningful support.

Principle Three: Led by Lived Experience

Children's "voices" and lived experiences are diverse and communicated in multiple ways. Views, perspectives, needs, and motivations are embodied in children's speaking, emotions, movement, behaviours, body language, play, arts, and drawing, to name a few. However, for a child's lived experience and "voice" to be heard, educators should actively engage in a "pedagogy of listening" (Rinaldi, 2021). Ultimately, as educators, we have to be interested in what neurodivergent and disabled children have to say, and we must recognise that the saying may not always be delivered through conventional means such as speech.

While the early education system increasingly promotes evidence-based practice and pedagogy, early educators should be research-curious and ensure that the evidence base meaningfully involves the perspectives and "voices" of neurodivergent and disabled children and adults. Early educators should draw upon disability and neurodivergent-led research to have a broader insight into the value of lived experiences on your developing pedagogy.

Principle Four: Honour's Holistic Learning, Development and Wellbeing

Adopting a holistic perspective when considering a child's learning, development, and wellbeing is essential. In educational inclusion, however, the focus can often be placed on identifying deficits, delays, or problems in a child's development. While there may be some scenarios where this is necessary, it also often overlooks the bigger picture for the child.

Neurodiversity-affirming practice commits to affording all children a holistic approach to understanding their learning, development, and wellbeing which includes:

Strengths & Interests: By recognising and valuing each child's unique strengths and interests, we can foster a supportive environment that encourages their individual growth, identity, and development. Instead of focusing solely on deficits, we acknowledge and embrace children's diverse skills and passions.

Traits: Understanding and appreciating the diverse traits that distinguish each child is vital in promoting neurodiversity. By accepting and empowering these traits, we create an inclusive space that values the diverse ways children navigate the world.

Honouring Differences: It is crucial to move away from asking "What is wrong?" with the child and instead ask "What is different?" This moves us towards a more curious approach to child development that can expand our viewpoint.

Needs: A holistic approach also involves considering and addressing each child's unique needs. By recognising that every child has specific requirements for optimal development, we can tailor support and accommodations to ensure they thrive and reach their full potential.

Principle Five: Resists Neuronormativity and Disrupts Ableism

Neurodiversity-affirming practice requires educators to resist neuronormativity and disrupt ableist practices. Neuronormativity, a set of norms, standards, and expectations reinforced throughout society, significantly impacts education. These norms centre a particular way of functioning, including thinking, feeling, communicating, and behaving. This way of functioning is often seen as the superior and right way (Wise, 2023, n.p.).

In education, neuronormativity is delivered through curriculums and frameworks. For example, they describe typical milestones or expect all children to learn similar ways. Neurodiversity-affirming practice embraces diversity and expands understanding of learning, development, and wellbeing. While such things can guide us, they are not considered a mandate for all children, including those diverging from typical development.

Similarly, ableism is the privileging of typically developing minds and non-disabled bodies, meaning that children who fall beyond these definitions can be subject to unconscious and conscious discriminatory practices that aim to normalise the child so that they fit into neuronormativity.

Principle Six: Embraces Diverse Pathways of Development

Neurodiversity-affirming practice acknowledges that child development is dynamic and varied, influenced by various intrinsic and external factors. It moves away from the idea that all children reach the same milestones simultaneously and in the same way. Instead, it embraces the concept of diverse developmental pathways, recognising that each child's journey is unique. For example, different communication identities and styles are welcomed, and the various ways children demonstrate their learning and development are validated.

The joy of diverse pathways lies in broadening understanding of diverse child development beyond what is considered typical or "normal". By reframing aspects of development previously perceived as problematic, early educators expand their inclusive practice, which is also increasingly compatible with neurodivergence and disability.

Principle Seven: Provides Children with Play-full and Rest-full Lives

Neurodiversity-affirming practice in early childhood recognises that central importance of having time to play and rest. Play, leisure, and rest form part of children's rights, which state that "every child has the right to rest, relax, play and to take part in cultural and creative activities" (UNCRC, 1989, Right 31). Unfortunately, the incorrect assumption is that children with developmental differences do not naturally engage in play. However, it is crucial to recognise that children have diverse play profiles and patterns, and we must refrain from labelling a child's abilities based on a limited understanding of the diverse play.

Furthermore, neurodivergent and disabled children often find themselves in environments and interactions that can be demand-heavy and sensory-overwhelming. This can impact learning, development, and wellbeing. Therefore, neurodiversity practice promotes the seven types of rest, ensuring that children can disengage and decompress from the busy neuronormative world. The seven types of rest are:

✦ Physical rest
✦ Mental rest
✦ Emotional rest
✦ Sensory rest
✦ Creative rest
✦ Social rest
✦ Spiritual rest

You can read more about the seven types of rest in Chapter 5.

Principle Eight: Prioritises an Ethics of Care

Neurodiversity-affirming practice upholds ethics of care, centring dignity, autonomy, presumed competence, and consent as fundamental practices.

Dignity means that neurodivergent and disabled children are treated fairly and sensitively throughout their experiences. Early educators are responsive to children's differences and needs and ensure they understand they are worthy of safety, security, professional love, and protection. By promoting dignity, early educators ensure children develop a strong sense of self-worth and confidence in their unique abilities.

Autonomy is about empowering children to have control over their own lives. In practice, this means providing opportunities for children to make choices and decisions about their activities, routines, and interactions. Supporting autonomy helps children develop critical thinking and decision-making skills, reinforcing their sense of agency.

Consent is integral to building trust and respect in early childhood settings. It involves seeking children's permission before engaging in activities and experiences that affect them, ensuring they understand and agree to what is happening. Practising consent teaches children about personal boundaries and respect for others, laying the foundation for healthy relationships.

Presumed Competence: educators should challenge biased assumptions about a child's unique abilities or competence based on their neurodivergence or disability. It involves presuming that every child has the potential to learn, grow, and contribute meaningfully and providing appropriate support and accommodations to help them realise their capabilities.

Principle Nine: Chooses Connection Over Compliance

Neurodiversity-affirming practice understands the importance of relationships and how connections to the important people in a child's life form the foundations of learning, development, and wellbeing. The early years phase is a time for play, exploration, discovery, and an opportunity for children to learn about themselves. The emphasis is not on compliance, for example, through school readiness, but on providing a child with the skills, knowledge, and tools to advocate for themselves and to access their learning in ways that are well-matched to their diverse developmental needs.

Principle Ten: Values Belonging Over Fitting-in

Every child occupying an educational space will do best when they feel a sense of belonging, knowing their similarities and differences are welcomed, understood, and seen as a celebratory aspect of the setting's culture. Neurodiversity-affirming educators ultimately want children and young people to feel they can be themselves rather than changing who they are to fit in. While differences are not always immediately understood, educators are curious enough to wonder why and ask questions that deepen their understanding of what is compatible with an individual child.

Adapted from Spectrum Gaming's Barriers to Education Project with Hanna Venton-Platz (2024).

REFLECTION

Now that you have read the principles, you can return to them as you read this book. Note down below any principles you already feel you are strong at delivering and those which you think you might need to learn more about:

BIBLIOGRAPHY

Crenshaw, K. 1989. Demarginalizing the intersection of race and sex: A Black feminist critique of antidiscrimination doctrine. *University of Chicago Legal Forum*, 139-168.

Rinaldi, C. 2021. *In Dialogue with Reggio Emilia: Listening, Researching and Learning*. Routledge.

United Nations. *Convention on the Rights of the Child*. Treaty Series, Volume 1577, November 1989, p. 3.

Wise, S.J. 2023. *We're All Neurodiverse: How to Build a Neurodiversity-Affirming Future and Challenge Neuronormativity*. Jessica Kingsley Publishers.

CHAPTER 1

INTRODUCING NEURODIVERSITY IN THE CONTEXT OF EARLY CHILDHOOD

STARTING POINTS

Neurodiversity has become more widely acknowledged in wider society and within the education system in recent years. It can also seem like a buzzword. Lots of educators have heard the term but there can also be uncertainty about what it actually means and why it is useful to early education. Additionally, there can be confusion about how the paradigm of neurodiversity can exist alongside current systems and processes that attempt to promote inclusion but often end up doing the opposite. As we progress through this book, you will have the opportunity to think about neurodiversity as an alternative to current approaches and also a way to resist failing systems and processes.

It can be useful to think about your current understanding, and once you have finished the book, this is a self-audit that you might return to:

I have heard of the term Neurodiversity and can define it				
Very Confident	Confident	Unsure	Not Confident	Not Confident at All

I would define neurodiversity as:

DOI: 10.4324/9781003323211-2

I know the difference between neurotypical conforming and neurodivergent				
Very Confident	Confident	Unsure	Not Confident	Not Confident at All

I would define neurotypical as:

I would define neurodivergent as:

I can give an example of neurodiversity-informed and -affirming practice				
Very Confident	Confident	Unsure	Not Confident	Not Confident at All

An example of neurodiversity-informed and -affirming practice is:

INTRODUCTION

Imagine you wanted to cultivate your outdoor area with the children and create a space where plants can grow and thrive. You take a trip to a garden centre, and the children each select the plants they are most drawn to. When you return to your setting, you read the care instructions and realise that the plants need different conditions and care to thrive. You map out your garden area, teaching the children that some plants must be placed directly under the sun while others need shade. Some of the plants chosen will need regular watering, while others are better in dryer conditions. You realise that some plants can thrive in proximity to each other while others may need more space. You explain to the children that it is important that you get the right balance so that

10

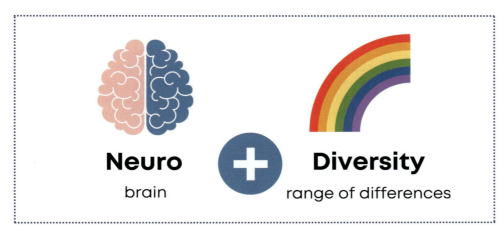

FIGURE 1.1 NEURO+DIVERSITY

FIGURE 1.2 PLANTS

the plants form an ecosystem or community in which they can all grow together. At that moment, you would be describing the process of biological diversity. Each plant is unique in the garden; each plays a specific role, and each contributes to that plant community's overall richness and balance. If you noticed that the plants were not thriving, you would change the conditions it exists in, not the plant itself. You wouldn't punish the plants for not growing according to your expectations, you would think about how to adapt your care of the plant.

This analogy is comparable to our brain and body development (henceforth minds and bodies), and neurodiversity is the term used to describe this process. Just like various plants are expected within biodiversity, different minds and bodies are expected within the societies in which we live. And if we switched plant out and replaced it with the word brain, the message remains the same. Human difference contributes to the balance and wellness of our communities and societies. This is not a particularly radical idea, yet embracing human differences is one of the most difficult challenges we face within our humanity.

NEURODIVERSITY AND EARLY CHILDHOOD EDUCATION

Neurodiversity is particularly relevant to early childhood education and care because of the understanding that "early experiences affect the development of brain architecture" (The Science of Early Childhood Development, 2007). While we may not always see this physical architecture or know of the child's specific neurodevelopmental pathway, the care and environment we provide for children will inevitably impact their lived experiences and lifespan development. Through our early interactions, and tuning into children's unique development, differences, and needs, we have the opportunity to provide developmentally compatible and meaningful experiences that help them to thrive. While this is the ideal scenario, unfortunately neurodivergent and disabled children can often find themselves in especially incompatible environments. Furthermore, their development, ways of playing, and learning can be framed as deficient, problematic, or broken, and so the onus is placed on the child to change who they are to fit in rather than on changing the environment.

Understanding that our approach to early childhood education shapes children's self-perception and worldview can feel like a big responsibility, especially as we help form part of the child's foundations. Yet, developing an understanding in diversity frameworks, educators can support children to develop into autonomous, self-determined individuals, driven by intrinsic motivation and competent in advocating for themselves. While these goals may seem ambitious, starting with such strategies sets the foundation for the necessary changes in education.

adapted from Luke Beardon's Golden Equation autism + environment = outcome. Beardon, L., 2021. Avoiding anxiety in autistic adults: A guide for autistic wellbeing. Hachette UK.

FIGURE 1.3 THE GOLDEN EQUATION

NEUROINSIGHT

TEACHING NEURODIVERSITY

We embed differences as part of our ethos. We do this by talking about how our brains enable us to do things, and how people do things differently. For example, we accept that some children need to move at *together times*, embrace communication styles and support play preferences. We don't explicitly say neurodiversity within teaching although we would if it felt relevant. We aim for them to understand themselves and their needs in time for school.

We celebrated **Neurodiversity Week** with the children, talking about brains and we planted seeds together. We didn't know what they were or what we would get but we will nurture them and change the environment for them to grow.

The biggest impact of embracing difference is supporting the parents and carers to understand their child's strengths and interests"

Katie York
Early Years Teacher and Deputy Manager

COMPANION RESOURCE

Neurodiversity Celebration Week takes place in March each year and consists of webinars, advocacy talks and information sharing. You can access the website at: www.neurodiversityweek.com/

NEURODIVERSITY DICTIONARY

Neurodiversity comes with its own set of terminologies, which helps us understand the landscape of human differences. It can, at first, feel slightly overwhelming to be confronted with newer language to describe different minds and bodies. However, it can be useful when you want to offer a more neutral set of words that do not stigmatise those whose minds and bodies diverge from what is socially constructed as "typical" or "normal":

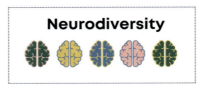

According to Wise (2023), neurodiversity refers to the variability of human minds and bodies and all the unique ways people can exist, think, act, process, feel, and function.

Neurodiversity is a neutral term that refers to all human minds. It includes everyone. It is a simple fact that the human population is diverse in our minds and bodies just as we are diverse in our ethnicity, gender, sexuality, and physical ability.

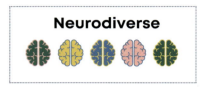

Neurodiverse is a term that encompasses the variability of individuals representing neurodiversity. While some may mistakenly think of it as describing an individual, such as "a neurodiverse child", it refers to a collective group.

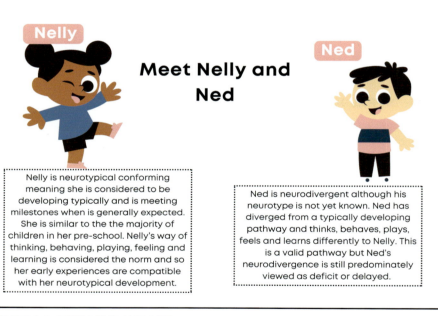

Meet Nelly and Ned

Nelly is neurotypical conforming meaning she is considered to be developing typically and is meeting milestones when is generally expected. She is similar to the the majority of children in her pre-school. Nelly's way of thinking, behaving, playing, feeling and learning is considered the norm and so her early experiences are compatible with her neurotypical development.

Ned is neurodivergent although his neurotype is not yet known. Ned has diverged from a typically developing pathway and thinks, behaves, plays, feels and learns differently to Nelly. This is a valid pathway but Ned's neurodivergence is still predominately viewed as deficit or delayed.

FIGURE 1.6 MEET NELLY AND NED

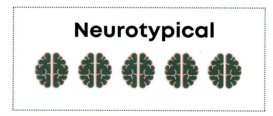

FIGURE 1.7 NEUROTYPICAL

NEUROTYPICAL

Neurotypical refers to those children whose minds and bodies conform to typically developing expectations. They represent the neuro majority of people whose development appears to follow a similar pathway. We live in a society that privileges those who conform to a neurotypical pathway, which is often framed as the "ideal" or "normal" way of developing.

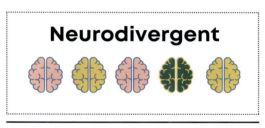

FIGURE 1.8 NEURODIVERGENT

NEURODIVERGENT

Neurodivergent refers to those children whose development diverges from what is considered typical or normal. However, the concepts of what is considered "typical" or "normal" are socially constructed, meaning that humans determine the standards by which "normal" is measured. Neurodivergence is usually a lifelong difference, such as being autistic. We live in a society that views these differences solely as something that needs to be fixed, reduced, or overcome. However, neurodivergence is its own way of being and should be respected.

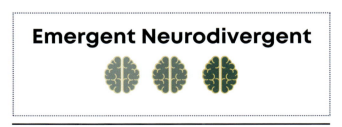

FIGURE 1.9 EMERGENT NEURODIVERGENT

EMERGENT NEURODIVERGENT

For those working in the early years, you will support children at the beginning of their developmental journey. They may or may not be on a diagnostic pathway but are emerging into their neurodivergence. Remember, it is not our role to diagnose children, but we should be alert to their possible development pathways.

Similarly, a person can identify as neurodivergent at any time, with or without a diagnosis. For some individuals, it might take time to realise they are neurodivergent or they realise later in life that they have masked (hidden) their differences.

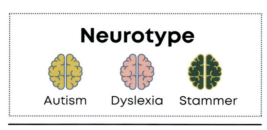

FIGURE 1.10 NEUROTYPE

NEUROTYPE

Neurotype refers to the type of neurodivergence you are referring to. For example, you may talk about the autistic neurotype or dyslexic neurotype.

Keepsake

It is important to remember that while we may use the language of neurodiversity to offer a more neutral stance on human difference, it is ultimately down to the individual or those with direct caring responsibilities to decide upon the terminology that most suits their situation.

NEUROFACT: NEURODIVERSITY IS A NEUTRAL TERM

One of the ways neurodiversity and neurodivergence have been misused is to focus only on the strengths and celebratory aspects of human difference. While it is great to re-address the balance from a deficit approach, this, too, can be quite harmful as it can lead to "toxic positivity" or an exclusion of those with higher support needs. Neurodiversity and neurodivergence are designed to be neutral terms. We are simply affording a balanced view and understanding of all children, including those with developmental differences.

PRESS PAUSE

- ✦ How many of these terms are familiar to you?
- ✦ Did you understand these terms, or are the definitions new to you?
- ✦ Why might neutral language to describe human differences be beneficial in early childhood practice?

NEUROMYTH: THERE IS SUCH A THING AS A NEURODIVERSE CHILD OR A CHILD WITH NEURODIVERSITY

Neurodiverse is a collective term, meaning it refers to a group of people, not a singular person. If a group of people who are both neurodivergent and neurotypical are in a room, that is a neurodiverse group (typical should not be viewed as the dominant group but so often is positioned this way). If you are in a room of neurodivergent people, that is a neurodivergent group. Why does this matter? From a linguistic point of view, diversity refers to a property of groups. It requires variability between more than one thing. In addition, neurodiversity scholars point to how terminology can often be co-opted by the mainstream without any depth of understanding, meaning that we risk tokenistic use and practices of neurodiversity frameworks. For example, a setting may say they use neurodiversity-affirming approaches but then confuse and mix up terminologies for example, "I support children with neurodiverse conditions" instead of "I support a neurodivergent child". *There is, of course, some consideration when thinking about language.* First, does the language matter if the practices are good? Second, we should empower neurodivergent people to define themselves in a way that suits them, including the children we care for and educate. Language is often emotive and holds deeply personal connections. Our choices for defining ourselves should not be overly policed or corrected without understanding their rationale. Third, if the neurodiversity framework, specifically those aligned to the neurodiversity movement, becomes too fixated on correct language use, there is a risk of it becoming too dogmatic. Yes, neurodiversity is a fact, but how it is represented among communities and cultures should always be up for discussion and understanding.

LANGUAGING MATTERS

There can be a tendency to think that placing too much emphasis on how we speak about and towards different groups of people can take us down the route of being too politically correct, followed by a fear of using the "wrong" language as you attempt to assimilate new ways of languaging. However, Shahvisi (2023) argues that we should aim for justice-oriented language as a way of demonstrating our commitment to and practice of inclusion. Justice-oriented language refers to speaking in ways that are non-stigmatising and promote fairness and equity. Additionally, languaging in this way demonstrates respect for individual and collective preferences. For example, autistic people tend to prefer identity first language (autistic person) as opposed to person-first language (person with autism) due to the recognition that autism forms part of a person's identity, and is not an addition to it (Flowers et al., 2023). However, it is also important to recognise that language preferences are nuanced and complex, and preferences in general can be quite personal to the individual and hold a variety of meanings. For example, a person may emphasise the importance of having their name pronounced correctly because they may have encountered countless times where it has been mispronounced, or someone has shortened their name rather than learnt how to say it. Someone else might not see this as quite so important because they haven't encountered countless mispronunciations. The point being made here is that language is personal to the person, and we should be careful not to assume someone's preferences without first checking in.

PRESS PAUSE

✦   Do you have any language preferences in relation to your own identity?
✦   What does it mean to you when people respect your language preferences?
✦   How does it feel when your language preferences are not respected?

When we use language thoughtfully, we can shift social realities and aim for practices that include rather than exclude people (Nee et al., 2021). The reason the language of neurodiversity is useful is because it offers an alternative to current stigmatising language. Think of the example of *special needs*. What makes someone's needs *special*? Are those with *special needs* treated especially well? What makes *special needs* different from human needs? How helpful is creating the binary of special/normal through language? Many disability and neurodiversity advocates reject the term *special needs* because it is often considered a term that negatively labels adults and children with developmental differences and disabilities, and in some cases can be used as a slur. Instead, there is a linguistic shift to neurodiversity-affirming language which humanises the lived experience of neurodivergent individuals.

Let's take a look at some other examples of neurodiversity-affirming language:

Special Educational Needs	Support Needs	All children will have different needs at different times. They do not need to be differentiated from typical to special. It might also be more beneficial to be specific, for example; developmental, emotional, social, basic or educational needs.
Disorder, Impairment, Condition	Differences and Needs	Neurodivergent and disabled communities do recognise that there are lived experiences that can cause impairments, illness and difficulties. The rejection of these terms relates to neurodivergence and general cognitive functioning as immediately being perceived as disordered or impaired. The use of differences and needs offers more balance.
A person with a disability	A disabled person	Disabled and neurodivergent communities often favour identity first language (disabled person) as opposed to person-first language (a person with a disability). This is often because communities want to destigmatise words, and by placing it first, it provides a standpoint that it does inform identity and lived experience. Again, always ask, as this can differ.
Suffering from . . .	Is . . . has . . .	Never assume the suffering of another or project this onto someone.
Non-verbal as an umbrella term for those who do not use mouth words to speak	Non-speaking/ minimally speaking/ unreliably speaking	This term can cause a lot of confusion. Generally, if someone does not use mouth words, they would be referred to as non-verbal. However, non-speaking individuals have argued that this is inaccurate because non-verbal means not relating to or understanding words. Non-speaking people do understand spoken words and language but may respond in a different way, for example, through signs, or vocalisations.
High- or low-functioning	Fluctuating capacity or support needs	Functioning labels can be problematic because they can be based on presumption and not always provide an accurate description of lived experience. Functioning can vary depending on many factors, and to assign a label without recognising the variation is unhelpful. For example, someone may be high-functioning one day, and low-functioning the next. It is more helpful to consider "support needs" but do remember these can also be variable. However, support needs are more balanced if it does not situate the problem with the child.

The type of language used about and towards certain groups can have an impact on how such group are then treated. As feminist activist Catherine MacKinnon states, "Speech Acts. Acts Speak" (Mackinnon, 2013). While the focus of this book is on children who are neuro-divergent and disabled, it is also important to acknowledge that children as a group, first and foremost, are often spoken about in ways that can be discriminatory and derogatory. For example, have you ever wondered why we use "childish" as an insult, and what message this conveys about the ways we feel about children? This is referred to as a form of adultism which can be "understood as the oppression experienced by children and young people at the hands of adults" (LeFrançois, 2014). As adults, we often dictate children's experiences with the language that we use to describe their experiences, and to label children. One such question that comes up about neurodiversity is why a shift in language matters.

As we begin to consider the different neurotypes and disabilities that fall under the neurodivergent umbrella, you will notice some subtle shifts in language that are more justice-oriented. As you refer to the Neurodivergent Umbrella, what shifts in language do you notice, and why do you think they matter? And what difference do you think such language shifts could make to the ways in which we speak about different groups?

NEURODIVERGENT UMBRELLA

The concept of the neurodivergent umbrella was introduced by Sonny Jane Wise (2023) to advocate the inclusion of all types of minds and bodies. According to Wise, any situation where your brain or physical development differs from socially constructed norms can be categorised as neurodivergent and/or disabled. The very point in the neurodiversity frame-work is to reduce exclusion of those most marginalised based on their neurotype or any other personal or social identity marker. The central idea of their argument is to emphasise that being different does not inherently imply being deficient or abnormal. Although the following list is not exhaustive, it demonstrates that neurodivergence aims to acknowledge variations in our neurodevelopmental pathways and the existence of such shouldn't result in our marginalisation or exclusion from society. For example, Wise refers to acquired neu-rodivergence, such as experiencing adversity or mental illness, which can alter brain and body development. The neurodivergent umbrella can be useful when having discussions with parents x carers about the different possible pathways a child might take, and provides an opportunity to think together about what they may mean for an individual child. For example, you can talk about the unique developmental experiences a child may encounter, or how development may appear different.

COMPANION RESOURCE

Visit the Anna Freud website for a Guide to Neurodiversity in the Early Years (Murphy, 2023): www.annafreud.org/resources/under-fives-wellbeing/a-guide-to-neurodiversity-in-the-early-years/

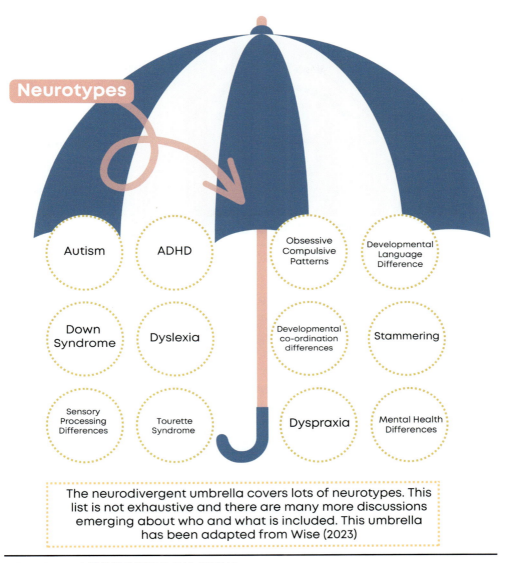

Neurotypes

Autism

ADHD

Obsessive Compulsive Patterns

Developmental Language Difference

Down Syndrome

Dyslexia

Developmental co-ordination differences

Stammering

Sensory Processing Differences

Tourette Syndrome

Dyspraxia

Mental Health Differences

The neurodivergent umbrella covers lots of neurotypes. This list is not exhaustive and there are many more discussions emerging about who and what is included. This umbrella has been adapted from Wise (2023)

FIGURE 1.11 NEURODIVERGENT UMBRELLA

THE COMPONENTS OF NEURODIVERSITY

Imagine you want to build a house, you would first need to begin with strong foundations. Neurodiversity as a concept is that strong foundation. Next you would need a team to build that house, that team represents the neurodiversity movement. It can only exist if there are people who help to build the house through creating a scaffold, or framework.

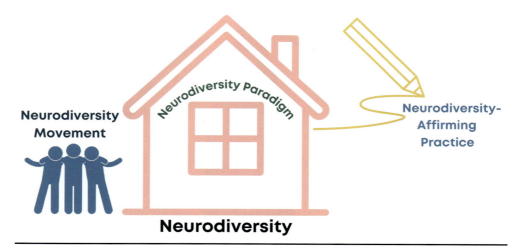

FIGURE 1.12 THE COMPONENTS OF NEURODIVERSITY

The house represents the framework. It is from this strong foundation, framework, and movement of people that neurodiversity can be delivered through neurodiversity-affirming practice, in the table below:

Neurodiversity	Neurodiversity is considered to be a biological fact similar to biodiversity. It is important to recognise that the infinite variety of ways in which bodies and minds develop can be beneficial to our human sustainability and thriving if we live in a world that adapts to the multitude of ways in which we present our humanness.
Neurodiversity Paradigm	The Neurodiversity Paradigm (or framework) is a specific perspective on neurodiversity that views human diversity as a valuable and expected component of humanity. This framework rejects the idea that you have to meet certain criteria to be considered "normal" and rejects the socially constructed ideas of normalcy. The framework positions itself through social justice, recognising that power dynamics impact your experiences of privilege and oppression.
Neurodiversity movement	The neurodiversity movement is a social justice movement that aims to advocate for the societal inclusion of those who are neurodivergent and/or disabled. It aims for equity and access along with a deeper understanding of human difference that is informed by the "voices" of those with that lived experience.

Neurodiversity-affirming education	Neurodiversity-affirming education has been encouraged, which "caters to the naturally occurring variability of humanity" (Aitken and Fletcher-Watson, 2022, n.p.). The premise of this approach is that our early childhood spaces are not a "one size fits all" but should adapt to various strengths, traits, differences, and needs of children.

NEURODIVERSITY

WHAT DOES NEURODIVERSITY MEAN TO YOU IN EARLY CHILDHOOD?

"I think embracing differences is something we naturally embrace because of the unique child. I think neurodiversity as a framework becomes even more relevant as they enter the school system that seems to reject that uniqueness".

"For me, it has been most useful for teaching children about differences. There are so many ways now in which we can help children to understand their brains and bodies".

"It's basically the unique child but more encompassing of children who are perhaps not included in our everyday documents".

"It has been a way to connect with parents so that they can see we do not see their child as broken".

"It feels like a refreshing antidote from Ofsted, and this constant obsession with turning children into numbers. I have found SEND so . . . I dunno . . . boring. It makes inclusion seem procedural rather than meaningful".

Early Years Educators and Childminders

CONTEXTUALISING NEURODIVERGENCE

Neurodivergence and Disability are not the same thing, but they are interconnected. There are different views on how these two terms are connected. For example, some neurodivergent people also identify as disabled because they see their specific neurotype as having disabling features. However, others may not associate neurodivergence with disability as they see their neurotype as a difference. Regardless, disability itself is rooted in a recognition that the societies we live in can make our human differences and mind and body experiences challenging and inaccessible.

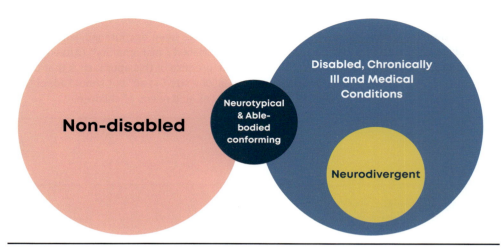

FIGURE 1.13 CONTEXTUALISING NEURODIVERGENCE

NEURODIVERSITY INFORMED TO BECOME NEURODIVERSITY AFFIRMING

This book introduces the concepts of being "neurodiversity informed" and "neurodiversity affirming". The focus of this chapter is to provide you with a solid

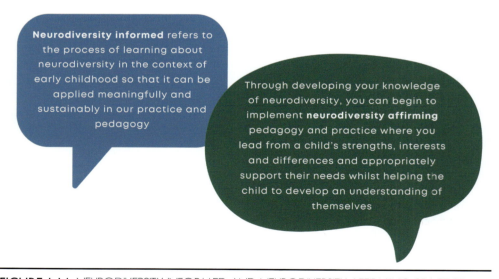

FIGURE 1.14 NEURODIVERSITY-INFORMED AND NEURODIVERSITY-AFFIRMING PRACTICE

understanding of what neurodiversity means, particularly in the context of early child-hood. Without this foundational knowledge, it becomes challenging to effectively apply neurodiversity principles in practice. As you gain insight and understanding, you'll reach a point where you can actively integrate neurodiversity understanding into your professional approach. This transition marks the shift towards practicing in a way that not only acknowledges neurodiversity but also actively supports and affirms it. This is important because there has been the emergence of neurodiversity lite which is the process where neurodiversity is used in superficial ways, but makes little difference to children's experiences.

NEURODIVERSITY AND INTERSECTIONALITY

Audre Lorde (1982) who was a feminist American writer, philosopher, and activist states that

> our struggles are not confined to single issues, as our lives are complex and interconnected. In other words, when you are thinking about children who are neurodivergent and/or disabled, you will also be thinking about the ways their other identity markers will shape, and inform their individual and collective experiences. For example, you might take into consideration the child's developmental differences and their social class as you consider access to resources and support.

In your understanding of neurodiversity and neurodivergence, it is crucial to explore children and families experiences through the lens of intersectionality. Intersectionality originates from the work of Black feminist scholars, including Kimberlé Crenshaw (1989), arguing that markers of difference such as gender, race, social class, and others overlap to reflect broader structures of oppression and privilege; for example, a Black autistic child may experience bias towards their autism, but you would also need to consider the ways in which racism further compounds this bias. According to the Black Child SEND report (Wheeler et al., 2024), parents x carers have repeatedly reported concern about the ways in which racism can impact their children receiving safe and compassionate support. Additionally, when Black and/or minoritised Global Majority parents x carers advocate for their child, they are subject to racist tropes such as being considered aggressive, difficult or hard to work with (p. 20).

In early childhood settings, recognising the intersecting identities of children is crucial, encompassing aspects like ethnicity, social class, gender, neurodivergence, and disability. Viewing these identity aspects in isolation is limiting because it can lead to overlooking the specific discrimination that a child or family might be experiences; a holistic approach acknowledges the interconnectedness of various identity markers.

Examples of Intersectional Bias

Gender	A female is late diagnosed as autistic because her autistic traits in pre-school were overlooked on the basis that autism is a male neurotype.	Research has found that females are often diagnosed later as autistic compared to males due a lack of awareness of female presentation of autism, and the lack of information (Lockwood Estrin et al., 2021). If as an early educator, you are not made aware of how gender influences autistic traits, you will be less able to identify differences and needs early.
Social class/ Living in an under-resourced area	A child resides in a postcode area where funding has been cut and no longer has access to targeted or specialist therapeutic services despite needing a higher level of support. Children living in a postcode area that is considered more affluent still have this access.	The Nuffield Foundation (Hutchinson, 2021) found that support for children with developmental differences and needs is decided upon a "postcode lottery" in which those in under-resourced area receive less support and less funding. If your setting is located in an under-resourced area, it means that needs may escalate as a result of poorly matched support.
Racialised identity/Ethnicity	A Black child who has sensory processing differences, is non-speaking and is demand avoidant. He is labelled as defiant and naughty, despite these being traits of autism. This diagnostic overshadowing delays access to the right support.	Campaigner Marsha Martin, who runs Black Mama's UK, has highlighted that support services for neurodivergence and disability often lack cultural awareness and this can lead to delays in support for children who are minoritised Global Majority (Wheeler et al., 2024). Similarly, a lack of information can lead to misdiagnosis or misunderstanding of children's developmental differences and needs. Hamilton and Showunmi (2023) highlight instances where unconscious biases contribute to the mislabelling of Black and Brown children as misbehaving, showcasing the intersection of racism and ableism in shaping perceptions and behaviours.

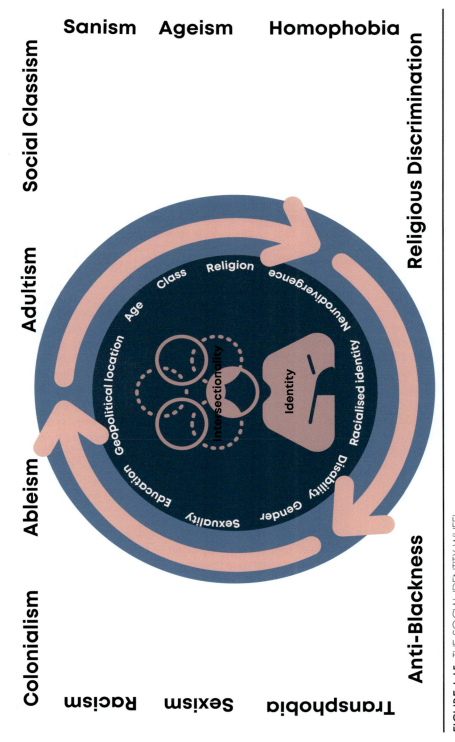

FIGURE 1.15 THE SOCIAL IDENTITY WHEEL

ACTIVITY: MY SOCIAL IDENTITY PORTRAIT

Across our lifespans, we are shaped by our identities in many different ways. Using the below intersectionality wheel, consider the reflection questions in relation to your own social identity portraits

- ✦ The part of my identity that I am most aware of on a daily basis is . . .
- ✦ The part of my identity that I am the least aware of on a daily basis is . . .
- ✦ The part of my identity that was most emphasised or important in my family growing up was . . .
- ✦ The part of my identity that I wish I knew more about is . . .
- ✦ The part of my identity that makes me feel discriminated against is . . .
- ✦ The part of my identity that provides me the most privilege is . . .
- ✦ The part of my identity that I believe is the most misunderstood by others is . . .
- ✦ The part of my identity that I feel is difficult to discuss with others who identify differently is . . .

It's essential to avoid reducing intersectionality to a mere listing of categories, as it goes beyond tallying up oppressions. Instead, it involves recognising the interconnected dimensions of oppression and understanding that collective action is needed to dismantle these experiences (Shahvisi, 2023). For instance, stating individual forms of oppression in a comparative manner can lead to a dangerous tit-for-tat mentality, disregarding the collective effort required to address diverse dimensions of privilege and power. Similarly, when addressing issues of oppression and discrimination, it's counterproductive to engage in what some term the "oppression Olympics". Comparing oppressions, such as responding to racism with claims of working-class struggles, misses the point that intersectionality seeks to address the complexity of overlapping identities and experiences.

PRESS PAUSE

Marianna Souto-Manning (2017) addresses play issues in early childhood, stating that the right to play is highly racialised in a society that often denies childhood(s). She discusses how Black boys, in particular, often have their play constructed as a problem. For example, it might be considered too loud, boisterous, or aggressive (think of the linguistic utterances when describing Black and white children's play). Considering the interlocking dimensions of the developmental profile, class, and culture, we can see how the child's play is further problematised. For example, to play while Black, autistic, and working class comes with risks.

- ✦ Have you ever considered the role of anti-racism in early childhood education?
- ✦ Have you noticed how different children are subject to labels based on their racialised identity or other identity markers?

PLANTING SEEDS FOR NEURODIVERSITY

One of the most crucial commitments you can make when incorporating neurodiversity into your everyday practice is to teach children about the concept. Below are some ideas for introducing neurodiversity to children:

Inspired by Katie York in the first Neuro Insight, you may draw upon the plant analogy and **plant seeds** with the children, while teaching them about the different care conditions of each. This can then be used to talk to children about the different ways in which we grow and develop, and how we need different things to thrive. You might then ask children about the things that make them unique, and what they think helps them to feel heard and understood. You can use symbols or a visual timeline to support all children's understanding.

Incorporate inclusive **neurodiversity literacy** into your setting. For example, you may have books about neurodiversity, or consider how neurodivergence and disability is represented. Authors James and Lucy Catchpole review the quality of representation in children's books over at https://thecatchpoles.net/.

To ensure accessibility, you should also offer multi-modal literacy, including books that have alternative and augmentative opportunities such as the use of symbol stories or sensory stories. For example, Joanna Grace, the founder of Sensory Projects, provides advice on implementing sensory stories. You may also find Neuroclastic's Neuroinclusive stories useful, one of which includes Room for All of Us. You can access this at www.neuroclastic.com.

Take a **teach all** approach when thinking about support for children who are neurodivergent. For example, you might decide to introduce visuals, or signs for a child who is minimally or non-speaking. Ensure that you think about the ways you are teaching all children about different forms of communication which can foster inclusion. For example, a non-speaking child and speaking child can use a choice board together to decide what type of play they want to engage in.

Embrace children's curiosity about difference and give them the language, and resources to be inclusive. Children notice differences, and the teaching they have in their earliest years can be the difference between forming a bias towards that difference, or developing understanding and compassion. For example, if children begin to label neurodivergent negatively based on what they have heard from adults, this is a "teachable moment" to give the child neurodiversity-affirming language. Imagine:

Child: "Teacher, Hattie is being silly again during story time and not sitting still."
Response: "Hattie, you like to wiggle and move when you are listening to the story. Bobby, why don't you try some wiggles too. It can help us to focus."

CRITICISMS OF NEURODIVERSITY

Like any other paradigm, neurodiversity is not without its criticisms and it is useful to recognise that there are some current limitations that need to be addressed. Below is an outline of some of the criticisms that may need to be considered:

A LACK OF INCLUSIVITY

There is concern that the neurodiversity movement largely advocates for those with lower support needs or who most closely align with neurotypicality. For example, those whose main form of communication is speech over those who are non-speaking. Parents of neurodivergent and disabled children, in particular, have expressed concern that it privileges those without co-occurring or complex difficulties and can often invalidate some of the very real challenges of raising a neurodivergent or disabled child (Russell, 2020). It is important to remember that parents are constantly battling the medical and education systems for support and may be reluctant to adopt a framework that doesn't appear representative of their child. Neurodiversity advocates often counter this as not being true, but I would say that if parents say they do not see it, we must believe them and work with them to ensure greater representation.

REPRESENTATION

Morénike Giaw Onaiwu (2020) was inspired to write an article about the neurodiversity movement called "I, too Sing Neurodiversity". Onaiwu was inspired by Langston Hughes' (1926) poem "I, too" in which he acknowledges that the reality of being a Black man is to devalued in his own homeland, but who refuses to have his hopes erased for an equitable future. For Black and Brown people in the neurodiversity space, they are often confronted with whiteness being centred or considered the default. Onaiwu's piece is compelling in that she clearly outlines how in theory "neurodiversity is a radical and inclusive space, a figurative home for the growing numbers of individuals around the globe who identify as neurodivergent" (2020, p. 58). Yet it fails to meaningfully represent Black and Brown children, and adults. When speaking at a conference where there was a Global Majority panel, she and fellow panellists were subjected to racist overtones from white attendees who took issue with the fact that whiteness was not considered the default. The Neurodiversity movement needs to take account of this. You will see all-white panels, literature, research, and whiteness has become the default. To address this, it needs to reposition itself within disability justice (Berne et al., 2018), which is more salient to the intersecting legacies of oppression, including how race, age, gender, and class (to name a few) shape your experiences. You can download a copy of the Disability Justice Principles in the book downloads.

AUTISM CENTRED

There is no denying that neurodiversity has become a synonym for autism. While this should not be the case, Autistic advocacy is having its moment, and a lot of good is emerging from this specific area of advocacy. So, while we absolutely need to expand our understanding of neurodiversity, the work that is happening here can potentially offer some blueprints for what is needed in other areas.

PARENT X CARER SOLIDARITY

When a child has developmental differences and needs, our relationships with parents and carers require careful maintenance and nourishment. Research consistently shows that parents and carers feel like they are in battle when it comes to securing the right support

Parent Partnership

When parent partnership is rooted in advocacy, it can be a powerful approach. However, parent partnership can also be misinterpreted as a surveillance approach whereby the setting (early years, specialist etc) defines what partnership should "look" like and how parents x carers should engage. While partnership should be equitable and balanced, it can sometimes be delivered in a way that situates the educator or specialist in a position of power and the parent x carer becomes at the receiving end of their "gifted" expertise. Standard parent partnership can lack the nuance of the complex "battles" parents x carers must currently encounter to secure meaningful support for their children. Parent partnership can also become misused as a way of pursuing normalisation. Parent partnership can often feel insufficient as a way of describing advocacy within neurodiversity and disability affirming practice.

Parent Solidarity

Parent solidary recognises that parenting is a social justice area recognising that parenting itself is a diverse experience where parents can face marginalisation and oppression. In practice parent solidarity is a side-by-side approach that involves being alongside parents x carers and recognising the specific power dynamics that often place parents x carers under surveillance and judgement, particularly in systems of normalisation and ableism. Parent solidarity approaches value the lived experience and personal expertise of the child and their family. The educator or specialist understands that they are a troublemaker as opposed to an upholder of the current oppressive SEND system. Educators and specialists actively dismantly parental and carer tropes, instead choosing compassionate soliarity.

FIGURE 1.16 THE DIFFERENCE BETWEEN PARENT X CARER PARTNERSHIP AND PARENT X CARER SOLIDARITY

for their child, and they often have to engage in processes that position their child as a problem to be fixed (Murphy and Harrison, 2022). Early educators should develop effective partnerships with parents to support a child's learning and development, but we should also recognise ourselves as their allies, and neurodiversity-affirming practice is about being in solidarity with parents and carers who may need our support in different ways. For some parents and carers, they may already be aware that the system is broken, and will be actively fighting against it while other parents or carers may need time and space to process their unique experience, and be met with patience as they figure out how they will advocate for their child. As you progress through this book, you will be given provocations and ideas for being in solidarity with your parents and carers.

CHAPTER CONCLUSION

As you come to the end of this first chapter, you may have a mixture of feelings surrounding the topic of neurodiversity. I often remind myself, and others, that the more we learn, the less we know – and that is a good thing. Uncomfortable feelings can emerge when a subject area feels almost too complex to untangle (which neurodiversity is). This can be made harder when we are trying to integrate this into outdated processes and systems that are still very much in place (we will explore some of the challenges in implanting neurodiversity-affirming practice in Chapter 2).

As we venture through these chapters on neurodiversity-affirming practice and weave our way through to play and development, this first chapter serves as those foundations that you can return to and it can guide you to be curious about different ways of doing early childhood education. A shift in approach can at times feel difficult to navigate, especially as you align this with the expectations of the 0–25 SEND Code of Practice (DfE, 2015). It is important to remember that neurodiversity-informed and -affirming practice can add an additional layer to your everyday practices rather than steer us away from what we must and should do from a statutory and legal point of view.

ACTIVITY – CHAPTER KEEPSAKES

Across this first chapter, think about what your keepsakes are, and note down the following:

✦ One thing you will start doing
✦ One thing you still stop doing
✦ One keepsake you will share with others
✦ One thinking knot that requires further exploration

BIBLIOGRAPHY

Aitken, D. and Fletcher-Watson, S. 2022. *Neurodiversity-Affirmative Education: Why and How?* British Psychological Association.

Beardon, L. 2021. *Avoiding Anxiety in Autistic Adults: A Guide for Autistic Wellbeing.* Hachette UK.

Berne, P., Morales, A.L., Langstaff, D., and Invalid, S. 2018. Ten principles of disability justice. *WSQ: Women's Studies Quarterly*, 46(1), 227-230.

Crenshaw, K. 1989. Mapping the margins: Intersectionality, identity politics, and violence against women of color. In M.A. Fineman, *The Legal Response to Violence Against Women*. Routledge, p. 91.

Crenshaw, K. 2013. Mapping the margins: Intersectionality, identity politics, and violence against women of color. In M.A. Fineman, *The Public Nature of Private Violence*. Routledge, pp. 93-118.

Department for Education (DfE). 2015. *Special Educational Needs and Disability Code of Practice: 0 to 25 Years*. Department for Education.

Flowers, J., Dawes, J., McCleary, D., and Marzolf, H. 2023. Words matter: Language preferences in a sample of autistic adults. *Neurodiversity*, 1, 1-11.

Hamilton, P. and Showunmi, B. 2023. Helping young children to think about race in the early years. Anna Freud Centre. www.annafreud.org/media/17815/anna-freud-anti-racism-booklet-early-years230123-final.pdf.

Hughes, L. 1926, 2001. I, too. In A. Rampersand (ed.), *The Collected Works of Langston Hughes*, Volume 1. University of Missouri Press.

LeFrançois, B.A. 2014. Adultism. In T. Teo (ed.), *Encyclopedia of Critical Psychology*. Springer.

Lockwood E.G., Milner, V., Spain, D., Happé, F., and Colvert, E. 2021. Barriers to autism spectrum disorder diagnosis for young women and girls: A systematic review. *Review Journal of Autism and Developmental Disorders*, 8(4), 454-470.

Lorde, A. 1982. *Learning from the 60s. In Sister outsider: Essays and speeches*, 1st ed. Crossing Press, p. 134.

MacKinnon, C.A. 2013. Speech acts. Acts speak. In *Butterfly Politics*. Harvard University Press.

MacKinnon, C.A. 2017. *Butterfly Politics: Changing the World for Women*. Harvard University Press.

Murphy, K. (2023). A guide to neurodiversity in the early years. Anna Freud Centre.

Murphy, K. and Harrison, E. 2022. The weight of waiting: The impact of delayed early intervention on parental self-efficacy. *British Journal of Special Education*, 49(1), 84-101.

Nee, J., Macfarlane Smith, G., Sheares, A., and Rustagi, I. 2021. Advancing social justice through linguistic justice: Strategies for building equity fluent NLP technology. In Equity and Access in Algorithms, Mechanisms, and Optimization (EAAMO '21). Association for Computing Machinery, New York, 1–9. https://doi.org/10.1145/3465416.3483301.

Neurodiversity Celebration Week. n.d. Neurodiversity Celebration Week. [Online] www.neurodiversityweek.com/

Nuffield Foundation. 2024. The level of support offered to children with special educational needs is decided by a postcode lottery. [Online] www.nuffieldfoundation.org/news/the-level-of-support-offered-to-children-with-special-educational-needs-is-decided-by-a-postcode-lottery

Rinaldi, C. 2006. *In Dialogue with Reggio Emilia: Listening, Researching and Learning.* Routledge.

Russell, G. 2020. Critiques of the neurodiversity movement. *Autistic Community and the Neurodiversity Movement*, 28(7), 287–300.

Shahvisi, A. 2023. *Arguing for a Better World: How to Talk About the Issues that Divide Us.* Hachette UK.

Shonkoff, J.P. 2007. *The Science of Early Childhood Development: Closing the Gap Between What We Know and What We Do.* National Scientific Council on the Developing Child. Center on the Developing Child. Harvard University. [Online] https://developingchild.harvard.edu/resources/the-science-of-early-childhood-development-closing-the-gap-between-what-we-know-and-what-we-do/

Souto-Manning, M. 2017. Is play a privilege or a right? And what's our responsibility? On the role of play for equity in early childhood education. *Early Child Development and Care*, 187(5–6), 785–787.

The Guardian. 2024. UK Black children face cultural barriers in accessing help for autism and ADHD. [Online] www.theguardian.com/education/2024/mar/31/uk-black-children-cultural-barriers-accessing-help-autism-adhd

Wheeler, R., Agyepong, A., Benhura, C., Martin, M., and Peter, M. 2024. Accessing special educational needs and disabilities (SEND) provision for Black and mixed Black heritage children: Lived experiences from parents and professionals living in South London. Global Black Maternal Health.

Wise, S.J. 2023. *We're All Neurodiverse: How to Build a Neurodiversity-Affirming Future and Challenge Neuronormativity.* Jessica Kingsley Publishers.

Reference website

www.spectrumgaming.net/ Barriers to Education Project

CHAPTER 2

THE ROLE OF ABLEISM IN EARLY CHILDHOOD

STARTING POINTS

Before addressing ableism in early childhood education, it is helpful to consider broader attitudes towards disability and neurodivergence. The following statements and questions are designed to provoke thought and encourage a deeper exploration of how discrimination and prejudice against disabled and neurodivergent individuals are perpetuated.

Do you agree or disagree with the following statements? Why or why not?

- There is no such thing as a "normal" brain (agree/disagree).
- Some disabilities or neurotypes are better or worse than others. For example, it is better to be dyslexic than autistic (agree/disagree).
- Neurodivergent and/or disabled people should be pitied (agree/disagree).
- Neurodivergent and/or disabled people sometimes use their differences and difficulties as an excuse (agree/disagree).
- Neurodivergent and/or disabled people are inspirational (agree/disagree).
- Disabled and/or neurodivergent people need to learn to overcome their differences and difficulties (agree/disagree).
- Educators should seek out opportunities to learn more about neurodivergent people through first-person accounts (e.g., social media, books, blogs, podcasts, etc. by neurodivergent people) (agree/disagree).
- I would be embarrassed to admit if I had a learning disability, such as dyslexia (agree/disagree).
- If someone uses a different kind of speech than I do (such as typing on a keyboard, using a speech-generating device, picture cards, and so on), I would be less likely to try to communicate with them (agree/disagree).
- I believe that neurodivergent people's brains work differently because there is something wrong in their brain (agree/disagree).
- Spoken language should be prioritised over other forms of communication when teaching neurodivergent children to communicate (agree/disagree).

DOI: 10.4324/9781003323211-3

+ Neurodivergent and/or disabled people just need to work harder to fit in (agree/disagree).
+ Neurodivergent people should learn social skills in order to fit in with their peers (agree/disagree).

Yes or No Questions

+ Do you consider how you will navigate the environment, communicate with others, or have your needs understood when going about your daily life? Why or why not?
+ If someone referred to a specific neurotype, such as autism, ADHD or dyslexia, would you be able to name strengths and traits as well as needs or difficulties?
+ Have you ever referred to a disabled or neurodivergent person as having superpowers or being inspirational because they have succeeded despite their differences and needs?
+ Do you think that neurotypical conforming and non-disabled people should see beyond a person's disability or neurodivergence?
+ I would feel uneasy if someone stopped a person from flapping their hands
+ I support organisations that want to find a cure for different neurotypes, such as autism.

The above questions are something for you to personally reflect on and return to at the end of this chapter. You may find your attitude changes in relation to some questions or makes you think more deeply about whether you think in ableist ways. These questions are not meant to shame the reader, but to act as a provocation to highlight that ableism is present in our every life, attitudes and behaviours.

You can read more about these questions and reflections in the companion resources. Questions adapted from:

Schuck, R.K., Choi, S., Baiden, K.M., Dwyer, P., and Uljarević, M. 2024. The Neurodiversity Attitudes Questionnaire: Development and initial validation. *Autism*, 0(0). https://doi.org/10.1177/13623613241245756 and Bridges Learning Center. https://bridgeslearningsystem.com/

INTRODUCTION

KEY TERM

Ableism is a form of prejudice and discrimination that specifically disadvantages disabled and neurodivergent people, often based on the belief that they should strive to to fit into ideas of normalcy to be considered valuable and productive to society. Ableism is systemic, meaning it is ingrained in societal structures, beliefs, and attitudes, portraying disabled and neurodivergent individuals as inherently inferior to non-disabled and typically conforming people.

Ableism happens at an **institutional, cultural** and **individual** level.
Systemic describes what relates to or affects an entire system. For example, attitudes towards disability span society as a whole.

Ableism is often seen as a societal issue unrelated to early childhood education. Yet, this form of discrimination begins early, affecting specifically those identified as disabled or neurodivergent. However, as you will see, ableism eventually harms everyone. This chapter will focus on ableism in early childhood, but it is crucial to understand its broader impact and the implications of attitudes and beliefs about disability and neurodivergence.

Ableism is a deeply entrenched part of society, happening around us every day. Disability and neurodivergence are often only accepted if individuals can pass as "normal" – in other words, if their disability or neurodivergence is subtle or concealed enough not to impose on others. This places an intense burden on disabled and neurodivergent people to assimilate to fit in. **This is ableism.**

Similarly, when a disabled or neurodivergent person exceeds expectations, they become a form of inspiration or are considered to have "superpowers". Think of the sympathy-fuelled headlines about someone overcoming or winning against their disability. Disability activist Stella Young refers to this as "inspiration porn", where disabled people become objects of inspiration – for example, being considered brave for expressing joy amidst the tragedy of being disabled. **This is ableism.**

You may also have been drawn into videos or stories about someone taking pity on a disabled or neurodivergent person and treating them kindly and altruistically. For example, a non-autistic child choosing to play with a non-speaking autistic child, which then finds itself on the internet for people to coo over. In this scenario, the message is clear: disabled and neurodivergent people are not considered equal, so when "normal" people interact and engage with them, it is seen as a good deed and one that must be promoted. **This is ableism.**

Our society assumes that the "normal" way to live is to be able-bodied and neurotypical. As a result, ableism often emerges without us realising it on an intuitional, cultural, and individual level. Examples include;

Institutional	✦ Designing a building with no ramps or lifts for wheelchairs.
	✦ Failing to make information available in an accessible format, such as Braille or British Sign Language (BSL).
	✦ Choosing a non-disabled job candidate over a disabled one because you think a disability will make someone less productive.
	✦ A failure to make the workplace adjustments that people with neurodivergent and/or disabled people need.

	✦ A failure to employ and promote disabled people. ✦ The segregation or exclusion of disabled and/or neurodivergent children and adults in education. ✦ Inequitable access to healthcare, especially if there are other marginalised characteristics such as ethnicity and gender. ✦ The failure to make buildings, events, and activities accessible to everyone. ✦ The failure to build an inclusive and accessible education system for children. ✦ Applying labels to children in education, i.e. special educational needs in order for them to access their education. ✦ A lack of adaptive technology.
Cultural	✦ The failure to value disabled and/or neurodivergent people's lives or views about what they believe is best for them. ✦ Emphasis on independence, not being reliant on others, and coping individually with life's daily demands. ✦ Appearance and beauty standards. ✦ Lack of representation in media, literature, popular culture, and curriculum. ✦ Tropes and stereotypes of disability. ✦ Ableist language that further stigmatises disabled people. For example, "st*pid", "id8ot", and "insa@ne". ✦ Parenting practices and quality is often presented as normative is best creating tragedy narratives when a child is disabled and/or neurodivergent. ✦ Having awareness and acceptance days or weeks with little change to the barriers of ableism.
Individual	✦ Feeling pity or shame towards a disabled or neurodivergent person. ✦ Assuming suffering in an individual as a result of being disabled and/or neurodivergent. ✦ Promoting neuronormativity, for example telling someone that they "don't look disabled" as a compliment. ✦ "Inspiration porn" whereby a disabled or neurodivergent person is considered inspiration solely for living a life as a disabled or neurodivergent person. ✦ Promoting saviourism about those who care for and educate neurodivergent/disabled people. For example, thinking a parent is courageous for raising a disabled child. ✦ Centring those who choose to support those who are neurodivergent and/or disabled

	✦ Non-disabled saviour trope in which a "normal" person helps someone with a disability and it is replicated across popular culture in many forms. We see it in the trend for "inspirational" videos of a disabled person.

Adapted from: Baglieri, S. and Lalvani, P. 2019. *Undoing Ableism: Teaching About Disability in K-12 Classrooms*. Routledge.

BELIEFS AND ATTITUDES

When I first read about ableism and its many examples, I felt upset and defensive. As an early childhood inclusion specialist, it seemed like an attack on my and others' good intentions. However, untangling the complex web of ableism requires sitting with the discomfort of recognising these well-intentioned but harmful impacts. Unfortunately, when a disability or neurotype is noticeable, whether through appearance or behaviour, general attitudes often range from pity and negativity to superiority and rejection. For example, the disability charity Scope found that three out of four disabled people had experienced negative attitudes or behaviours towards them in the past five years (Moss and Frounks, 2022). Similarly, children who are disabled or neurodivergent are not always accepted by their typically developing peers. Research by Babik and Gardner (2021) found that across cultures, disabled and neurodivergent children encounter negative attitudes, bullying, social exclusion, and isolation. These negative attitudes eventually become internalised, leading children and young people to develop negative perceptions of themselves, such as believing they have a "bad brain" (Hodge, Rice, and Reidy, 2022; Humphrey and Lewis, 2008). This is often referred to as internalised ableism. While some of the examples shared across this initial part of the chapter may refer more broadly to ableism, it is also important to consider how children begin to internalise this messaging and how they are exposed to pressures to fit in.

NEUROMYTH: THERE IS SUCH A THING AS NORMAL

"Normal" is a seemingly harmless label often used interchangeably with words like average, ordinary, typical, and standard. Historically, it began as a mathematical concept to describe angles and then later used to measure human characteristics such as height and weight. The "normal distribution" described the range where the most people could be found. For instance, young adult women typically range from 5ft 1 to 5ft 6 in height, leading to the belief that those in the majority group represent the correct or ideal way to be. Consequently, everything was designed for someone with average characteristics. For example, since the average person walks on two legs, steps became the standard way to move between different heights. Yet, not all people walk using two legs; they may wheel or require mobility aids, so steps become a barrier to access.

While average characteristics are common, this idea has also perpetuated the belief that there is an ideal or normal way to be, including how one should behave. Societies create dominant representation through customs, social expectations, media and unwritten rules, so those who act outside these norms are considered non-ideal and abnormal. In many cases, deviating from expectations could result in negative perceptions and, at the extreme, pathologisation, such as being considered disordered when you process the world differently to those considered typical or normal. Over time, "normal" has become a universally accepted term, underpinning much of what is deemed acceptable in society and our institutions. For example, in early childhood, development is defined by milestones, or "what to expect when", even though it can be very variable. Although cultural variations exist on the idea of normal, it ultimately creates a division between normal and abnormal or educationally "typical" or "special".

Moreover, definitions of normal often stem from specific groups. For example, characteristics of white people are frequently used as the dominant standard, leading to the perception that Black characteristics are less desirable. This perpetuates a biased and exclusionary view of what is considered normal. Similarly, non-disabled characteristics are described as normal, whereas disabled people are considered to deviate from this.

According to Chaney (2022), normal standards have shaped much of our history and still influence the design of our institutions, such as education in modern times. Yet, the idea of normal is known to be inaccurate and exclusionary. Furthermore, it reinforces prejudice about race, disability, gender, and social class. She states: "in the end, what is most common or usual across humankind is diversity and difference" (2023, n.p.).

PRESS PAUSE

What does "normal" mean to you?

✦ How might you have described a "normal" person when you were a child? What colour skin do they have? What abilities? What do they physically look like? How do they speak? In what language?
✦ What is your earliest memory of realising that people were different to you? How did you feel about those people? Did you feel better than them, or did you feel less than?
✦ Who did you see represented in books, television, and society?
✦ Did you know anyone who did not conform to the generally accepted notion of "normal"? How were these people viewed or treated?

You might notice in your answers that you too have specific ideas about what is considered normal and what is not. We begin to internalise these ideas in our childhoods, meaning that early childhood education must teach respectfully about differences and needs across human development. This will help to break down barriers and create opportunities for diversification rather than normalisation.

NORMAL DEVELOPMENT VERSUS
HEALTHY DEVELOPMENT

One of the issues that has arisen in education is that normal development is often used interchangeably with healthy development. However, they hold different meanings and contexts. Normal is a social construct that has been agreed upon by scientists and researchers over the last 200 years, and is often generalised to entire populations, meaning that variations or deviations from this are considered abnormal.

In child development, normal development usually refers to children who progress through neuronormative milestones to a prescribed and desired outcome. Outcomes are ultimately designed to prepare children for the schooling system, and for later economic value and productivity. Children who conform or fit into ideas of normalcy usually access greater opportunities because the education system privileges this way of being. However, as you will go onto see time and time again across this book, there is no such thing as normal development.

Healthy development, on the other hand, is a crucial aspect of a child's early experiences. The Harvard Center for the Developing Child describe three foundations for healthy development. They state:

From these foundations, it is clear that healthy child development is not solely the result of internal factors, but is influenced by external experiences, including (1) compatible relationships and interactions, (2) safe and secure environments, and (3) the meeting of basic and fundamental needs such as movement and nutrition. Furthermore, healthy development is not the absence of disability or neurodivergence. Conflating normal and healthy development can be unhelpful because it cultivates the idea that children should strive to be normal to be considered healthy. Health is not a fixed characteristic and is very fluid across the lifespan for all humans. For example, a disabled child may be experiencing healthy development whereas a so-called normal child may have a range of unhealthy developmental experiences.

Cognitive scientist Victoria Hedlund at Goldsmiths University, London, stated:

healthy development is a dynamic process across the lifespan. Educators will be thinking about physiological health for example, the underlying functions of the brain and body including the role of the nervous system, stress and the sensory systems. If a child is, say, autistic, the educator may need to adjust their expectations based on how the autistic nervous system works. To simply suggest there is something wrong with the underlying functions is inaccurate because scientists do not know enough about those functions to definitively state this. Hence why lived experience is always vital in building a clearer picture. You will also be thinking about fluid healthy development acknowledging that life is not linear and the environment, life choices and the meeting of needs will be variable. Think again of the autistic child thriving when surrounded by people who understand her autistic ways of being versus the autistic child who has every aspect of themselves denied in particular environments because they are not considered normal. It is not the autistic brain that is causing unhealthy development, rather it is the environment. And finally, healthy development should always be considered in terms of lifelong health and quality of life. What decisions are being made now for the child that will serve their development in the future. It makes little sense to think that every child will respond to the same experiences, and so the education system needs to expand its understanding of healthy development along with expectations and how they perceive a child's abilities . . . or disabilities.

An example of healthy development being perpetuated as normal development is health visitor childhood assessments. While health visiting is an integral and hugely beneficial system, it does not escape the ableist foundations. At a recent conference, I was approached by two health visitors who shared their reflections on realising that some of the standardised child development tools such as the Ages and Stages Questionnaires (ASQ) do not account for disabled or neurodivergent pathways of development, and this has significant implications on how a parent may come to see development that does not meet the ASQ standards. While they understood their responsibility to identify early concerns and risks to development, they had come to consider that categorising development in normal or pathological ways is in itself very limiting to human diversity.

ABLEISM IN EDUCATION

Parekh (2023) asserts that education is crucial for teaching children the skills they will use throughout their lives. Similarly, Ken Robinson (TED Talk, 2016) emphasises that education is meant to help individuals discover their strengths. Unfortunately, for many children, especially those with marginalised characteristics, education can become a place of adversity, reinforcing how they do not fit in. Supporting a child to reach their individual goals is critical, but the skills, knowledge, and opportunities to learn must be compatible with the variations of learning and development.

ABILITY AND ABLEISM

One of the most pervasive aspects of ableism in education is the focus on ability. Any person who has been through the schooling system will be all too familiar with the various aspects of measurement used to determine whether or not they fit into normal, average, and typical expectations. Moreover, these measurements cultivate competition between peers, creating a Good Level of Development and progress and the best level of progress and development.

Standardised measures such as exams and tests and their results often become internal dialogues about whether we are smart or not. For many children, school is either a place of opportunity or adversity. For example, I remember being at secondary school, and each year, the children with the best literacy results would be rewarded with a book voucher and a trip to a local bookshop. I never won. I vividly remember being furious and feeling that I was being punished for being "thick". Access to books could have also been an opportunity to engage in literacy, but it felt like widening rather than closing the ability gap.

Accordion to Parekh (2023), critically examining the issues with ability in the education system is difficult because it would require an entire rethink of the current core values of education and how children come to understand themselves. Ken Robinson once said: "education is the place where you are meant to find out what you are good at" (Ted Talk, 2016), but doing this via ability grouping ends up having the opposite effect on so many children, particularly those with marginalised characteristics. The reason this is relevant to early childhood education is that ability priming begins very early through the promotion of competition. For example, the definition of a milestone is a race to get from point a to b. Evans, K. and Bloem, M. (2024). Parents often are under pressure to prove that their child is able, and so will highlight those skills or knowledge that are considered valuable.

Early educators must be aware of the pressures that come from a focus of ability in schooling because of the emphasis that they are getting children school ready. A key question to ask is what you are actually getting children ready for? And does this readiness account for meaningful inclusion? School readiness is a huge agenda which shapes the paradigms and curriculums that are used, and unfortunately such things are also underpinned by ableism. Let's now explore how.

ABLEISM IN EARLY CHILDHOOD

Ableism is baked into experiences of conception, pregnancy, birth, and early childhood. It spans parenting, early childhood education, and school readiness. For example, when prospective parents pick up their first parenting books, they are likely reading descriptions of neuronormative development with disability and neurodivergence described as the worst-case scenario. They may meet with health visitors whose assessment procedures only deem typical and non-disabled development healthy. Parents may not share a child's diagnosis when looking for childcare for fear that they will be rejected, and similar early education settings may decline a place, thinking they cannot meet a child's needs if they are disabled or neurodivergent. Once attending an early childhood setting, children are then cared for and educated via a neuronormative play-based paradigm, and prescribed outcomes are set for the end of this educational phase, meaning that some children are already set to fail before their early childhood experiences have even begun.

Ableism in early childhood environments is especially harmful because it can be both widespread and subtle, often going unnoticed. Many settings claim to be inclusive because they can identify developmental differences, but they may inadvertently focus on making children conform to typical behaviours. This approach can unintentionally reinforce ableism by not fully embracing and valuing each child's unique qualities and needs. For example, a child who stammers may have their spoken language corrected, which begins to make them self-conscious about their stammer.

NEUROINSIGHTS

REFLECTION ON NEURODIVERSITY

In my journey to understand neurodiversity, I have had to unlearn a lot of what I was taught and that does not always feel comfortable. I have always been such an advocate of school readiness and was very invested in ensuring that the children we sent up to school became a good reflection on my setting. Afterall, I feel like we get blamed if the child does have developmental delays or behavioural issues. It was difficult realising that my ego was so involved in this process. I am still figuring that out to be honest. However, what I have changed my view on is that unreadiness itself can be a form of resistance to neuronormativity. Sometimes I think children just refuse to be rushed. And in England where my setting is based, our children are going into formal environments as young as four. I don't think I have ever truly faced how bad that is for human flourishing. And so my transition reports have changed as a result: I am no longer trying to please the next setting. I am just trying to cultivate understanding no matter where they are in their development.

Early Years Educator

Educators in early childhood should avoid assuming that disability and neurodivergence are inherent problems with the child. This perspective can put children in an impossible situation, implicitly and explicitly teaching them to reject who they are. Our very existence is rooted in our minds and bodies (Campbell, 2009), so it is misguided to say that a child succeeds despite their differences or disabilities, as if they have somehow separated their mind and body to achieve success. This mindset can lead to the harmful practice of masking, where a child feels compelled to hide their true self to fit an unrealistic standard of normalcy.

In Chapter 1, you were introduced to an analogy illustrating the diverse conditions necessary for plant growth, serving as a way for understanding the varied differences and needs of children. Nonetheless, over the past decade, there has been a trend towards practices that restrict children's access to creative and flexible care and education, opting instead for a rigid "one size fits all" approach. The predominant aim for many children becomes compliance and conformity to the demands of the schooling system, ultimately ensuring they are deemed productive and valuable citizens.

Children who resist and push against these pressures, notably usually those who are neurodivergent and disabled, become increasingly denied access to a fair and equitable educational experience. As an Early Years Educator, it can be frustrating to be continually subjected to the contradictions in Early Childhood Education (ECE) and Educational Inclusion policy. On the one hand, we are told of the importance of inclusion, equity, and accessibility and, on the other hand, we are primed to deliver care and education through outdated and traditional methods (Symeonidou, Loizou, and Recchia, 2023). For example, you may have heard of the term "integration" which refers to the expectation for children to change who they are in order to fit into a prescriptive education system. This implicitly communicates that the problem is still very much considered to be within the child. Many early childhood settings will be using interventions that train children to behave more typically or normally without realising that it may be entirely at odds with that child's unique developmental pathway. As we progress through these chapters, it will become glaringly obvious that the most precious and biggest thing up for grabs for this agenda of normalcy is children's play. Thus, expanding upon Chapter 1, we must consider what underpins this need for the neurodiversity paradigm and how that will leave us feeling much less tangled up in these contradictions.

THE MEDICALISED MODEL OF DISABILITY IN EDUCATION

The predominant perspective on neurodivergence and disabilities is often framed by the medical model. This model views these differences as abnormalities that need to be prevented, fixed, or cured (Marks, 1997). The widespread adoption of this model can lead to the public perceiving disability and neurodivergence as something sad and shameful (Chapman, 2020). The medical model itself remains relevant especially as there are lived experiences that may require treatment, and cure. The issue arises when the medical model is the only lens through which human differences are perceived. Furthermore, the medical model translates into education whereby the focus is often on prevention, intervention, and normalisation.

Medicalised perspective	Educationally this translates . . .
Disability and/or neurodivergence is considered solely the result of an impairment, deficit, or limitation across physical, sensory, intellectual, or emotional developmental domains.	. . . as having delays, difficulties or lacking in abilities in comparison to peers. For example, a child using sign language rather than speech is considered lacking in speech ability which is prioritised.
Disability and/or neurodivergence is inherent within the individual; for example, there is something "wrong" with the individual.	. . . to labelling certain undesirable traits. For example, a child who does not sit still is considered defiant rather than realising they need movement to focus.
There are two distinct categories of either being normal or pathological.	. . . as either typical or special. For example, a child defined as having special educational needs (SEN) which assumes delay and difficulties but does not account for differences.

Disability and/or neurodivergence is understood as something to be eliminated, fixed, or cured.	. . . to a child being normalised, or subject to early intervention to secure neuronormative outcomes. For example, a neurodivergent child has to join a small group intervention that promotes neuronormative whole body listening skills such as sitting still, providing eye contact, and having quiet hands.
Disability and/neurodivergence is the cause of a poor quality of life and positive outcomes.	. . . to integration, segregation, exclusion, and isolation based on undesirable traits, even those that provide the child with intrinsic motivation. For example, a child who enjoys repetitive play is encouraged to engage in activities that are less motivating in order to socially fit in.
Fails to take into account the social, political, and historical contexts within which neurodivergent and/or disabled children exist.	. . . to attributing learning gaps to social factors such as poverty but not recognising the under-resourcing of public services and funds to certain areas and communities. For example, believing that being from a lower social class caused poor language skills.
It focuses on reducing or fixing the impairment or, to the extent possible, rendering the individual more "normal".	. . . to interventions, strategies, and approaches that take a "neurotypical gaze". For example, child development documents that include neuronormative outcomes.
Adapted from Baglieri, S. and Lalvani, P. *Undoing Ableism*. Taylor & Francis. Kindle Edition, p. 22.	

ABLEISM RED FLAGS AND GREEN FLAGS

When a medicalised model dominates education it leads to children being viewed as deficient, delayed, and deficit. One way this shows up is by labelling any development that does not fit into neuronormativity as a "red flag". However, it might be more beneficial to identify our practices and approaches as "red flags" to be able to identify how these are ableist. The table below provides some examples.

Red flag	Ableism	Green flag
Developmental Milestones which only address neuro-typical or non-disabled development.	Believing that children who do not meet these milestones do not fit into our early years' spaces and classrooms. Using "Red Flags" to describe any development that does not meet milestones.	Ensuring that all children are described through a holistic and strengths-led paradigm (strengths, interests, differences and needs). Rejecting that all child development follows the same developmental pathways or trajectories and embracing divergent and diverse pathways.
Positive reinforcement.	Providing reinforcement to children **only** when they conform to neurotypical standards.	Providing meaningful feedback and commentary on children's unique developmental profile. Rejecting the behaviourist notions of positive reinforcement and instead focusing on affirmation and encouragement. Developing an understanding of neurodivergent traits and viewing these through a capability lens, for example, stimming as a source of joy.
"Play-Based" Interventions that train children to behave in neurotypical and non-disabled ways.	The child is expected to mask or conceal aspects of themselves that they know are not accepted. The children begin to develop internalised ableism.	Inclusion practices that cultivate self-esteem, enjoyment, and wellbeing. For example, special interest groups for autistic children.
Prescribes to outdated and dehumanising language to describe neurodevelopmental differences and disabilities.	Continues to use pathologised language such as ASD Assume difficulty, challenge or suffering. For example, "the child suffers from a stammer".	Reframes language to be justice orientated meaning that it recognises community preferences. For example, using the term autism as opposed to ASD.

ACTIVITY

Read the following short case studies. These refer to real but anonymous statements made about children's play and development in recent years. In most cases, educators were seeking advice about how to eliminate or reduce particular behaviours in children. Once you have read through them, ask yourself the following:

- ✦ What would you consider to be the problem or issue with the following children's play and/or development?
- ✦ Would you consider these helpful or harmful ways to talk about children's play and development?
- ✦ Does any aspect of the case study show evidence of ableist thinking or practice? If so, how?
- ✦ How might some of the statements within the case studies be reframed to reflect neurodiversity-informed and affirming pedagogy and practice?

I am the key person to an autistic child who refuses to make eye contact during social interactions, making it difficult to engage in cooperative play. I have set a target for the child to make eye contact for up to 60 seconds during a shared play experience. I will also set up some play experiences that require turn-taking and paying attention, which might help.

I am working alongside a speech and language therapist (SLT) who is helping me redirect a child's play. The child is obsessed with playing with the trains and doesn't seem to want to play with anything else. The SLT has suggested I remove the trains and replace them with other toys to encourage a wider repertoire of play interests. This will hopefully lead to more purposeful ways of playing.

The child's play is not appropriate. She is three years old but still seems to be in the exploratory and sensory stage of playing, similar to what you might observe with a two-year-old. She also loves to run and move a lot. She is not yet sitting down to play in more socially acceptable ways with her peers. We tell her "no" and to "stop" a lot. I have raised this as a "red flag" on her development chart.

The child's play is fleeting, meaning they do not play in any play for very long. They seem just to want to spin all the time. We just leave her to it because she seems happy but not quite sure what else to do.

The child ruins play for all the other children when we are outside. The moment the door is opened, he is off running, jumping, pushing, climbing, and wants to have his hands and feet in everything. It is not safe, and we spend most of our time telling him to be careful.

What if I told you that none of the children's play, learning, or development in the above examples is inherently wrong? As educators, however, we might find some of these behaviours or traits frustrating, unruly, or confusing because they don't align with what we have been taught to expect. Nevertheless, it's not the child who is at fault but rather the broader guidance on child development that suggests all children must neatly fit into predetermined developmental milestones that promote neurotypicality as the gold standard. These milestones are often expected to be reached by the time children enter formal schooling, sometimes as young as four years of age. Our notions of play and child development are often underpinned by an ableist mindset which is the belief that typical and non-disabled development is superior and the *right way to be*. Almost everything within early childhood education is geared towards this way of thinking and being, meaning that despite our best efforts to be inclusive, we are often thwarted by an incompatible paradigm that encourages us to "fix" children's play and development rather than to diversify our understanding of it.

If you skip to the end of this chapter, you can see the above examples reframed.

NEUROINSIGHTS

ABLEISM AND SPECIALIST PRACTICE

SPECIALISTS ARE FIGURING OUT THEIR ABLEIST PRACTICE TOO

I recently met a speech and language therapist, Alice Hill, who was such a refreshing specialist to speak to because they were open about their previous ableist practice, and in sharing their own ongoing journey in becoming neurodiversity-affirming. Alice shared the following insights:

"I realised how ableist my views used to be. This wasn't the intention, but I can see now that they were. I really did used to think it was my job to minimise autistic and other neurodivergent traits, and to help the child appear more neurotypical. The thing that started my neurodiversity-affirming journey was when my friend mentioned they joined an autism inclusivity group. I decided to join it too and it was the first time I directly heard from autistic voices and started to understand the importance of their lived experience. I admit that, at first, I was very defensive and did not want to hear some of what was said. I had been practicing for years in ways that I thought were

(continued overleaf)

(continued)

helpful, and it was hard to hear that many of them caused unintended but real harm and distress. One day I decided to be brave and ask the autistic people in the group what they wanted from a speech therapist. This is where I heard about Gestalt language processing. And I also really started to embrace communication in all its forms, and not valuing spoken language above all else."

Here are some of the things Alice did to shift towards neurodiversity-informed and affirming practice:

- ✦ Changing language to be more neurodiversity affirming.
- ✦ Looking for all the ways a child does communicate and embracing and encouraging these (instead of focusing on what they are yet to do).
- ✦ Stopped making comparisons to neurotypical conforming children and using age equivalents.
- ✦ Presuming competence and stepping away from assessing language comprehension in a formal way.
- ✦ Advocating for children and families because there is true belief that to be neurodivergent is not a deficit, it is a difference.

Alice Hill
Speech and Language Therapist
Destination Communication

ABLEISM HARMS US ALL

Have you heard about the canaries in the coal mine?

The classic example of an animal sentinel is the domestic canary, used in the early twentieth century to alert miners of deadly carbon monoxide in the coal mines. The miners brought these caged canaries with them into the mines. Because the birds are small and have particularly sensitive respiratory systems, the poison kills them more quickly than it would a human being, leaving the coal miners enough time to save themselves. I remember learning about the miners' canary, shaken by the images of these starkly bright yellow birds, tiny, fragile, beautiful - caged in the dirt and the lightlessness of those mines.

Shalaby, Carla. Troublemakers. The New Press. Kindle
Edition, p. xxi.

The above quote is designed to get you to think about fact that both the miners and the canaries face danger, but it is the canaries who are first harmed. Shalaby is trying to point out that ableism harms us all but it is usually neurodivergent and disabled children who suffer first. Consider the below statements about how ableism might impact you too . . .

Now consider the following:

◆ Have you ever felt the deep well of anxiety when needing to ring into work sick, or have you forced yourself up and out because you fear judgement, and for your livelihood?

◆ Have you ever referred to yourself as stupid or non-academic because you didn't perform well in exams or tests?

◆ Have you ever worn shapewear to make your body or appearance more acceptable?

◆ Do you feel shame when you choose rest over heading to the gym or being active?

◆ Have you ever felt like expressing your needs has been perceived as you making an excuse?

◆ Have you ever turned up somewhere well ahead of time through fear of being late?

◆ Have you ever sat in a workspace that is loud, too bright, and over-stimulating and tolerated it knowing you will later have a headache and fatigue?

◆ Have you ever been referred to as difficult for setting a boundary or expressing a need?

◆ Have you ever worn clothes that are entirely uncomfortable, but did not want to stand out?

◆ Do you say yes or agree to things even if you don't want to do them?

Ableism places expectations on all humans to endure suffering in order not to stand out. The status quo – which basically is things staying the same – can only stay the same if we all just accept things. If you think back to your school days, you might remember that to question, answer back, or give cheek was not acceptable. As children and young people, we were generally expected to conform and it is hard to shake that mentality as adults. However, there are children who answer back, who say no, who give cheek, who resist every attempt to normalise them. Neurodivergent and disabled children stand out in our education system because they are so loudly and visibly different to the norm. Historically, this was a bad thing, but perhaps it is time we hear their warnings? As Shalaby concludes: "The child who deviates, who refuses to behave like everybody else, may be telling us – loudly, visibly, and memorably – that the arrangements of our education systems are harmful to human beings. Something toxic is in the air, and these children refuse to inhale it. It is dangerous to exclude these children and silence their warnings" (Shalaby, 2017).

THE NEURODIVERSITY PARADIGM IN EDUCATION

In contrast to the medicalised model, the neurodiversity paradigm aims to present a more nuanced perspective on neurodevelopmental variation. It highlights the traits and strengths associated with different neurotypes to offer a more holistic perspective. For instance, past autism research has been criticised for being too biased towards impairments, leading to a fixation on cure or normalisation (Happé and Frith, 2020). A Neurodiversity Paradigm seeks to address this bias by offering new insights into neurodivergent and disabled ways of going through a process of de-pathologisation.

KEY TERMS

Disablement is the state of being disabled or the experience of becoming disabled. Disablement recognises that external factors often adversely contribute to disability. For example, a person in a wheelchair trying to access a building without ramps is disabled by the absence of ramps rather than the disability itself.

Enablement is the action of giving someone the means to be able to access or participate in daily life by addressing and removing potential barriers, for example, enabling access for people with different physicalities, such as ramps, handrails, visuals, instructions etc.

Neurodiversity	Educational, this translates . . .
Neurodivergence and/or disability is viewed as a natural and expected part of human variation.	. . . to an education system that is not standardised or "one size fits all" but is dynamic and varied in its educational offer.
Disability and/or neurodivergence is understood through a holistic profile of interests, strengths, traits, differences, and needs.	. . . to affording all children the same holistic understanding and not relying on a deficit approach to those with developmental differences and disabilities.
It is understood that neurodivergent and/or disabled people experience disablement as a result of barriers to inclusion and systemic ableism at an institutional, cultural, and individual level.	. . . to educators understanding that accessibility, adaptations, and affirming practices are key to enablement.
It rejects the idea of normalcy and is understood to be a socially constructed concept within educational frameworks and curriculums. For example, developmentalism promotes neuronormative and staged development, excluding a range of marginalised characteristics.	. . . to accepting diverse child development and a commitment to expanding knowledge and evidence base to include neurodivergent and disabled development. This is intersectional and accounts for other marginalised characteristics such as class, ethnicity, and gender.
Neurodivergent and/or disabled people are considered experts in their own lives.	. . . to meaningfully gathering the views and perspectives of children through different means.

Lived experience is prioritised in neuro-divergent and/or disabled people's lives, meaning that their traits, differences, and needs are understood in a meaningful context.	. . . into child-led practice, where children are supported to understand their traits, differences, and needs and are not en-couraged to conceal or mask their needs to fit in.
Approaches to inclusion and pedagogical practices are rooted in attunement and affirmation rather than prevention, inter-vention, and normalisation. For example, interventions and programmes are re-viewed for ableism.	. . . to developmentally meaningful inclu-sion practices and the use of programmes that help a child or children to understand different ways of learning, playing, and de-veloping.
Quality of life and outcome measures fo-cus on autonomy, self-advocacy, engage-ment, wellbeing, and belonging.	. . . to practices that centre joy and en-gagement within an early years setting, and opportunities for children to learn about themselves and to form a positive self-identity.
There are clear ethics of care, including consent, dignity, and responsiveness.	. . . to children being able to make choices about decisions that affect them. They are not made to feel ashamed about their differences.
The neurodiversity paradigm model does not deny the existence of difficulties and needs. Rather, they are understood within a broader context, meaning that a person's strengths are always the starting point.	

PLANTING SEEDS FOR NEURODIVERSITY

To combat ableism, educators can begin to deconstruct current practices and build a new.

Creating **safe spaces** for conversations about ableist practices is essential to mak-ing gains in neurodiversity-affirming practices. This means fostering an environment where discussing neurodiversity and ableism is done with compassion, not through shaming. It might be quite confronting to have a practice called out in the moment and so you may wait for an appropriate time and place to hold space for the discussion. The person will want to feel that you are an ally rather than against them, and so ensuring that it is a shared dialogue where both perspectives are heard can be a useful gateway for negotiating practices. For example:

> *Our circle times are always so engaging for children but I wonder if you share the same thoughts about expecting children to provide eye contact when speaking. We have some children who are neurodivergent and might find that uncomfortable. Could we adjust this expectation so that all children can engage in a way that feels comfortable to them?*

Be prepared to **model alternatives** where possible. It might be that you want to collaborate with colleagues, parents, carers, or specialists to think about neurodiversity-affirming practice. However, if you already know of alternatives, or have ideas, be open in sharing them.

Abandon the pursuit of developmental norms. And instead look for what is developmentally meaningful to the child. It might not always make immediate sense, and you may be required to do some neurodiversity digging to find contexts to certain traits, ways of learning, and behaviours, but by moving away from a one-way mentality, you open up the possibility for all the diverse ways children learn and develop.

Signpost and give it time for processing. Anti-abelist practice does not occur rapidly, and often requires individuals or collectives to grapple with complex ideas. As humans, we tend to hold our knowledge tightly and when contradictory information arises, it can threaten our knowledge base. Providing links to blogs, podcasts, videos, and research can provide the person with time to figure out how they feel. Simply saying "we shouldn't do it this way" doesn't take the practice to new places, you have to be prepared to back yourself up.

Focus support on helping children to better understand themselves. Remember that neurodivergent and/or disabled children will be consciously and unconsciously subject to messaging that who they are does not fit into ideas of normalcy. While it may feel that we are helping them by enforcing neuronormativity, it can have undesirable consequences on wellbeing and mental health such as masking or fatigue at meeting incompatible demands.

Have a setting policy for neurodiversity and anti-ableism. A key question that early educators will often ask me is how to communicate their commitment to becoming neurodiversity-affirming. Settings may be anxious to claim they are ND affirming when there is so much practice to unpack, and adapt, but that does not mean to say you cannot outline this journey via a policy. It also helps in aiding discussions with families and specialists to provide rationale for some of your decisions.

COMPANION RESOURCE

Neurodiversity-affirming practice and anti-ableism policy: https://www.canva.com/design/DAFzk5Daqmw/PYKOiGmwZjTIDvWg_gMOVw/view?utm_content=DAFzk5Daqmw&utm_campaign=designshare&utm_medium=link&utm_source=editor

NEUROMYTH: SPECIAL NEEDS IS LESS OFFENSIVE THAN SAYING DISABILITY

I recently heard a non-disabled Disability and Inclusion Office proclaim to a group: "I am the disability officer but I do not like to use that word". This is a very powerful statement because what it suggests is that the person views disability as a dirty or bad word. Ultimately, they view disability as bad (even unconsciously). This is ableism in action. While this person's intentions were good, the impact on a room that included disabled people was palpable. It reminds disabled people that to be accepted, our disabilities must be made invisible enough not to cause discomfort and instead, we have to be subjected to dressed-up words. You may have heard several of these words yourself . . .*differently abled*, *handi-capable* and the often confused one . . . we come again to *special needs*. Disability can be defined in many ways, but this one from a disabled activist is much better than those that focus purely on the person as an impairment: "Disability is a holistic experience, so it must have a holistic definition. Disability is not just a physical diagnosis, but a lived experience in which parameters and barriers are placed upon our lives because of that diagnosis" (Imani Barbarin as cited in Ladau, 2021). The key aspect of this definition is the recognition that you are not just disabled by your individual diagnosis or physicality, but by the environment around you. A disabled person knows the problem does not purely reside within themselves. For example, I recently walked into a building and saw a disabled lift. As I walked past, I noticed a sign saying, "If you want to use this lift, please come upstairs and let reception know". The world is disabling. And so those who claim ownership of that identity and lived experience do so because they recognise that being disabled isn't individualised, but connected to a much larger network of ableism and disablism. Furthermore, special educational needs is a policy-based term related to your learning and functioning as per age-related norms. Many disabled people have zero "special educational needs".

ABLEIST INTERSECTIONS

Ableism should not be thought of in isolation from other forms of discrimination as it is often upheld by other systems of oppression. For example, ableism and racism often overlap to compound further the ways a person is marginalised. When thinking about children's lived experiences, it is useful to consider the different intersections and how this might translate into everyday life. Below is an outline of key discriminatory intersections to be aware of:

ABLEISM AND ADULTISM

In her child-friendly summary, Eloise Rickman (2024) explains that adultism is the unfair treatment of children by adults. While the term isn't new, it is increasingly recognised as a way to describe the injustices children face. For instance, children often don't get enough chances to share their views on important issues like climate change that affect them now and in the future. Rickman notes that there's a power imbalance between adults and children in most of their interactions, such as between a child and a parent or a child and a teacher.

Adultism, like ableism, is based on a power imbalance. In ableism, typical and non-disabled people are seen as superior to disabled and neurodivergent people. Similarly, in adultism, adults are seen as superior to children. Both forms of discrimination rely on the idea of deficiency. For example, our education system often views children as just preparing for the next stage, rather than valuing their current stage. When ableism and adultism intersect, children face even greater challenges.

In her book *It's Not Fair*, I was interviewed by Rickman. We discussed how ableism reinforces the idea that disabled and neurodivergent children are less competent than so-called normal children. Combined with adultism, these children are often treated as if they are younger or helpless, without a voice. The presence of neurodivergent and disabled children in educational spaces is a form of resistance because they rarely conform to neuronormative expectations. Carla Shalaby, who wrote *Troublemakers*, reminds us that this non-conformity is not defiance but a signal that the education system doesn't always accommodate diverse childhoods.

I recall an instance in a reception class where a teacher repeatedly spoke harshly to a five-year-old child with ADHD. The child was constantly reprimanded. At one point, the child asked, "Who do you think you are talking to?" This was an assertion of their right to be treated with dignity. Instead of acknowledging this, the teacher punished the child for being impolite, failing to model the very respect they demanded.

ABLEISM AND RACISM

Have you ever heard someone say, "I don't see colour", intending to convey that they are accepting and inclusive of everyone? If you are a white or white-passing person, your skin colour might not be something you think about often because it's frequently presented as the dominant or "normal" way to be. However, for Black or Brown individuals, their skin colour significantly impacts their daily experiences. They are constantly reminded of their colour and how it affects their lives. Recognising this is crucial because ignoring race and racism diminishes their profound impact on society.

Similarly, have you heard someone say, "I don't see someone's disability"? This statement, like the one about colour, often comes from a place of discomfort with certain identity markers. However, it can inadvertently minimise the realities and challenges faced by people with disabilities. Both ableism and racism perpetuate the idea that there is an ideal or "right" way to be, typically characterised as white, able-bodied, Western, middle-class, and cisgender.

Gloria Ladson-Billings (2021) describes children of colour as experiencing an "ongoingness" of educational debts. This means they often face greater discrimination and receive less culturally informed education. For children with special educational needs (SEN), these challenges are even more significant. They are more likely to be excluded, mislabelled, and misdiagnosed, which can delay the support they need.

It is important to approach these topics with empathy and an open mind. Recognising and valuing people's diverse identities and experiences helps create a more inclusive and understanding society. Let us strive to see and appreciate each person's unique qualities, rather than ignoring them.

PARENT X CARER SOLIDARITY

Fisher (2024) sums up the pressures on parents x carers perfectly in this social media post:

> We are told to standardise our children. We compare and contrast, from the off. We buy books of expectations which tell us when they are meant to first smile (6 weeks) and roll (4 months). And when they don't do it on time, we fret. We worry about what that might mean, and what we could do about it – can you compel a baby to smile? What if they are just feeling serious?
>
> We're told about the standards everywhere, the developmental milestones. Do they have a pincer grip yet? Are they showing an interest in letters? Can they button their coat themselves? Childhood becomes a long list of things they should be doing now – and therefore things they aren't doing yet"

(n.p.)

Stacey (2024) argues that failing to uphold societal standards of ableism is often seen as failing to be a good parent. When a child is naturally rebellious, non-conforming, or behaves outside societal expectations, it is not just the child who is scrutinised; the parents' or carers' abilities are also questioned. This scrutiny can pressure parents to enforce compliance in their children so that they fit in. For example, parents may go along with certain intervention practices despite finding them ill-fitting for the child. A parent shared with me the fear they had at nursery pick-up each day as they knew it would be their child who had caused mischief or playful chaos. The parent deep down knew this wasn't a misbehaving child but a child who loved the freedom to play.

It is important to reflect on the ways that ableism can also chip away at a parent's self-efficacy which is the belief one has about their capability in the role of being a parent or caregiver. I often describe it to educators as a Jenga tower. While it may appear to stand tall and sturdy, our deficit-based interactions or ableist focus can lead to the toppling of their confidence. When a child has developmental differences, this can come from different angles as well.

Alternatively, it may also lead parents to realise that their child's non-conformity might reflect the family dynamic. In other words, rebellious children can awaken rebellious parents x carers who also begin to push against the system. It is part of the reason that parents x carers will often describe a fight for support, or going to battle because they are literally battling ableist systems, perhaps sometimes without realising it.

One way parents respond to the pressures of ableism is by opting to homeschool or "unschool" their children. This can be as much about necessity than choice; for example neurodivergent children face greater risk of exclusion or segregation. Although this approach is less common during early childhood, the experiences during these formative years can greatly influence parents' understanding of their children's needs. Early childhood teaches us that children thrive on play, self-directed learning, nurturing relationships, and respect for their unique developmental paths. These elements become a blueprint for parents and caregivers to support their children's growth and wellbeing.

CONCLUSION

Ableism is a complex topic, especially for the second chapter of a book that challenges current approaches to inclusion. However, to affirm neurodiversity, educators must begin dismantling practices that uphold a medicalised model of disability and other forms of discrimination. The good news is that much of what has been discussed in this chapter can be easily adapted to be more affirming. Increasingly, neurodivergent and disability-led initiatives are offering meaningful alternatives and new ways of practice that can be as rewarding for educators as they are for children. Ultimately, anti-ableist practices can lead to better holistic development opportunities for all children.

ACTIVITY - CHAPTER KEEPSAKES

Across this first chapter, think about what your keepsakes are, and note down the following:

✦ One thing you will start doing
✦ One thing you still stop doing
✦ One keepsake you will share with others
✦ One thinking knot that requires further exploration.

END OF CHAPTER FOLLOW-UPS

I am the key person to an autistic child who refuses to make eye contact during social interactions, making it difficult to engage in cooperative play. I have set a target for the child to make eye contact for up to 60 seconds during a shared play experience. I will also set up some play experiences that require turn-taking and paying attention, which might help.

I am a key person to an autistic child who has a preference for lowered eye contact. However, they will socially interact via side-by-side play, pointing, and touch. To encourage cooperative play and shared experiences, I have set a target to engage in parallel play, and to mirror his communication preferences so that he knows they are honoured and affirmed. I have built upon his current interests to plan play experiences that are intrinsically meaningful to him. I also recommend to him to look where feels comfortable.

I am working alongside a speech and language therapist (SLT) who is helping me redirect a child's play. The child is obsessed with playing with the trains and doesn't seem to want to play with anything else. The SLT has suggested I remove the trains and replace them with other toys to encourage a wider repertoire of play interests. This will hopefully lead to more purposeful ways of playing.

I am working with a speech and language therapist (SLT) who is aware that I take a neurodiversity-informed and affirming stance, and has been keen to collaborate with me on support that is compatible with the child. We have agreed to enable and build upon his interest in trains, and make train play available across other activities and experiences. We have also began building invitations and provocations into his train play. For example, including books on trains, and different types of trains. As his key person, I do not get to decide what is/isn't purposeful, rather I look at what is meaningful to the child.

The child's play is not appropriate. She is three years old but still seems to be in the exploratory and sensory stage of playing, similar to what you might observe with a two-year-old. She also loves to run and move a lot. She is not yet sitting down to play in more socially acceptable ways with her peers. We tell her "no" and to "stop" a lot. I have raised this as a "red flag" on her development chart.

The child is intrinsically motivated by exploratory and sensory play. This includes running and moving, and so this is reflected in her planning to ensure she is able to have these developmental needs supported. We have limited "no" and "stop" language and instead incorporated "let's" and "how about" when there are potential risks in play. This is not considered a "red flag" on her developmental chart, and embodied learning is entirely expected in the earliest years.

The child's play is fleeting, meaning they do not play in any play for very long. They seem just to want to spin all the time. We just leave her to it because she seems happy but not quite sure what else to do.

> *The child enjoys moving from space to space, and appears motivated by movement. We have started to join in with her spinning, and planning for other proprioceptive and vestibular opportunities.*

> *The child ruins play for all the other children when we are outside. The moment the door is opened, he is off running, jumping, pushing, climbing, and wants to have his hands and feet in everything. It is not safe, and we spend most of our time telling him to be careful.*
> *The child has a preference for outdoor play where there is more freedom and less demands. They are showing increasing capacity with the whole body gross motor, and they benefit from sensory and physical opportunities.*

BIBLIOGRAPHY

Babik, I. and Gardner, E.S. 2021. Factors affecting the perception of disability: A developmental perspective. *Front Psychol.* 12, 702166.

Bae, B. 2009. Children's right to participate: Challenges in everyday interactions. *European Early Childhood Education Research Journal*, 17(3), 391–406. doi:10.1080/13502930903101594

Baglieri, S. and Lalvani, P. 2019. *Undoing Ableism: Teaching About Disability in K-12 Classrooms*. Routledge.

Campbell, F. 2001. Inciting legal fictions: "Disability's Date with Ontology and the Ableist Body of the Law". *Griffith Law Review*, 10, 42–62.

Campbell, F. 2009. *Contours of Ableism: The Production of Disability and Abledness*. Springer.

Campbell, F.K. 2012. Stalking ableism: Using disability to expose "abled" narcissism. In D. Goodley, B. Hughes and L. Davis (eds), *Disability and Social Theory: New Developments and Directions*. Palgrave Macmillan UK, pp. 212–230.

Chaney, S. 2022. Am I Normal?: The 200-Year Search for Normal People (and Why They Don't Exist). Profile Books.

Chapman, R. 2020. Neurodiversity, disability, wellbeing. In H. Rosqvist, N. Chown, and A. Stenning (eds), Neurodiversity Studies. Routledge, pp. 57–72.

Chapman, R. and Botha, M. 2023. Neurodivergence-informed therapy. *Developmental Medicine & Child Neurology*, 65(3), 310–317.

Crompton, C.J., Hallett, S., Axbey, H., McAuliffe, C., and Cebula, K. 2023. "Someone like-minded in a big place": Autistic young adults' attitudes towards autistic peer support in mainstream education. *Autism*. 27(1), 76–91. doi: 10.1177/13623613221081189.

Evans, K. and Bloem, M. (2024). *What to make of developmental milestones*. The Informed SLP. Retrieved April 21, 2025, from https://www.theinformedslp.com/review/what-to-make-of-developmental-milestones

Fisher, N. 2024. Standardised children. Substack. [Online] https://naomicfisher.substack.com/p/standardised-children.

Foucault, M. 1977. The political function of the intellectual. *Radical Philosophy*, 17(13).

Gassam Asare, J. 2022. What is white saviorism and how does it show up in your workplace? Forbes. [Online] www.forbes.com/sites/janicegassam/2022/09/30/what-is-white-saviorism-and-how-does-it-show-up-in-your-workplace/.

Happé, F. and Frith, U. 2020. Annual Research Review: Looking back to look forward–changes in the concept of autism and implications for future research. *Journal of Child Psychology and Psychiatry*, 61(3), 218-232.

Hodge, N. and Runswick-Cole, K. 2013. "They Never Pass Me the Ball": Disabled children's experiences of leisure. *Children's Geographies* 11(3), 311–325. doi:10.1080/14733285.2013.812275.

Hodge, N., Rice, E.J., and Reidy, L. 2022. "They're told all the time they're different": How educators understand development of sense of self for autistic pupils. *Disability & Society*, 34(9-10), 1353-1378.

Humphrey, N. and Lewis, S. 2008. What does "inclusion" mean for pupils on the autistic spectrum in mainstream secondary schools?. *Journal of Research in Special Educational Needs*, 8(3), 132-140.

Ibrahim, I.M. 2020. Becoming Anti-Racist: Fear, Learning, Growth. #BlackLivesMatter. Twitter, 7 June. [Online] https://x.com/AndrewMIbrahim/status/1269423199273525250?lang=en.

Ladau, E. 2021. *Demystifying Disability: What to Know, What to Say, and How to be an Ally*. Ten Speed Press.

Ladson-Billings, G. 2021. *Critical Race Theory in Education: A Scholar's Journey*. Teachers College Press.

Lalvani, P., Broderick, A.A., Fine, M., Jacobowitz, T., and Michelli, N. 2015. Teacher education, in exclusion, and the implicit ideology of separate but equal: An invitation to a dialogue. *Education, Citizenship and Social Justice*, 10(2), 168-183.

Lewis, T.A. 2022. Working definition of ableism – January 2022 update. Talila A. Lewis. [Online] www.talilalewis.com

Marks, D. 1997. Models of disability. *Disability and Rehabilitation*, 19(3), 85-91.

Michalko, R. 2008. Chapter twenty-three. In: S.L. Gabel and S. Danforth (eds), *Disability & the Politics of Education: An International Reader*. Peter Lang, pp. 401-420.

McNair, L.J. 2022. The relationship between young children's transitions and power: "Why are all the doors locked? I don't feel free . . . I am not in charge of me anymore". *Children's Geographies*, 20(5), 661–673.

Moss, C. and Frounks, A. 2022. *Attitudes and Disability: The Experiences of Disabled People in 2022*. Scope.

Nutbrown, C., Clough, P., and Atherton, F. 2013 *Inclusion in the Early Years*. Sage.

Parekh, G. 2023. *Ableism in Education: Rethinking School Practices and Policies*. Routledge.

Rickman, E. 2024. *It's Not Fair: Why it's Time for a Grown-up Conversation About How Adults Treat Children*. Scribe Publications.

Robinson, K. 2016. Do schools kill creativity? TED Talks. [Online] www.ted.com/talks/ken_robinson_do_schools_kill_creativity.

Schuck, R.K., Choi, S., Baiden, K.M., Dwyer, P., and Uljarević, M. 2024. The Neurodiversity Attitudes Questionnaire: Development and initial validation. *Autism*, 28(11), 2821–2833.

Shalaby, C. 2017. *Troublemakers*. The New Press. Kindle Edition, p. xxi.

Siuty, M.B., Beneke, M.R., and Handy, T. 2024. Conceptualizing white-ability saviorism: A necessary reckoning with ableism in urban teacher education. *Review of Educational Research*, 0(0). https://doi.org/10.3102/00346543241241336.

Slee, R. 2019. Belonging in an Age of Exclusion. *International Journal of Inclusive Education*, 23(9), 909–922. doi:10.1080/13603116.2019.1602366.

Slee, R. and Allan, J. 2001. Excluding the included: A reconsideration of inclusive education. *International Studies in sociology of Education*, 11(2), 173–192.

Stacey, P. 2024. *How to Do Life with a Chronic Illness: Reclaim Your Identity, Create Independence, and Find Your Way Forward*. Jessica Kingsley Publishers.

Symeonidou, S., Loizou, E., and Recchia, S. 2023. The inclusion of children with disabilities in early childhood education: interdisciplinary research and dialogue. *European Early Childhood Education Research Journal*, 31(1), 1–7.

University and College Union (UCU). n.d. Everyday Ableism. [PDF]. [Online] www.ucu.org.uk/media/11222/Everyday-Ableism/pdf/Everyday_Ableism.pdf

Watson, K. 2023. Fear and othering in the inclusive early childhood classroom: remnants from the past. *European Early Childhood Education Research Journal*, 31(1), 8–21.

Refence website

www.sense.org.uk/information-and-advice/life-with-complex-disabilities/ableism-and-disablism/

PUT IT INTO PRACTICE
ABLEISM AUDIT

NEURODIVERSITY ZONES OF PRACTICE AND THE ABLEISM AUDIT

THE NEURODIVERSITY AFFIRMING ZONES OF PRACTICE

Murphy, K (2025). Neurodiversity-Affirming Practices in Early Childhood: An Empowering Guide to Diverse Development and Play. Routledge.

Cathy Nutbrown reminds us that inclusion is a state of becoming rather than a state of being (2016). It is important to recognise that before becoming neurodiversity-affirming, we must become informed about neurodiversity and its implications. The zones of practice help you to map where you currently are and where you might want to be. Please note: this is a rework of Andrew M. Ibrahim's *Becoming an anti-racist: fear, learning, growth framework (2020)*. It is critical to acknowledge that ableism is rooted in anti-Blackness, eugenics and racism (Lewis, 2022). We cannot address neurodiversity without acknowledging how systems of power and oppression operate to marginalise certain groups of people.

Ibrahim, I. M. Learning a lot and striving to be better. Created this visual mental model as a way to help keep myself accountable (Adapted from one I had seen for #COVID a couple months ago.) Becoming Anti-Racist: Fear, Learning, Growth. #BlackLivesMatter. 1:17 AM · Jun 2020. Tweet.

Nutbrown, C., Clough, P., & Atherton, F. (2013). Inclusion in the early years. Sage.

Lewis, T. A. (2022). Ableism 2020: An updated definition. Talila A. Lewis.

FIGURE AA. I NEURODIVERSITY-AFFIRMING ZONES OF PRACTICE

DOI: 10.4324/9781003323211-4

Comfort Zone

Protecting yourself from change

Currently prioritises **what you know** over what **could be gained** from **neuro+disability-affirming practice.**

Becomes defensive and fragile over existence of ableism potentially taking things personally.

Rejects systemic ableism and other forms of discrimination such as racism and classism

Conformity to **outdated language & tropes.**

Obedience to "experts" & **belief in a dependency model.**

Saviour mentality.

Knows current approach is flawed but has become accustomed to it.

Continues to engage with SEND processes because you feel you must **"navigate the system"**

FIGURE AA.2 THE COMFORT ZONE

Curiosity Zone

Letting the light in on new ways of thinking

Curious by neuro+disability affirming practice but **fearful of getting it wrong.**

Cautious of **information overload but** experimenting with new ways of thinking.

May find **neurodiversity-affirming** practice **too progressive** or unlikely to lead to change.

Defensive when new knowledge contradicts what you thought you knew.

Defiantly holding onto outdated language and terminology.

Feelings of **fragility**

Cognitive dissonance as you process the contractions of **educational inclusion.**

Overwhelmed by the realities of **ableism**

Blaming & Judging others.

Experimenting with *neurodiversity lite & white*

Being **performative.**

Venturing towards **problem-solving conversations.**

FIGURE AA.3 THE CURIOSITY ZONE

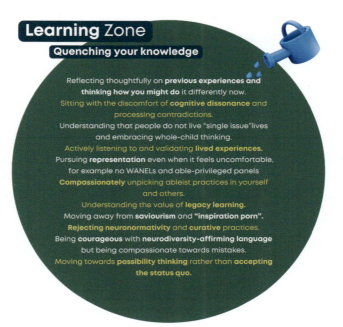

FIGURE AA.4 THE LEARNING ZONE

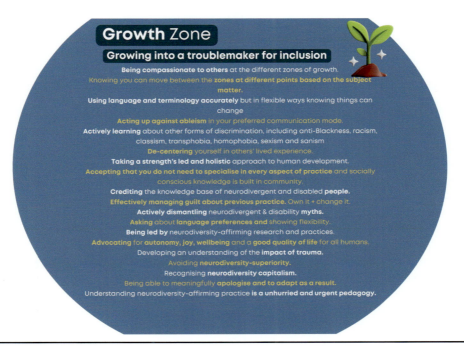

FIGURE AA.5 THE GROWTH ZONE

COMPANION RESOURCE

You can refer to my website: www.eyfs4me.com

Neurodiversity-aware	Neurodiversity-lite	Neurodiversity informed	Neurodiversity affirming
Being neurodiversity-aware refers to the growing understanding of the concepts and ideas of neurodiversity.	Neurodiversity-lite refers to individuals utilising neurodiversity ideas and concepts who still need to fully understand the foundations and principles of the approach and movement. It is important to have a deep and nuanced understanding of neurodiversity to apply informed and affirmed practices. It is important not to assume that someone is utilising neurodiversity-lite as opposed to being on a journey of learning and understanding.	If we view neurodiversity as a journey, it is important that we first spend time becoming informed about the concept, movement and approach. This will take time, and will involve lots of new learning and ways of being.	Neurodiversity-affirming practices emerge from us becoming more informed about developmental differences. In our everyday beliefs and practices we affirm, empower and embrace difference, while supporting and adapting to address areas of need.

A useful starting point in moving towards neurodiversity knowledge is to begin to unpack ableism within your early childhood practices. It is not a comfortable thing to do, but it is a necessary part of the journey. The list below is not exhaustive but has been generated from the many discussions I have had with early childhood settings and educators who have been interrogating their so-called inclusive practices. The purpose of these discussions has been to consider to what extent they may be considered ableist but to also consider the nuance in why we choose to do the things we do. Some of these examples are also drawn upon from my own practices, and ones that I have had to deconstruct and move on from. And so now, it is your turn. I would recommend doing the following:

1. Read through each ableist example, along with the anti-ableist stance.
2. Highlight any that stand out to you. For example, a few may jump out because you totally agree that they are ableist, or others you may feel uncomfortable (or even defensive about).
3. Also bookmark those that you do not fully understand, and you might want to conduct more research on why they are considered ableist. Those with an asterisk have recommended readings in the signposting section.
4. Next go through the list again, and think about your neurodiversity zones of practice, highlighting those that you still are getting to grips with (comfort zone), those that you want to know more about (curious zone), and those that you think you are already dismantling (learning and growth zones).
5. This is an activity you can keep returning to throughout the book, and in collaboration with colleagues. The purpose is for you to think about the examples I have provided but it may also generate examples from your own practice. Good Luck!

EDUCATORS HOLD CURRENT KNOWLEDGE TOO TIGHTLY MEANING THAT THE OUTDATED AND ABLEIST ATTITUDES, BELIEFS AND PRACTICES REMAIN THE STATUS QUO

Ableism example and alternative stance	Comfort Zone	Curious Zone	Learning Zone	Growth Zone
Ableism example: "The child would not sit still during circle time so the practitioner held them down on their lap". The setting is beginning to recognise that they can learn alternative ways of supporting children rather than prioritising what they already think they know is best.				

Ableism example: "Ableism is just another woke thing to contend with. Children are too young even to be impacted by this stuff". Ableism and disablism are understood as a significant threat to childhood development, and educators are actively exploring how they translate into everyday care and education practices.				
Ableism example: "The child can now give eye contact so the intervention has worked", despite the fact that the child remains uncomfortable with eye contact. The setting is developing an understanding of the harms of their practice and beginning to consider alternatives.				
Ableism example: The setting continues to use autism spectrum disorder because this is the medical definition. The setting is beginning to understand the power of how language is used and considering possible reframes so that there is neutral and non-assuming language. For example, to assume that to be autistic also means to be disordered.				
Ableism example: The setting consistently chooses training from organisations that do not have representation.				

The setting is beginning to explore representation in the training and professional development they engage with. This includes asking about representation at conferences and training events. The setting is keen to learn from an intersection of neurodivergent and disabled educators and advocates.				
Ableism example: *The setting only refers to neurotypical and non-disabled research and information.* The setting is actively moving towards being informed by neurodivergent and disability-led research. It draws upon lived experience sources and ensures that this takes into account intersectionality.				
Ableism example: *The setting says that they do not see colour, and so do not see the relevance of this in their inclusion support for a neurodivergent child.* The setting understands the interplay of ableism and racism. It is making efforts to understand how experiences will differ for children and families based on their identity markers, such as racialised identity, gender and social class.				
Ableism example: *The setting continues to use corrective interventions as they believe they must*				

69

make sure they fit in at school. The setting actively challenges the idea of normalising children and works closely with schools to ensure that the children's differences and needs are understood.				

LANGUAGE IS NOT JUSTICE-ORIENTATED AND DEHUMANISES NEURODEVELOPMENTAL DIVERSITY AND DISABILITY

Ableism example and alternative stance	Comfort Zone	Curious Zone	Learning Zone	Growth Zone
Ableism example: *When speaking to parents, the educator referred to developmental differences as "red flags".* The setting is adopting humanising language and moving away from pathologising language. For example, continuing to use the term disorder when talking about autism. They also talk to children, parents and specialists about language preferences.				
Ableism example: *The setting state that the child might be suffering from ADHD.* The setting generally uses identity first language (dyslexic person) as opposed to person-first language (person with dyslexia) but also checks in with individual preferences.				

Ableism example: *The educator says that all children with SEN have superpowers.* The setting does not reinforce neurodivergent and disability tropes, for example, stating that disabled children are inspirational or to be neurodivergent is to have a "superpower". The setting understands that these tropes can be harmful and suggest that children need to be viewed as inspirational or superpowered to be considered valuable.				
Ableism example: *The educator explains to the parent that they know better as they have taken a course in developmental language disorder, and so what they are saying about their child's lived experience cannot be accurate.* The setting prioritises lived experience as a way of understanding neurodivergence and disability. They spend time listening to families and are open to thinking differently about difference. They understand that they will not always *"know best"*.				
Ableism example: *The setting says that they must describe children on their "worst days" in order to secure support.* The setting commits to understanding children on their best days, and thinks about what is needed to help them have good days as opposed to worst days.				
Ableism example: *The educator described the child's development as abnormal.* The setting consistently questions whether their language could be discriminatory or harmful and seeks to reframe language into neutral terms.				

RELYING TOO HEAVILY ON A PATHOLOGY FRAMEWORK

Ableism example and alternative stance	Comfort Zone	Curious Zone	Learning Zone	Growth Zone
Ableism example: *The setting only believes children can be supported through intervention, and not through high-quality care and education.* The setting understands that anti-ableist high-quality care and education are the foundations for children to flourish. They do not prescribe to interventions that claim to correct, fix or cure children of their problems.				
Ableism example: *Educator believes that medicalised and clinical knowledge cannot be challenged is fact.* The setting understands that medicalised and clinical knowledge can be biased or motivated by the pathology framework, and does not always account for lived experience.				
Ableism example: *The setting decides to start training the children ready for school by setting up the early years space as a classroom.* The setting understands that current understandings of school readiness are rooted in ableist compliance and do not take into account the diversity of childhood(s).				

Ableism example: *Only supporting children when they reach crisis point, or only planning for need rather than holistic development.* The setting fundamentally believes that all children are entitled to joy, flourishing, pleasure, and wellbeing. They do not allow children to reach crisis point before responding to their to learning and development needs.				
Ableism example: *The setting has a display up which lists all the symptoms of common forms of neurodivergence.* The setting promotes a holistic understanding of child development and wellbeing and explores traits and differences as well as needs.				
Ableism example: *Only utilising child development documents that frame children with developmental differences as a problem without drawing on a wide range of sources.* The setting explores developmental diversity and draws upon a range of sources to understand child development. They are not limited by prescribed milestones and outcomes.				

CURRICULUM, RESOURCES AND PRACTICES UPHOLD ABLEISM

Ableism example and alternative stance	Comfort Zone	Curious Zone	Learning Zone	Growth Zone
Ableism example: *Display and visuals in setting represent diversity, but then children are expected to conform to same practices.* The setting is beginning to recognise that tokenism can be harmful in representation and aims to ensure the setting meaningfully reflects children's identities and lived experiences.				
Ableism example: *Any development that does not fit into typical development has a red flag next to it.* The educator no longer writes about children in deficit ways, for example, using "red flags" to describe development.				
Ableism example: *The setting uses a small steps document that has broken down typical development despite this still promoting one developmental pathway.* The educator actively challenges and questions neurodivergent and disabled children being erased from child development documents, or considered an afterthought.				
Ableism example: *When asked about professional development, the practitioner says there is no point in attending autism training as there are no autistic children in the setting.* The educator learns about a range of inclusive approaches even if they do not have children experiencing particular				

differences or disabilities. They understand, however, that expanding inclusive pedagogies is an ongoing area of development.				
Ableism example: *Despite being give valuable advice about a child, the setting is reluctant to follow it because it would require a change in practice.* The educator views change as a positive and does not feel threatened by having to adapt practices.				
Ableism example: *A setting refuses to put in a reasonable adjustment because it would not be fair on other children.* The setting understands equality, equity ad inclusion and intentionally teaches these concepts to children so they understand why traits and needs are accommodated differently.				
Ableism example: *"Children do not see differences, they are too innocent to understand all that stuff".* The setting teaches neurodiversity and disability justice to children understanding that children recognise differences and disabilities and benefit from developing an understanding and respect of differences.				
Ableism example: *Thinking it will make things worse for the child for them to know they are neurodivergent and so keeps it from them without exploring all perspectives.* In collaboration with the family, the setting helps children to understand their strengths, differences, traits and needs, and holds all neurotypes and disabilities as equal and valuable so that children develop a positive self-identity.				

Ableism example: *Having a special needs table where all children who are neurodivergent or disabled are expected to sit.* The educator avoids inadvertently or openly group children based on neurotypical and non-disabled abilities. For example, "Take those children outside while the rest of us do this activity".				
Ableism example: *An educator says "No, all children must complete the task in the same way".* The educator adapts practices and activities to suit divergent pathways of development.				
Ableism example: *Having golden rules and praising children for doing them even though they are clearly finding it difficult.* Positive reinforcement is avoided as it can often reinforce neurotypical skills. Instead, settings use intrinsically motivating experiences to support the child's access to the environment, curriculum and learning.				
Ableism example: *The child is put on time out for not sitting still during the intervention group.* Applying the setting do not apply to intervention strategies that don't appear suited or matched to the child's individual need. For example, expecting a child to sit in small group activities to practice good listening.				
Ableism example: *The child is taken out of the room regularly to take part in an intervention programme and is often taken away from their self-directed play.*				

Decisions about the most suitable environments are made based on what is most meaningful to the child rather than segregating children who do not fit in or comply.				
Ableism example: *A practitioner saying that there is no point in planning an activity because the child won't be able to do it anyway.* The setting presumes competence in all neurodivergent and disabled children understanding that children should have opportunities, exposure and scaffolds for all learning.				
Ableism example: *The child is expected to tolerate sensory input to get used to sensory play despite it causing lots of distress.* The setting understands the unique sensory blueprints of each child and attempts to ensure a balanced environment that can accommodate variations in sensory needs.				

OBSERVATION, ASSESSMENT, AND REFERRAL

Ableism example and alternative stance	Comfort Zone	Curious Zone	Learning Zone	Growth Zone
Ableism example: *Children planned for on separate paperwork, rather than expanding current planning systems.* The setting attempts to include children in everyday planning systems so that it becomes a habit to be flexible and adaptive in practices.				

Ableism example: *Continuing to use Individual Education Plans and ABC Behaviour charts.* The setting explores tools and resources that take an anti-ableist approach and questions those that narrow children to either their deficits or assumes that their behaviours and expressions are just surface based.				
Ableism example: *Not challenging the system, for example, unnecessary requirements for "evidence" that a child needs support.* The setting appropriately questions and challenges processes that lead to unnecessary paperwork, or evidence, especially that which attempts to stage the child.				
Ableism example: *Goals are focused on enforcing neurotypicalism, for example, sitting still, eye contact, responding to adult prompts, exchanging visuals for needs to be met.* The setting is exploring neurodiversity-affirming goals, and considering how they help the child to become confident and have self-belief and self-esteem.				
Ableism example: *Infantilising a child's development based on a neurodivergence or disability: "The child is three years old but falls under the band 0-11 months".* Children are not staged within the setting or infantalised. Support needs descriptions are used to acknowledge the unique profile of the child.				
Ableism example: *Standardising development through SMART goals rather than child-centred goals.* Goals are affirming and unique to the child, and do not become a measure of neurotypicalism				

SPECIFIC PRACTICES

Ableism example and alternative stance	Comfort Zone	Curious Zone	Learning Zone	Growth Zone
Ableism example: *"Our setting has a SEND cap so that we do not have too many children at one time".* Capping of children identified as SEND is avoided, and an assessment of need is always carried out to make a decision that is in the best interests of the child.				
Ableism example: *"The child has too many meltdowns during the day, and so we have had to ask the parents to find alternative provision".* Children are not excluded based on their neurodivergence or disability. For example, excluding a child who is dysregulated due to sensory overwhelm.				
Ableism example: *"Upon finding out the child is autistic, the setting said they could not offer a place".* A diagnostic identity or disability does not result in a child being denied a place in the setting.				
Ableism example: *"The child would not sit still during circle time so the practitioner held them down on their lap".* Physical intervention is not used to control or direct a child. Under exceptional circumstances, it will be used to ensure safety.				
Ableism example: *"The child was introduced to a social story about the importance of providing eye contact*				

when talking to peers and not interrupting". The setting does not use social stories inappropriately, for example, to correct behaviours or make the child more compliant to "fit in".				
Ableism example: "The child was not allowed to have their drink unless they provided the correct symbol". The setting avoids Picture Exchange Communication Systems (PECS) or any visual system that requires transactional communication, for example, "you must do this to get this".				
Ableism example: "The child is told to use their words despite being minimally speaking". The setting embraces whole-body communication and understands that speech is not the only mode of interaction.				
Ableism example: "The goal for the child is to fade visual supports as they need to learn to use their words, despite the success of visuals". The setting focuses on autonomy, including self-advocacy, expressing needs in preferred communication modes, and knowing how to ask for help over independence, which suggests that children should just be able to do things independently of helpful supports.				
Ableism example: "The child is taken away from their play and carried to the intervention group". The setting uses consent procedures to ask for permission from children, for example, "Would you like to join the circle time? Yes or no?".				

Ableism example: *"The child is being taught to accept play initiation from peers during solitary play".* Play is not used to rectify or coerce a child into neurotypicalism. For example, using play to improve neuronormative social skills.				
Ableism example: *"The child has a special interest in trains, and so we made them less available so that the child is forced to pay with something else".* Children's play is not sabotaged or unnecessarily redirected to promote "normal" play skills.				
Ableism example: *"The child is told to stop hand flapping as it disrupts other children during story and song time".* The setting understands whole-body listening and engagement and learns about children's unique whole-body profiles including stimming.				
Ableism example: *"The child has been naughty all day and has now been placed on the rain cloud. He can try again tomorrow to be on the shining sun".* Public behaviour systems are not used, and children are not publicly shamed for behaviours that may or may not be beyond their control.				
Ableism example: *"Children who have had good attendance are being rewarded with a picture book at the end of term".* Compliance awards are not used as they discriminate against disabled, neurodivergent, and medically unwell children				

Ableism example: *"We have introduced a sticker system for good behaviour. Once the children earn five stickers, they will get a reward".* The setting avoids relying on extrinsic rewards where behaviour and engagement are based on reward transactions. Meaningful feedback, praise, and motivators are used instead.				
Ableism example: *"We have a calm down box that children can use when they are worked up".* Self-regulation is understood to be a process of matching your energy state to the task at hand. Children are not constantly told that they need to be calm as this is not the goal.				

It is likely that some of the examples in Ableism 101 have made you feel uncomfortable or defensive. It is entirely expected that you will feel this way because it brings to attention how much ableism is baked into the education system. Have a look through the list again, but this time, choose a few that feel uncomfortable and conduct some research about why this may be ableist. In addition, come up with some ideas for adapting it to be more anti-ableist or replacing the practice with an alternative.

CHAPTER 3

THE MYTH OF UNIVERSAL CHILD DEVELOPMENT

STARTING POINTS

In Chapter 1 and 2, you explored neurodiversity and the impact of ableism on early childhood education. Across this chapter, you will consider how ableism influences and can limit our understanding of diverse child development.

As an Early Years Educator, you often observe and assess developmental milestones and are therefore required to have sufficient knowledge of child development. The below task aims to help you reflect on which developmental milestones are prioritised in early childhood as desirable or typical versus autistic milestones.

1. Note down the possible developmental milestones or expectations you might have of a typically developing child of pre-school age (3–4 years). You can choose to explore communication & language (C&L), personal, social, and emotional development (PSED), or physical development (PD). You do not need to do this from memory and can refer to child development documents, and online searches.

2. Now repeat this task, but think about the possible developmental milestones or expectations you might have of an autistic child of pre-school age (3–4 years) who is using delayed echolalia.

DOI: 10.4324/9781003323211-5

REFLECTION QUESTIONS

✦ Which set of milestones were easier to note down?
✦ What key differences did you identify between the milestones?
✦ If you referred to child development documents and online/physical resources, how useful were they in describing both a typically developing child and an autistic child?
✦ What might you need to consider when applying neurodiversity-affirming practice to neurotypical developmental milestones?

At the end of this chapter, you'll revisit this starting points task to reflect on how your understanding of autistic child development has grown.

INTRODUCTION

One of the greatest myths of early **childhood development is that all** children are travelling down **a universal developmental pathway**

FIGURE 3.1 DEVELOPMENTAL PATHWAYS

A NOTE ON THIS CHAPTER

As you explore this chapter, you'll notice the focus is on the autistic neurotype. There are a few key reasons for this:

✦ A significant amount of advocacy and research is currently being led by autistic people and their allies. We can learn valuable insights about autism and use neurodiversity-affirming frameworks to apply to other neurotypes and disabilities.
✦ Child development is a vast and dynamic field with many developmental pathways. Covering every neurotype or disability in one chapter would not do it justice.

Additionally, a crucial aspect of neurodiversity-affirming practice is grounding our understanding in lived experiences whenever possible. While my specialisation is in inclusion, I cannot speak for or specialise in every neurotype or disability. The early years sector requires collaborative action to develop comprehensive knowledge and understanding of a range of neurotypes and disabilities.

Instead of attempting to cover everything, I have focused on the latest insights into autistic development to highlight the possibilities of developmental diversity. While I will also touch on other neurotypes and disabilities, this chapter, like the rest of the book, invites you to explore beyond these pages and use lived experience frameworks to inform your understanding of child development. It serves as a springboard for exploring other neurotypes and disabilities through a neurodiversity-affirming lens.

TUNING-IN TO CHILD DEVELOPMENT

In your daily interactions with children, you consciously and unconsciously observe them, tuning-in, and attempting to make sense of their play, learning, and wellbeing development. This process is greatly enhanced by your continuous learning and professional dialogue, which helps you to identify familiar patterns amongst children and their developmental sequences. Over time, you likely start noticing these patterns, such as hearing their babbled and first attempts at words. Through your close relationships, you may also notice developmental sequences, such as a child progressing from crawling to shuffling to pulling herself upright, taking those first risky but exhilarating steps, and eventually walking and adventuring. These observations, alongside your professional learning, form your understanding of developmental milestones and, generally, what to expect when. This is referred to as developmentalism and is the lens through which Early Years Educators learn about the typical stages and sequences of child development. This usually forms the basis of the child development guidance we use to observe, assess and plan for children progress. However, issues can emerge when the focus is solely on what is considered typical.

DEVELOPMENTALISM

FIGURE 3.2 TRADITIONAL PIONEERS OF EARLY CHILDHOOD

KEY TERM

Developmentalism refers to the leading theoretical approaches that promote the idea that childhood is a universal experience during which all children progress through uniform, linear, and progressive stages towards a state of completion called adulthood (Play Wales, 2021).

According to Gabriel (2021), developmental psychology emerged as a dominant framework for studying young children's development in the early 20th century. The majority of early childhood educators will hear about well-known learning and development theories through their professional training and qualifications. Developmental psychology explores how humans grow, develop, and adapt at different life stages, with developmental psychologists dedicated to helping children reach their optimal potential. This includes understanding developmental "norms", milestones, stages, and supposed delays or gaps within development.

The likes of Jean Piaget (1896–1980), John Bowlby (1907–1990), and Lev Vygotsky (1896–1934) have endured as pioneers who continue to shape the landscape of early childhood education today. Afterall, pioneers such as these have been instrumental in raising an understanding of the importance of the first few years of life. We can value the legacies and contributions of these pioneers while recognising that our understanding of childhood also needs to continue to evolve. To truly embrace the diversity of childhood experiences, we must move beyond some of their outdated and limited perspectives.

The dominance of developmental psychology in early childhood raises two distinct issues. First, Souto-Manning and Rabadi-Raol (2018) argue that traditional notions of quality, including the theoretical evidence base in early childhood education and development, are exclusionary. They are predominately based on white, monolingual (standard English), and monocultural (western) values and experiences which often use deficit paradigms to describe the developmental paths of many minoritised children. For example, Black and Brown children are frequently subject to stigma related to their so-called speech abilities (Nair and Farah, 2024). Early childhood "best practice" to this day is haunted by word-gap myth which suggests that affluent children use more words than those from socially deprived areas despite this research being exposed as racist and discriminatory (Cushing, 2023). Broughton (2022) states that children's experiences are often understood through "white theorising", meaning that white scholarly perspectives are prioritised and generalised across all development. This not only impacts children who form part of the global majority, but extends to neurodivergent and disabled children also.

KEY TERM: GLOBAL MAJORITY

Global majority refers to people who are Black, Asian, brown, dual heritage, indigenous to the global south and/or have been racialised as "ethnic minorities" (Campbell-Stephens, n.d.).

While developmentalism can be argued to provide valuable insights into how children might develop, it mainly focuses on typical, non-disabled traits and generalises these to all children. This becomes problematic when assessing diverse children's development, as it may lead to assumptions of deficits, delays, or failures if they don't follow the expected stages seamlessly. For instance, Jean Piaget's stages of cognitive development describe how children's thinking evolves: from the Sensorimotor stage (birth to 2 years), where learning is based on sensory experiences and actions; to the Preoperational stage (2 to 7 years), marked by symbolic thinking; the Concrete Operational stage (7 to 11 years), involving logical thinking about concrete events; and the Formal Operational stage (12 years and up), characterised by abstract reasoning. However, stage theory is increasingly criticised for not accounting for individual differences. For example, suppose a child remains in the Sensorimotor stage longer than stated or shows has a dominant preference for a particular stage. In that case, it might be wrongly viewed as a delay rather than a different but valid developmental approach.

Ultimately, for early educators to embrace intersectional and neurodiversity-affirming practices, they need theories and ideas that recognise and respect the diverse ways children learn and develop. This underpinning theory must be translated into child development guidance and professional development.

CHILD DEVELOPMENT GUIDANCE

Access to reliable child development guidelines is crucial. They should provide reassurance and deepen your understanding, enabling you to support each child's growth effectively. I recall my first role as an Early Years Educator, and coming to rely heavily on illustrated guides to child development, and books that provided ways to support through to the next steps. For typical and non-disabled pathways, such tools can be invaluable.

Yet, you might also encounter less familiar development pathways – instances where a child's development diverges from the expected norm. In principle, this variation should spark curiosity because a fundamental understanding of child development in early years is that children are unique, developing at a pace and rate that is meaningful to the individual. For reasons I will explain, we currently utilise a "red flag" model for any child development that does not fit the norm.

TYPICAL CHILD DEVELOPMENT

In early childhood settings, curriculum and child development guidelines often favour neurotypical children who are typically developing and non-disabled. This approach suggests that this group represents the ideal way for children to learn and grow. Unfortunately, it overlooks children's diverse developmental journeys, inadvertently implying that deviations from this norm should be normalised rather than embraced and supported. This emphasis on a universal developmental pathway can limit our ability to appreciate the richness and variety in child development fully.

DISORDERED DEVELOPMENT?

KEY TERM

Developmental neurotype or disability refers to differences that are present from birth or become apparent in early childhood and are lifelong. In this chapter, autism is referred to as a developmental neurotype because it is present from birth and is lifelong.

In the early years, children exhibit a variety of neurotypes. Some children will follow a typical developmental pattern, others may already have a recognised disability, and some may have developmental differences which suggest neurodivergence. Developmental neurotypes such as autism, ADHD, or dyslexia are present from birth, although the point at which these may be identified, assessed or diagnosed can vary. Furthermore, many traits can overlap, co-exist, or indicate an environmental influence such as trauma. In other words, understanding an individual child's developmental profile can be complex so having access to child development guidance that is dynamic, encompasses diversity, and is inclusive is critical.

As an Early Years Educator or caregiver, you often play a pivotal role in observing the initial traits of neurodivergence. For instance, you might be reflecting on whether a child could be autistic because you notice they:

◆   avoid eye contact
◆   engage in repetitive play
◆   use echolalia to communicate
◆   struggles with unexpected changes.

Although it is not your job to clinically diagnose children, you need to ensure they get the right support in a timely manner and to support the process if diagnosis becomes necessary. Currently, the above traits would be considered as "red flags" or warning signs of being autistic rather than as traits or indicators of difference. This is due to the exclusion of differences in child development:

1.   Developmentalism does not adequately account for neurodiversity.
2.   The health system still predominantly views developmental neurotypes through the pathology paradigm, focusing on the child's behaviours as symptoms or "warning signs" (although gradual changes are happening with this).
3.   The education system is reliant on the health system in a lot of ways to understand developmental neurotypes meaning the pathology paradigm gets translated to early childhood practice.

In contrast, neurodiversity-affirming advocates view developmental neurotypes as indicators of natural variations and human differences. This is not to say that autistic children will not encounter delays, difficulties, or challenges within their development, but the pathology paradigm does not capture the holistic experiences. To understand why autism is viewed so negatively in education, we must consider how it is currently understood and diagnosed in the health system, and then consider how this then translates into our child development knowledge.

UNDERSTANDING HEALTH PERSPECTIVES OF AUTISM

Diagnosing Autism

Most countries produce best practice guidelines for diagnosis of any kind, including developmental neurotypes such as autism. These guidelines outline the desired approach for consistent identification, assessment, diagnosis, and support within the health service. The National Institute for Health and Care Excellence (NICE) (2021) currently provides guidelines in the UK. While subtle changes can be seen across guidance around diagnoses, such as the increased use of word difference (as opposed to impairment) and identity-first language (autistic person as opposed to person with autism), information and advice related to autism remain very deficit-focused. As autism is a developmental neurotype, meaning it is present from birth and often first identified in early childhood, parents and carers will be subject to this deficit approach to autism early on. This can either be counteracted in the way we deliver early education or reinforced if we solely rely on health guidelines.

To receive a formal diagnosis, a child must meet specific criteria outlined in the Diagnostic and Statistical Manual of Mental Disorders (DSM-5), categorising their condition as autism spectrum disorder (ASD). The diagnostic process typically results in a report detailing the child's impairments, deficits, symptoms, and severity levels. Deficits must be found in:

1. persistent deficits in reciprocal social communication and social interaction;
2. restricted, repetitive patterns of behaviour, interests or activities;
3. symptoms must be present in the early developmental period;
4. symptoms cause clinically significant impairment in social, occupational, or other important areas of functioning;
5. these disturbances are not better explained by intellectual disability or global developmental delay.

The significance of autism is based on social communication differences and specific, repetitive patterns of behaviour. For either criterion, differences are described in three levels:

- ✦ Level 1 – requires support
- ✦ Level 2 – requires substantial support
- ✦ Level 3 – requires very substantial support.

Children or adults do not receive a levelled diagnosis; for example, you are not diagnosed as Level 2 ASD. Rather, the significance or severity is considered in persistent deficits in reciprocal social communication and social interaction and restricted, repetitive patterns of behaviour, interests, or activities.

Seeking a diagnosis can be crucial for parents and caregivers to understand their children's health and development, and any difficulties or challenges should not be ignored. However, the current diagnostic process is based on an outdated view of autism. It often focuses on deficits, failures, or how a child or adult deviates from being neurotypical, rather than capturing the full range of autistic experiences. If autism is understood this way in medical terms, these perceptions can also influence early education, leading to an outdated view of autistic child development. The same can be said for almost all other neurotypes and disabilities.

UNDERSTANDING AUTISM AS DEVELOPMENTAL DIVERSITY

KEY TERM

Developmental diversity approaches are the recognition that individual variations and differences in developmental neurotypes occur beyond biological underpinnings but are also influenced by other factors.

According to Jim Sinclair (1999), "Autism isn't something a person has, or a 'shell' that a person is trapped inside. There is no normal child hidden behind autism. Autism is a way of being. It is pervasive; it colours every experience; every sensation, thought, perception, emotion and encounters every aspect of existence" (p.1). If early educators apply neurodiversity-affirming practices to their understanding of child development, they can use a developmental diversity approach. Like neurodiversity, developmental diversity recognises that variations in development and functioning are natural and valuable parts of human diversity (Leadbitter et al., 2021). Specifically, developmental diversity views autism through a broader ecological lens, rather than just defining it biologically as brain and behaviour deficits. It also considers what is meaningful to the individual and how they interpret their differences (Hens and Goidsenhoven, 2023). If this approach were applied to health and education, our general understanding of developmental differences, neurodivergence, and disabilities could also be transformed. For example, compare the following deficit-definitions and descriptions versus neurodiversity-affirming definitions and descriptions. What differences do you notice between the two descriptions and why do you think these different ways of describing autism matter?

DEFINING AUTISM

Medicalised and diagnostic definition	Neurodiversity-affirming and neutral definition
Autism spectrum disorder (ASD) is a developmental disability caused by differences in the brain. It is characterised by	Autism is a lifelong neurodevelopmental difference and disability of the body and mind. It is characterised by differences,

impairment, deficit, symptom and severity (American Psychiatric Association. Diagnostic and statistical manual of mental disorders. 5th ed. Arlington, VA: American Psychiatric Association, 2013).	traits, symptoms and fluctuating capacities (Hammon, 2024).

CRITERION 1: PERSISTENT DEFICITS IN RECIPROCAL SOCIAL COMMUNICATION AND SOCIAL INTERACTION

Medicalised and diagnostic definition	Neurodiversity-affirming and neutral definition
Deficits in social-emotional reciprocity, ranging, for example, from **abnormal** social approach and **failure** of normal back-and-forth conversation; to reduced sharing of interests, emotions, or affect; to failure to initiate or respond to social interactions.	**Differences** in social-emotional reciprocity can include varied social and communication preferences, hyper- or hypo-empathy, alexithymia, and a monotropic communication style compared to a polytropic one. The double empathy problem may also be relevant (Milton et al., 2022).
Deficits in nonverbal communicative behaviours used for social interaction, ranging, for example, from **poorly integrated verbal** and **nonverbal** communication; to **abnormalities** in eye contact and body language or **deficits in understanding** and use of gestures; to a **total lack** of facial expressions and **nonverbal** communication.	**Differences** in communicative behaviours used for social interaction for example, different communication identities including sporadic or lowered eye contact, neutral expression, high/low intonation, vocal, and bodily stims and interoceptive differences.
Deficits in developing, maintaining, and understanding relationships, ranging, for example, from **difficulties adjusting behaviour** to suit various social contexts; to difficulties in sharing imaginative play or in making friends; to absence of interest in peers.	**Differences** in developing, maintaining, and understanding relationships can arise from various factors. These include finding certain social contexts incompatible with autistic traits, experiencing interoceptive and alexithymia differences, and exhibiting divergent play patterns such as solitary or schematic play. Preferences for friendships may differ, with

	some individuals favouring parallel experiences. Additionally, special interests, inertia, and monotropic thinking styles can influence social interactions.

CRITERION 2: RESTRICTED, REPETITIVE PATTERNS OF BEHAVIOUR, INTERESTS, OR ACTIVITIES

Medicalised and diagnostic definition	Neurodiversity-affirming and neutral definition
Stereotyped or repetitive **motor** movements, use of objects, or speech (e.g., simple motor stereotypes, lining up toys or flipping objects, echolalia, idiosyncratic phrases).	Self-regulatory or repetitive **motor** or oral movements, use of objects, or speech (e.g., simple motor stims, lining up toys or flipping objects, echolalia, idiosyncratic phrases).
Insistence on **sameness**, inflexible adherence to routines, or ritualised patterns of verbal or nonverbal behaviour (e.g., extreme distress at small changes, difficulties with transitions, rigid thinking patterns, greeting rituals, need to take same route or eat same food every day).	Preference on **sameness**, and persistent desire for routines, or ritual patterns of verbal speaking or nonverbal non speaking behaviour (e.g., highly dysregulated at small changes, inertia, specific thinking patterns, greeting rituals, need to take same route or eat same food every day).
Highly restricted, fixated **interests** that are abnormal in intensity or focus (e.g., strong attachment to or preoccupation with unusual objects, excessively circumscribed or perseverative interests).	Highly specific, passionate fixated interests that have monotropic intensity (e.g., strong attachment to or preoccupation with unusual objects).
Hyper- or hyporeactivity to sensory input or unusual **interest** in sensory aspects of the environment (e.g. apparent indifference to pain/temperature, adverse response to specific sounds or textures, excessive smelling or touching of objects, visual fascination with lights or movement).	Hyper- or hyporeactivity to sensory input or specific **interest** in sensory aspects of the environment (e.g. sensory integration differences, interoceptive, vestibular or proprioceptive differences).

NEURO-AFFIRMATIVE HEALTH ASSESSMENTS

The reality is that for education itself to shift in its understanding of neurodivergence and disability, the health services also need to make this shift given that diagnosis is still relevant. Hartman et al (2023) suggest that "exploration of identity" is a more appropriate way to describe the process of understanding autism in an individual because

> a core central component of the process relates to supporting a person to make sense of their inner experiences (i.e. to begin the process of discovering their true sense of identity) and to integrate a person's inner experience with how they relate to other and with the world.

> (p. 248)

In other words, diagnosis should help the child or adult understand themselves and thrive. It should not be about proving that they are broken, deficient, or lacking. The way a neurodivergent and/or disabled child is perceived in their earliest years can shape how they perceive themselves as an adult. If health services continue to treat individuals as if something is wrong with them, they may go through life believing they are flawed. Therefore, we must carefully consider how we describe and conceptualise autism and other neurotypes in early childhood, including in how we describe their early development.

NEUROINSIGHT

HOLISTIC DEVELOPMENT

As a nursery Special Educational Needs Coordinator (SENCO), I was eager to ensure children received support at the right time and to improve my colleagues' awareness of early signs and symptoms. I downloaded a set of "signs and symptoms" posters from an educational website and created a display so everyone, including parents, could become more aware of what to look out for.

Looking back, I realise this approach was problematic. For parents of children who had already been identified or diagnosed, it served as a reminder of what we considered problems or delays. For those just becoming aware that their child might be on a different developmental path, it could incite unnecessary fear about a potential diagnosis.

Now, I take a different approach. I share holistic descriptions of various neurotypes. This fosters more meaningful discussions about what it means to be autistic, have ADHD, a developmental language difference, or a disability.

Early Years Educator

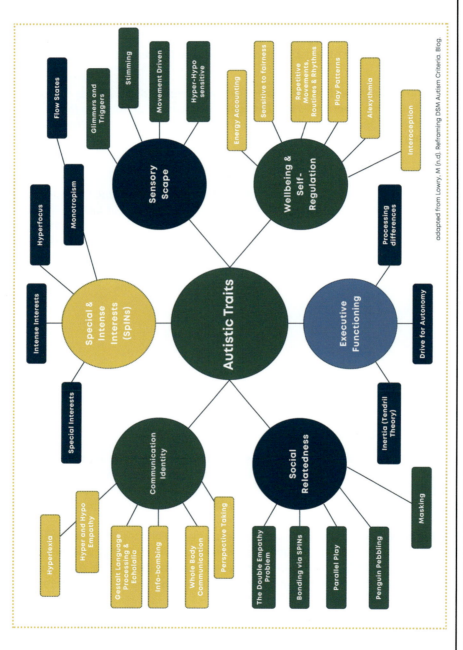

adapted from Lowry, M (n.d). Reframing DSM Autism Criteria. Blog.

FIGURE 3.3 AUTISTIC TRAITS AND NEEDS

UNDERSTANDING NEURODIVERSITY-AFFIRMING PERSPECTIVES OF AUTISM

Reimagining Autistic Child Development

When you read about or research most neurotypes, you will find that they are only described in deficit terms. The above neuro insight refers to a common practice where mind maps outline all the signs, symptoms, or difficulties of being neurodivergent. When early educators only have access to this information, it means they miss out on other valuable information about neurodivergence, which could equally support their practice and pedagogy. Take a look at the below Traits and Needs map for autism and consider:

- ✦ How many are familiar to you?
- ✦ Are there any traits and needs that you know less about?
- ✦ What impact do you think a focus on symptoms and deficits would have on your everyday early childhood practice?

NEUROINSIGHT

UNLEARNING

In my journey to understand neurodiversity, I've had to unlearn much of what I was previously taught, which has not always been comfortable. I was a strong advocate for school readiness, feeling that the children we sent to school should reflect well on my setting. I felt blamed if a child had developmental delays or behavioural issues. Coming to terms with my ego being so tied up in this process was challenging, and I'm still working through it.

What I've come to realise is that unreadiness can sometimes be a form of resistance to neuronormativity. Children may refuse to be rushed, especially in England, where formal schooling begins as early as four. I now recognise how detrimental this early pressure can be to human flourishing. Consequently, I've adjusted my transition reports. Instead of trying to meet the expectations of the next setting, I focus on fostering understanding and supporting each child at their own developmental stage.

Early Years Educator

PRESS PAUSE

1. How did you feel about the educators stating that school readiness felt like a reflection on the educator's abilities?
2. What do you think about unreadiness being a form of resistance against neuronormativity?
3. What do you think the implications are of rushing children through their childhood(s)?

NEURODIVERGENT TRAITS

Imagine if child development guidance drew upon neurodiversity-affirming research to further expand our understanding of developmental diversity. The autism traits and needs map likely includes things that you have not yet heard of in the context of early childhood yet could be instrumental in your support planning. Let's now explore a few traits and their implications for early childhood.

MONOTROPISM

Polytropic and Monotropic Processing

Nelly has a polytropic processing style, which means she can focus on several things or switch between tasks with relative ease. For example, if Nelly is playing and needs to wash her hands for snack time, she will be able to finish up her play and begin to process the next task of washing hands.

Ned has a monotropic processing style, which means he focuses quite intensely on a small number of interests or tasks, and may not notice things outside of his 'attention tunnel'. Ned may need more time to shift between tasks. For example, he may need further cues or reminders before snack time, or may need to hear things repeated.

FIGURE 3.4 MONOTROPISM VERSUS POLYTROPISM

Monotropism is a cognitive theory that describes how autistic and potentially other neurodivergent people focus their attention. It suggests that autistic individuals concentrate more energy and resources on fewer interests, tasks, or sensory inputs at a time than non-autistic people, who tend to spread their attention across multiple tasks, referred to as polytropic. Hartman et al. (2023) note that everyone has limited attention resources and uses different strategies to manage them so we should respect these differences. Monotropism has been used to explain the passions and intense interests that autistic people appear to develop. This theory, as described by Edgar (2023), highlights that when we embrace monotropism, we open up "possibilities for children who are monotropic to gain deep knowledge, new skills, and the engagement of flow states, which support sensory regulation and good mental health for monotropic people" (n.p.).

One of the key benefits of monotropism is that it does not pathologise autistic attention patterns or believe they need specific intervention. Instead, it encourages educators to develop practices that align with how autistic brains naturally work rather than trying to make autistic children more like their non-autistic peers.

NEUROMYTH: ATTENTION AUTISM (AA) SUPPORTS AUTISTIC ATTENTION

Attention Autism (AA), developed by Speech and Language Therapist Gina Davies, is an early intervention programme designed to help professionals and parents/caregivers support children in improving their engagement, attention, and communication skills. AA serves as both a framework and a set of skills for adults to foster better interactions with children. Through formal AA training, parents, caregivers, and professionals learn techniques to develop and share joint attention with children during sessions. The key to AA is creating sessions that offer an "irresistible invitation to learn" through novel experiences decided by the adult.

Attention Autism receives mixed responses from educators. While it can be a fun and engaging activity, children are not necessarily given a choice as to whether they want to engage or not, and they are not allowed to interact with the toys or resources to maintain the novelty, nor do they have a choice about what is included. Furthermore, the programme itself is based on typically developing attention patterns (polytropic), meaning that autistic children (usually monotropic) are expected to progress through stages where their attention can then be directed/re-directed by an adult, which could be argued as a form of compliance training.

Another issue with Attention Autism is that it has become the universal go-to for any child who is potentially autistic. Still, it only addresses one aspect of being autistic and, with ableist underpinnings, may not be the most appropriate choice for supporting attention. Early educators may be best finding alternatives that support monotropic "flow states".

Some settings have adapted aspects of Attention Autism by removing certain restrictions, such as enabling children to touch the items, and have used it as a shared sensory experience. For example, an Early Years Educator found that an autistic child who didn't enjoy direct sensory play benefited greatly from observing it. By focusing on visual sensory experiences, the child became deeply engaged and immersed. Similarly, another Early Years Educator used the bucket activity common in Attention Autism as a co-regulation activity where children could relax, enjoy the novelty items, and choose to attend to the experience in a way that suited them. Furthermore, they could play with the items, which only increased engagement and attention rather than reduced it.

Monotropism can be both beneficial and challenging. Monotropism generates intense energy towards a primary focus, often referred to as a "flow state", meaning that autistic children may show hyperfocus on a special interest, hobby, or deep knowledge. This can feel wonderful and joyful. On the flip side, it can be difficult to redirect attention when needed. Pulling away from a "flow state" can feel very difficult, even painful, and can lead to neglecting of other needs. For example, a child may be so immersed in play that they do not recognise hunger or the need to go to the toilet. Furthermore, they may find transitions difficult and need plenty of time to process and prepare for change.

PRACTICAL WAYS TO SUPPORT MONOTROPIC PROCESSING

Environment + Positive connections + Understanding + Time + Space = Happy Monotropic Flow States (Edgar, 2023).

Embrace passions, interests and fascinations. Although following children's interests is already a common feature of early childhood education, it can still be frowned upon when a child is neurodivergent, meaning they are more likely to be encouraged to move away from deep interests and passions to play more normally. Engaging in monotropic flow states can offer predictability and reassurance while cultivating skills and knowledge, so building on what is important to the child is important.

Embrace self-directed play in teaching and learning. According to Edgar (2023), children can become disengaged when they are pulled into adult-led tasks that seem dull, repetitive, or purposeless. By connecting activities to their interests and giving them more autonomy, children can become more self-directed, making their learning experiences more engaging and meaningful.

Slow transitions. Those with a monotropic processing style usually find it hard to switch tasks. Erin Human (2015) came up with Tendril theory, which explains that when a person is focused on something, their mind sends out a million tendrils of thought, expanding into all their thoughts and feelings. When it is time to switch tasks, Human explains that all those tendrils must be retracted, which can take time. Eventually, a person can shift to a new task. However, if the task switch is too abrupt, disruptive, or interruptive, it can feel like the tendrils are being ripped out, leading to an emotional or physical reaction.

This directly impacts the everyday transitions that a child encounters with a high demand to task switch multiple times. By taking a slow approach to transitions, those with a monotropic processing time can retract their tendrils to move between tasks, experiences, and activities with relative ease.

Minimise sensory noise. Many monotropic people experience the joys of entering a flow state, but reaching that point can be challenging. It can be disorienting to find an attention tunnel. Autistic inertia refers to the difficulty in starting or stopping a task, often because the conditions for being monotropic aren't quite right. For example, frequent interruptions or distractions can make it hard to enter a flow state. Similarly, unmet needs can leave a person feeling trapped between states. Ensuring that the environment is predictable, calm, and free of sensory noise can support the flow state.

NEUROMYTH: AUTISTIC CHILDREN HAVE NO OR LOW EMPATHY

Before discussing this myth, I will share an anecdote from my own autistic experience. As a child, I felt things very deeply and had heightened empathy. I could not cope with seeing pain or sadness in any other creature, human or animal. I remember distinctly, as a child, curling up into a ball of pain whenever I saw animal cruelty adverts on the television and launched a "Free the Donkeys" campaign because I was so upset that their fur was being caught on the fence wiring (it turns out they were well looked after donkeys). Empathy felt physically painful, but it also spurred me to action. My emotional responses, however, gained unwanted attention, and I remember being laughed at for getting so emotional or being told to calm down. As a young child, I learnt that it was considered abnormal to feel so deeply for other things, and so for many years, I masked this to the point where I was later accused of being unfeeling and cold. In fact, as an adult, I was often told I lacked empathy and must be "on the spectrum". It has taken me many years to recover and reconnect with my empathy and to see it as part of my autistic identity.

Many people mistakenly believe that autistic individuals lack empathy or have low empathy. To understand this misconception, it's important to distinguish between different types of empathy:

✦   cognitive empathy is the ability to understand another person's perspective and mental state;
✦   affective empathy is the emotional response to another person's experience;
✦   compassionate empathy drives one to help others in need.

(adapted from Henderson, Wayland, and White, 2023)

A lack of empathy is not a fixed trait in autism. While some may report lacking or having low empathy, others may have typical or heightened empathy. Heightened affective empathy has been reported in autistic people. This means they can feel things deeply when observing another person's emotions or experiences. This can extend to animals and even objects (object personification). However, this concern may not always be apparent in their behaviour, or an autistic person may have been told that feeling things so deeply is an unusual trait.

THE DOUBLE EMPATHY PROBLEM

The Double Empathy Problem (Milton, 2012 and 2014) challenges the outdated idea that autistic people lack empathy and theory of mind, which is the ability to understand and infer the thoughts, beliefs, intentions, and emotions of others. This long-held belief unfairly assumes that autistic people are deficient in empathy. In reality, autistic empathy and understanding of others vary based on numerous factors. The Double Empathy Problem suggests that social difficulties between autistic and non-autistic (allistic) people are a two-way issue. It highlights that empathy breakdowns can occur on both sides, creating an empathy gap. This reframes empathy issues as a matter of reciprocity, arising from the interactions and connections between people, rather than a deficiency solely within autistic individuals.

KEY TERMS

Reciprocity refers to the mutual exchange of actions, behaviours, or emotions, where one person's response is influenced by the other's actions, creating a balanced and responsive interaction. For example, if a person smiles or waves, that would invite a response to smile or wave back OR to respond with your own way of greeting someone.

Let us think about this from an early years perspective:

Nelly has a neurotypical communication style. Ned is atuistic and has a neurodivergent communication style. Sometimes, when Nelly and Ned play, they can experience some differences in how they interact.

I like to chat and I will give eye contact when I am speaking. I use my gestures to communicate and I like to talk about lots of different topics.

I repeat my favourite phrases and sounds. I prefer not to give eye contact, and I like to play alongside Nelly. I like playing with my diggers and that is mostly what I love to talk about.

Historically, it is Ned who would be perceived as having a deficit in his communication preferences, so Ned would have to work much harder to be understood. The Double Empathy problem (Milton et al., 2022) highlights that the problem doesn't lie with Ned. It is that both Nelly and Ned have different and equally valid communication preferences. They key to addressing The Double Empathy Problem is to support both children in understanding these differences.

Milton, D., Gurbuz, E., & López, B. (2022). The 'double empathy problem': Ten years on. Autism, 26(8), 1901-1903.

FIGURE 3.5 THE DOUBLE EMPATHY PROBLEM

PRACTICAL WAYS TO SUPPORT THE DOUBLE EMPATHY PROBLEM

Validate children's communication identities. Each person has a unique communication identity, reflecting their preferences for interacting and engaging with the world. Some children use spoken words, while others may prefer signs or visuals. Accents and body language will differ, and individuals may develop a unique vocabulary or favoured speaking methods. Communication styles vary: some speak quickly, others speak slowly; some use technology or objects of reference, others rely on expressive hand and arm movements. One of the great joys of communication is its vibrancy, variety, and dynamism, often requiring time to understand and connect with each other.

No single communication or interaction style should be promoted as the ideal communication method. All communication identities should be validated and supported to help each child engage with the world in a comfortable way.

Teach children about each other's communication identities. There is a tendency for autistic children's communication to be a target of intervention and correction so that they communicate in typical ways. This is an ineffective way to support a child. Instead, early educators should take time to teach all children about the richness of communication and the different ways children engage with the world around them. For example, "Mohammed you love to wave at your friends to say hello, but Harriett likes to give you a toy as way of saying hello. Isn't it amazing we can say hello to each other in different ways".

Ditch whole-body listening skills. While whole-body listening (such as sitting still, keeping "quiet hands", maintaining eye contact, raising hands, and not shouting out) is often seen as a practice that promotes good listening skills, it can be unhelpful for some children. There is a misconception that to demonstrate good listening, one must engage in specific visible actions. In reality, children listen and engage in various ways: some fidget, some look up or down, some remain still, and others need to move. Whole-body listening is not a true measure of listening ability but rather an indicator of compliance.

INTEROCEPTION

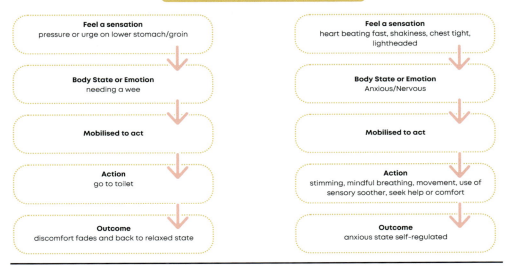

FIGURE 3.6 INTEROCEPTION

What does it mean when you feel butterflies or a grumble in your tummy? Interoception is the ability to notice a body signal or sensation and understand its meaning. By understanding the meaning, we can then choose an action to self-regulate. For instance, if you feel pressure in your tummy indicating the need to urinate, you would decide to go to the toilet. This sense develops over time and becomes intuitive as we become more in tune with our bodies.

However, due to general sensory differences, this intuition may develop differently in autistic children. Interoception involves recognising bodily urges like hunger or thirst and linking internal cues to emotions. For example, butterflies in the stomach might indicate needs or excitement, allowing us to respond appropriately.

Autistic children in your setting may have hyper- (over-responsive) or hypo- (under-responsive) interoception. For example, they may experience intense emotions and need more tailored co-regulation, or they may not recognise certain sensations and need scaffolded cues and reminders.

PRACTICAL WAYS TO SUPPORT INTEROCEPTION

Kelly Mahler suggests the following strategies for supporting interoception (n.d):
Interoceptive talk. One of the most significant things you can do to support growing awareness of interoception is to model interoceptive awareness. Making those connections between bodily sensations and feelings/behaviours can also help the child to make those connections. For example:

✦ "Oh my goodness, my hands feel so warm when you hold it."
✦ "Oh, my skin feels so comfortable when you're cuddling me."
✦ "My stomach is growling right now, whew, I must need some food."

Interoceptive Curiosity. You can also show curiosity about might be happening for a child. You may not always be accurate, but exploring options will lead you closer to understanding the child's internal experiences. For example:

✦ "Oh, I notice that you're crying, I wonder what's going on."
✦ "I wonder where you feel something in your body."
✦ "Do you feel something in your body?"

Interoception Validation. A child with interoceptive differences may sometimes feel out of sync with themselves and disorientated. By validating the child's experiences, it helps them to feel affirmed and understood. For example:

✦ "I hear you, it sounds like . . ."
✦ "How does this feel for you?"
✦ "Can you show me where?"
✦ "Let's figure this out together"

Adapted from: www.kelly-mahler.com/interoception-for-parents-and-caregivers/

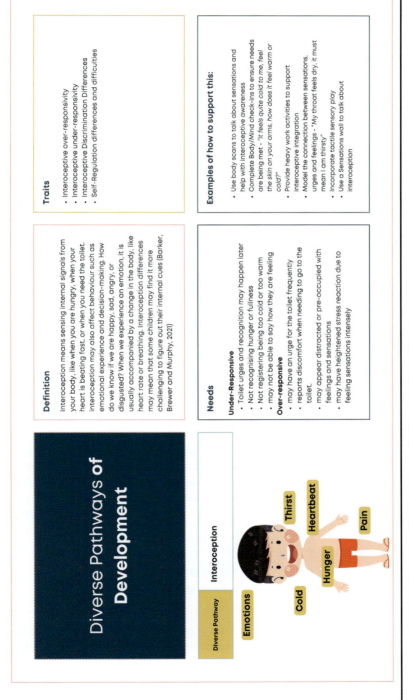

Diverse Pathways of Development

Diverse Pathway | Interoception

Emotions · Cold · Hunger · Thirst · Heartbeat · Pain

Definition

Interoception means sensing internal signals from your body, like when you are hungry, when your heart is beating fast, or when you need the toilet. Interoception may also affect behaviour such as emotional experience and decision-making. How do we know if we are happy, sad, angry, or disgusted? When we experience an emotion, it is usually accompanied by a change in the body, like heart rate or breathing. Interoception differences may mean that some children may find it more challenging to figure out their internal cues (Barker, Brewer and Murphy, 2021)

Traits

- Interoceptive over-responsivity
- Interoceptive under-responsivity
- Interoceptive Discrimination Differences
- Self-Regulation differences and difficulties

Needs

Under-Responsive
- Toilet urges and recognition may happen later
- Not recognising hunger or fullness
- Not registering being too cold or too warm
- may not be able to say how they are feeling

Over-responsive
- may have an urge for the toilet frequently
- reports discomfort when needing to go to the toilet.
- may appear distracted or pre-occupied with feelings and sensations
- may have heightened stress reaction due to feeling sensations intensely

Examples of how to support this:
- Use body scans to talk about sensations and help with interoceptive awareness
- Complete Body/Mind check-ins to ensure needs are being met – *"It feels quite cold to me, feel the skin on your arms, how does it feel warm or cold?"*
- Provide heavy work activities to support interoceptive integration
- Model the connection between sensations, urges and feelings - *"My throat feels dry, it must mean I am thirsty"*
- Incorporate tactile sensory play
- Use a Sensations wall to talk about interoception

FIGURE 3.7 DIVERSE PATHWAYS OF DEVELOPMENT FOR INTEROCEPTION

COMPANION RESOURCE

You can download the Diverse Pathways of Development tool on the companion website: https://www.canva.com/design/DAGMQmhzqF8/U3lcFCQldSY4nM4HLX6Hng/view?utm_content=DAGMQmhzqF8&utm_campaign=designshare&utm_medium=link&utm_source=editor

STIMMING

NEUROINSIGHT

STIMMING

I recently supported a practitioner who noted that her key child got great joy from hand flapping and would often do this as a form of expression. She had also read that engaging in self-stimulating behaviours was not socially acceptable, so perhaps she should discourage the child. We spoke at length about the importance of trusting her knowledge of the individual children, especially as the stimming had a clear function. We also unpicked how problematic the term "socially acceptable" can be when spoken about in the context of children who have developmental differences and disabilities. Social acceptance should not be about fitting in but existing within a society that accepts and adjusts to differences

Kerry Murphy
Author

Stimming, or self-stimulatory behaviour, is something every person engages in to some extent. For autistic and other neurodivergent individuals, however, it is often pathologised and seen as something that needs to be reduced or stopped. While it's true that stimming can sometimes result from dysregulation and may become self-injurious, this is only one aspect of stimming. Considering the broader context and understanding the full picture of stimming behaviours is important. Let's begin with a pathologised definition versus a neurodiversity-affirming definition:

PATHOLOGISED DEFINITION	NEURODIVERSITY-AFFIRMING DEFINITION
In the symptomatology of disorders, the practice of "odd, unusual, or repetitive behaviours" such as hand flapping and body rocking is referred to as stimming (Hammel and Hourigan 2013: 75).	In an alternate frame of reference grounded in neurodiversity, however, stimming is subject to a very different kind of interpretation. In this interpretation, such behaviours and expressions are embraced as meaningful, communicative,

Stimming is routinely cast as problematic, self-injurious, and targeted for reduction or elimination.	pleasurable, and even socially valuable for those who perform them – as manifestations of difference, not symptoms of deficit. Furthermore, everybody stims.

Examples of stims include

Tactile	Rubbing, feeling textures, fidgeting, stroking, petting, tapping
Vocal	Whistling, singing, humming, echolalia, throat clearing
Visual	Following moving objects, noticing colours, staring, gazing, being drawn to sensory items such as looking at lights
Cognitive	Singing in your head, scripting, daydreaming
Auditory	Listening over and over to certain sounds, music, enjoying clicking
Physical	Hand flapping, swaying, rocking, stepping on specific spots on the floor, knee bouncing, hanging upside down, swinging, spinning
Olfactory	Sniffing, putting nose to things, being comforted by certain smells

PRESS PAUSE
- ✦ Whether or not you are autistic, do you do any of the above stims?
- ✦ What are the range of reasons you might stim?

There are multiple reasons a child might stim, and your role as an Early Years Educator is to make sense of this through your observations and ongoing knowledge of the child's developmental profile. Some functions of stimming include (this is not an exhaustive list):

- ✦ Soothing
- ✦ Stimulating
- ✦ Expressing emotions
- ✦ Communicating
- ✦ Processing
- ✦ Indicating a need
- ✦ Socialising
- ✦ Self-regulating
- ✦ Co-regulating
- ✦ Play pattern

✦ Musicality
✦ Relief
✦ Joy or excitement
✦ Anxiety or nerves

PRACTICAL WAYS TO SUPPORT STIMMING

Embrace stimming as part of developmental diversity. Stimming is socially acceptable and forms part of children's development. When this is recognised, early educators
will show more curiosity about the stim rather than just trying to eliminate or reduce it.

Figure out the function. Through your observations and knowledge of the child, it is
important to identify the function where possible so you can understand this as part of
the child's holistic development.

Sensitively mirroring. Due to the recognition that stimming can also be communica-
tive, mirroring the stim can be a good way to connect with the child and have a shared
experience.

Provide stimming resources. Like any other interest, if a child shows a preference for
a particular way of stimming, think about how to support and develop it further. For
example, you may offer sensory items, visuals, space, or toys.

Identify if the child is stimming up or down. Due to the recognition that stimming can
be self-regulatory, it can be useful to consider whether stims will need regulating up
(doing more of it) and other stims might need regulating down (grounding).

Raise awareness. Stimming is a historically pathologised trait and it can be useful to
raise awareness to those who may see it as a concerning or unruly trait.

Safe stims should not be eliminated or stopped. Stimming is related to self-regulation, so stopping it also thwarts it.

Recognise stim strengths. Stimming can show some significant strengths in autistic
children's development. For example, a child who can spin on the spot for a prolonged
period may show strengths in their vestibular and proprioceptive sense.

GESTALT LANGUAGE PROCESSING

Gestalt Language Processing (GLP) is a form of language development that begins with
whole memorised phrases and gradually breaks down into single words. Typically, the basic
unit of language is a word. We build language by combining individual words to convey meaning. However, for Gestalt Language Processors, the basic unit is not a single word but a

"chunk" of language. For instance, a gestalt language processor might perceive the phrase "I'll be back" as a single unit rather than as separate words like "I", "will", "be", and "back". These chunks are known as gestalts or scripts. For those working in early childhood education, it is highly likely that you will encounter children who acquire language this way, and one of the earliest indicators is the use of delayed echolalia which refers to the repetition of words or phrases that are echoed after the fact. This could be minutes, hours, days, months, or weeks later. It is stage one of Gestalt Language Processing. The other stages are outlined below:

Stage One	Delayed Echolalia
Stage Two	Mitigation
Stage Three	Isolated single words
Stage Four	First sentences
Stage Five	Grammar
Adapted from: Leci, R and Kenway, S. 2023. *Gestalt Language Processing – An Introduction*. YouTube.	

According to Assistive Aware (Konyn, 2022) Gestalts are a valid part of language development. All children have some gestalts, even if they primarily begin speaking word-by-word. For example, most children (and adults) process "you're welcome" as a gestalt or script. They understand it as a single unit of meaning rather than thinking about the individual words "you", "are", and "welcome".

Understanding Gestalt Language Processing is important because historically, echolalia, has been pathologised and there has been suggestion that to repeat phrases or words holds no specific meaning. Yet Just Stimming aptly describes echolaia as "an unexpected treasure hunt. It is full of echoing, referencing, scripting, riffing, and rifting, storing and combining and recombining, patterning, quoting, punning, and swinging from hyperlexic memory to synesthetic connection. Words are my tangible playground" (n.p).

Research increasingly shows that all forms of language are valid and meaningful for children, even when their speech isn't literal. Recognising Gestalt Language Processing can involve noticing several key features:

✦ Gestalts are often tied to emotional experiences.
✦ They are linked to episodic memories and first impressions, shaped by holistic thinking.
✦ Gestalts can serve as a form of self-stimulation, such as through vocalisations or sounds.
✦ They may signal whether a child is feeling regulated or dysregulated.
✦ Gestalt language is rich in intonation, sometimes called "intonation babies".
✦ It can be either clear or unclear, like babbling or sing-song speech.

- ✦ It may be interactive or non-interactive, depending on the context.
- ✦ This approach highlights the many ways children communicate meaningfully, even when their language may seem unconventional.

PRACTICAL WAYS TO SUPPORT GESTALT LANGUAGE PROCESSING

Echolalia is still communication. Even if we don't understand a certain gestalt we should make an effort to acknowledge them with a friendly "yeah!" or repeat their phrase back to them. Gestalts are still meant to communicate wants, needs, opinions, questions, etc.

Don't take children's gestalts/scripts literally. Some gestalts might be quite confusing. It is often worth asking their family if they know where a certain gestalt came from and what they think it is meant to communicate.

Gestalts don't need to be corrected, ignored or stopped. In fact, young children need more gestalts. This is how young GLPs communicate. They need us to model more scripts they can use and eventually combine. If they only hear short one- and two-word phrases from adults, their communication skills won't progress.

Intonation really matters. GLP children are much more likely to pick up a gestalt if it has an intonation they find pleasing or interesting. Play around with trying different intonations as you like and see what clicks with the child.

Most importantly, don't worry and overthink it. Early Years Educators are already spinning dozens of plates day in and day out. For us to pick up and make use of new knowledge, it needs to be done over time, with support and proper training. We should always be reflective and open to changing the way we do things, but change in our practice or provision is best achieved at a sustainable pace. Don't feel like you need to be an instant expert or change your ways immediately.

Adapted from the blog: www.famly.co/blog/gestalt-language-processing-ecolalia-in-the-early-years

---

COMPANION RESOURCE

Embracing Echolalia and Gestalt Language Processing by David Cahn and Kerry Murphy (2023): https://www.famly.co/blog/gestalt-language-processing-ecolalia-in-the-early-years

MASKING

Another risk that we need to account for in our early childhood spaces is the development of masking in neurodivergent and disabled children. Masking is defined as: "the conscious or unconscious suppression of self and identity and the use of non-native cognitive in social strategies" (Pearson and Rose, 2023, p.3). In other words, it is performing traits and behaviours to fit in with social norms and expectations. For example, autistic children being taught that it is anti-social to not provide eye contact, and therefore forcing themselves to provide this in order to fit in. The environment may appear inclusive, but we also have to ask what is being required of children in meeting social rules and group "belonging". For many neurodivergent and disabled children, they are entering spaces that are incompatible with many of their ways of being, and so they need to adjust and adapt to those spaces which takes a huge amount of emotional, cognitive, and social labour. As an adult who masks a lot in social environments, I can say that it is one of the most frustrating and upsetting aspects of being neurodivergent. Throughout my childhood and upbringing, there were constant cues from people and spaces which told me "you do not fit in" and so I began to copy others around me. This impacted my relationships deeply, and I had a friend who would often complain that I would copy every aspect of her identity. I acutely recall trying to learn her behaviours and attitudes as I figured more people seemed to like her so that is what I must also be doing. When you think of your early childhood environment, a fundamental question you need to ask yourself is: how are you helping children to become who they are? While the research in this area is sparse in relation to young children, it is safe to assume that if our setting adopts a pathology framework where children are led to believe that they need to be fixed or corrected, they will begin to adapt their behaviours to suit the narratives of others. This is essential to their survival and wellbeing, and becomes a long-term coping mechanism seeing them through to adulthood. However, there are significant implications of masking over time, which impacts wellbeing and can lead to burnout, stress, and anxiety.

PLANTING SEEDS FOR NEURODIVERSITY

Take a more than one-way mentality. When thinking about what is typically expected, it is useful to ask yourself about the other ways in which the milestone or developmental steps can be achieved. For example, while some children may use mouth words to communicate, other children may have a different preference, such as signs, visuals or imitation. By taking a more than one-way mentality, you can think beyond narrow definitions of development.

Aiming for **meaningful milestones** rather than generalising all milestones to all children. Milestones often refer to typical points across development rather than neurodivergent and disabled development. When you reframe this, you can embrace children's developmental diversity.

Learn from **neurodiversity-affirming research** to develop an understanding of developmental diversity. In many cases, you will find alternative ways of framing historically pathologised neurotypes, for example, understanding monotropic attention versus polytropic attention.

More than one way mentality

Communicating	Mouth words & speech	Writing & Literacy	Sign language sign to speech	Stammer	Body language	Augmentatively i.e visuals
Paying attention	Stillness	Stimming	Montropically	Polytropically	Whole body listening	Reduced eye contact
Regulating	Resting	Calmy and compliant	Through movement	Stimming	Escaping retreating	Seeking
Playing	Solitary	Parallel	Pepetitive	Co-operatively & socially	Schematic	Via special interests
Moving	Co-ordinated and calmly	Embodied and using their whole bodies	With a movement aid or specialist equipment	Stimming	Quietly	Fidgeting, energetic or active

FIGURE 3.8 MORE THAN ONE MENTALITY

PARENT X CARER SOLIDARITY

While early educators refer to child development guidance, parents and carers also seek to understand their child's learning and development. They might turn to parenting books, seek advice from friends and family, or use social media, which has become a popular tool for sharing information.

Parents and caregivers also frequently encounter guidance that suggests there is a "right" or "ideal" way for children to develop, which can create added pressure. Many feel compelled to follow these ideals to avoid judgement of their parenting skills. For instance, I've worked with parents who want to "fix" their child's neurodivergence or change certain traits or behaviours. This is rarely because they are inadequate as parents or caregivers, but because they, too, are influenced by ableist messages. There is also the additional pressure that when a child does not conform to typical developmental norms, the quality of parenting can come under scrutiny, and there can be a lot of parental blame.

Assuming that all parents and caregivers want what's best for their children helps build a relationship based on mutual respect and collaboration. If a parent isn't ready to embrace developmental diversity because they want their child to fit in with conventional norms, it is important to adjust your approach. Work at a pace that suits them and be patient as they gradually understand and accept their child's unique developmental journey.

It is also important to recognise that when a parent expresses frustration or difficulty regarding their child's development, this is not necessarily a rejection of the child's neurodivergence or disability but speaks to the wider issue that parents and carers are not always equipped with the tools and information to do things differently.

Finally, it is important to think about how your setting's processes and procedures guide parents to take a celebratory approach to their child's development. So much of what is required is about measurement or monitoring of concerns. The general rule of thumb is that early educators should be strengths led, but you should also find ways to celebrate and acknowledge the diversity of development. For example, at age two years, children receive a progress check. If you read the guidance and approach to this check, you will know that it is important to identify any emerging concerns in early development but it should also be a time of celebration and acknowledgement of the child's developmental journey. You can look at a two-year-old celebratory check in the companion resources.

COMPANION RESOURCE

A celebratory check at age two: https://www.canva.com/design/DAGDOGAPo_k/ n2OOxxQsdUO-BfRTJdihmQ/view?utm_content=DAGDOGAPo_k&utm_campaign= designshare&utm_medium=link&utm_source=editor

TRANSLATING NEURODIVERSITY-AFFIRMING PRACTICE TO EDUCATION

In 2021, the early years sector saw the introduction of the Early Years Foundation Stage Framework reforms, which included updated non-statutory Development Matters (DfE, 2021).

This framework outlines developmental expectations from birth to age five. Some reasons for updating from the original Development Matters (DfE, 2012) were practical, such as creating a more accessible document to help educators focus more on interacting with children rather than sifting through complex documents to understand developmental milestones.

Another issue with the previous Development Matters was the emphasis on "ages and stages", which often resulted in a checklist approach. This led to multiple printed copies with highlighted developmental milestones, sometimes requiring a child to demonstrate a developmental statement at least three times in different contexts to be marked as achieved.

However, there is a consensus across the sector that rewriting Development Matters lacks ambition and diversity. Although intended to lay a strong foundation for a child's future, the document presents a narrow and reductionist view of child development. Ultimately, current child development documents focus on normalising and standardising children, guided by concepts from developmental psychology.

Recently, I spoke with a frustrated practitioner who had attended training from an autistic-led, neurodiversity-affirming organisation. She left the training in tears, feeling both anger and grief. For years, she had only heard autism described as a disorder, failure, disease, or diminished state. The tears reflected her sadness over how she had previously described and discussed children. They also signified relief, as she realised her new knowledge could benefit the children she supports. She viewed this training as an opportunity to reimagine her approach to child development.

The term "reimagination" resonated deeply with me. Often, we are taught to see socially constructed concepts as fixed and unchangeable. Yet, this practitioner began envisioning child development differently for her autistic children. We reviewed Development Matters and other child development documents together, noting our new perspectives outlined below.

Considered typical	Reimagined development	Non-pathologising explanation
By around 3 years old, the child should be able to shift from one task to another when their attention is directed by an adult. Using the child's name can help: "Jason, please stop now; we're tidying up."	By around 3 years, some children will shift from one task to another if you get their attention, for example, by calling their name. Other children may be more deeply immersed in a task and may need more time to shift from one task to another or may benefit from information about why the task shift is required.	Attention can be influenced by different cognitive experiences including: ✦ Understanding polytropic versus monotropic attentional tunnels (Duffus, 2023). ✦ Hyperfocus which refers to absorption in a task (Ashinoff and Abu-Akel, 2019). ✦ Desire for Autonomy to make own decisions about where to focus attention.

Start to develop conversation, often jumping from topic to topic.	Some children will start developing conversation, jumping from topic to topic, whereas others may have special or intense interests and can converse at length about a topic or interest.	✦ Understanding polytropic versus monotropic attentional tunnels (Duffus, 2023).
Develop pretend play: "putting the baby to sleep" or "driving the car to the shops".	Pretend play can be diverse, and different aspects may motivate children. For example, some children may like to role-play, such as "driving the car to the shops", whereas other children may like to set up play scenes, for example, setting up a doll house, but won't necessarily play dollies. They may copy actions or phrases they see and hear from their interests.	✦ Children may have different play patterns based on their neurotype (Conn, 2015). ✦ The child may use gestalts or scripts playfully rather than role playing conversation.
Start to say how they are feeling, using words as well as actions.	Children will begin to indicate their energy states and feelings through their preferred modes of communication. For example, words, actions, signs, and visuals. Some children will benefit from support to understand how bodily sensations relate to feelings.	✦ Children might have interoception differences meaning they need support to connect bodily sensations to feelings. ✦ Children might not have words for feelings and may express this in other forms of communications, such as pointing or using visuals.
By around 2 years old, is the child showing an interest in what other children are playing and sometimes joins in?	Depending on the child's neurotype will depend on their interest in others. Some children will show an interest in others play, others may prefer prolonged solitary play, or enjoy parallel play. Some children may prefer to play alongside adults for a longer period of time.	✦ Children may have different play patterns based on their neurotype (Conn, 2015).

We undertook this task to explore why policy-makers and early childhood specialists have struggled to create more inclusive definitions of learning and development. During our brief session, we focused on linking our observations to non-pathologising theories and explanations. This approach aimed to show that while practitioners may not need to know every aspect of diverse development immediately, they should be guided towards expanding their understanding and perspectives.

The reality is that research on neurodivergence and disability has often focused on identifying deficits and deficiencies, reinforcing a limiting view. This perspective can hinder our efforts to create truly inclusive practices that are developmentally meaningful for children. While this may seem discouraging, it is an opportunity for change. We stand on the brink of building something new. There is freedom in reimagining child development without diluting or narrowing it. It's time to embrace the idea that child development is chaotic, messy, complex, and wonderfully diverse.

CONCLUSION

In all the training I have done in recent years, the thing that always stands out is when I talk about the fact that not every child is travelling down the same developmental pathway. Once the words are uttered, it seems to break the spell. It is not something we didn't already know, but the lack of developmental diversity within our curriculums, frameworks, and guidance documents can lull us into believing there is only one pathway to follow.

This chapter has sought to challenge the notion of a one-size-fits-all approach to development by highlighting the richness of a specific developmental neurotype – autism. Acknowledging that differences and variations are a natural part of human growth opens up more opportunities to integrate these insights into our everyday practices and teaching methods. Embracing developmental diversity can enrich our work and enhance our understanding of how individuals grow and learn.

While this chapter has focused on autism, it hopefully serves as a springboard for thinking about other neurotypes and disabilities and other intersectional characteristics. Expanding developmental diversity within early childhood education would make our roles more rewarding, challenging, and dynamic.

ACTIVITY - CHAPTER KEEPSAKES

Across this first chapter, think about what your keepsakes are, and note down the following:

- ✦ One thing you will start doing
- ✦ One thing you still stop doing
- ✦ One keepsake you will share with others
- ✦ One thinking knot that requires further exploration.

ENDING POINTS

Throughout your training and qualifications, you've likely focused on typically developing children, using them as a benchmark for measuring all children's progress, including those who are neurodivergent or disabled. Child development documents often guide you to spot deviations from the norm with terms like "red flags", "alarm bells", or "checkpoints", leading to early intervention. While it's crucial to address developmental concerns, not all differences are delays – some are lifelong variations. The starting points task was an opportunity for you to think about your knowledge of milestones in autistic child development. Having read this chapter, have another go at this task, this time focusing on the autistic child.

Think about the possible milestones or developmental expectations you might have of an autistic child of pre-school age (3-4 years) who is using delayed echolalia.

Now reflect on the following:

✦ Having read this chapter, did you find it easier to note down milestones for the autistic child?
✦ What would you consider the implications of understanding diverse child development?

BIBLIOGRAPHY

Bakan, M.B. 2014. The musicality of stimming: Promoting neurodiversity in the ethnomusicology of autism. *MUSICultures*, 41(2).

Broughton, A. 2022. Black skin, White theorists: Remembering hidden Black early childhood scholars. *Contemporary Issues in Early Childhood*, 23(1), 16-31. https://doi.org/10.1177/1463949120958101.

Campbell-Stephens, R. n.d. Keynotes on the Global Majority Mindset. [Online] https://rosemarycampbellstephens.com/service-post/keynotes-on-the-global-majority-mindset/.

Cushing, I. 2023. Word rich or word poor? Deficit discourses, raciolinguistic ideologies and the resurgence of the "word gap" in England's education policy, *Critical Inquiry in Language Studies*, 20(4), 305-331. doi:10.1080/15427587.2022.2102014.

Duffus, R. 2023. *Autism, Identity and Me: A Professional and Parent Guide to Support a Positive Understanding of Autistic Identity*. Routledge.

Edgar, E. 2023. Embracing Autistic Children's Monotropic Flow States. ND Connection. https://ndconnection.co.uk/blog/embracing-autistic-childrens-monotropic-flow-states.

Gabriel, N. 2021. Beyond "developmentalism": A relational and embodied approach to young children's development. *Children & Society*, 35(1), 48-61.

Hammond, E. 2024. *S3 E29: The NeuroWild Shift for Neurodivergent Kids at School*. [podcast] NeuroWild. www.buzzsprout.com/1890886/14.

Hartman, D., O'Donnell-Killen, T., Doyle, J.K., Kavanagh, M., Day, A., and Azevedo, J. 2023. *The Adult Autism Assessment Handbook: A Neurodiversity Affirmative Approach*. Jessica Kingsley Publishers.

Hammel, A.M. and Hourigan, R.M. 2013. *Teaching Music to Students with Autism*. Oxford University Press.

Henderson, D., Wayland, S., and White, J. 2023. *Is this Autism? A Guide for Clinicians and Everyone Else*. Taylor & Francis

Hens, K. and Van Goidsenhoven, L. 2023. Developmental diversity: Putting the development back into research about developmental conditions. *Frontiers in Psychiatry*, 13, 986732.

Human, E. 2015. Tendril Theory. E is for Erin. [Online] https://eisforerin.com/2015/08/10/tendril-theory/.

Konyn, M. 2022. Gestalt language processing and AAC: Gestalts are a valid part of language. AssistiveWare. [Online] www.assistiveware.com/blog/gestalt-language-processing-aac.

Leadbitter, K., Buckle, K.L., Ellis, C., and Dekker, M. 2021. Autistic self-advocacy and the neurodiversity movement: Implications for autism early intervention research and practice. *Frontiers in Psychology*, 12. https://doi.org/10.3389/fpsyg.2021.635690.

Milton, D.E. 2012. On the ontological status of Autism: The "Double Empathy Problem". *Disability &* Society, 27(6), 883-887. doi:10.1080/09687599.2012.710008.

Milton, D.E. 2014. Autistic expertise: A critical reflection on the production of knowledge in Autism Studies. *Autism 18*(7), 794-802. doi:10.1177/1362361314525281.

Milton, D., Gurbuz, E., and López, B. 2022. The "double empathy problem": Ten years on. *Autism*, 26(8), 1901-1903.

Nair, V. and Farah, W. 2024. Beginner's guide to linguistic justice. Tapestry. [Online] https://tapestry.info/beginners-guide-linguistic-justice/.

Pearson, A. and Rose, K. 2023. *Autistic Masking: Understanding Identity Management and the Role of Stigma*. Pavilion Publishing and Media Ltd.

Sinclair, J. 1999. *Don't Mourn for Us*. Autistic Rights Movement UK.

Souto-Manning, M. and Rabadi-Raol, A. 2018. (Re)Centering quality in early childhood education: Toward intersectional justice for minoritized children. *Review of Research in Education*, 42(1), 203–225. https://doi.org/10.3102/0091732X18759550.

Reference websites

https://issuu.com/playwales/docs/playwork_guides_-_volume_1/20

https://juststimming.wordpress.com/

https://ndconnection.co.uk/blog/embracing-autistic-childrens-monotropic-flow-states

https://tapestry.info/wp-content/uploads/2024/07/A-Beginners-Guide-to-Linguistic-Justice-in-Settings-and-Schools.pdf

www.assistiveware.com/blog/gestalt-language-processing-aac

www.famly.co/blog/gestalt-language-processing-ecolalia-in-the-early-years

www.kelly-mahler.com/interoception-for-parents-and-caregivers/

CHAPTER 4

THE ROLE OF SELF-DIRECTED PLAY IN NEURODIVERSITY-AFFIRMING PRACTICE

STARTING POINTS

Take a look at the below terms:

Play-based	Child-led Play	Guided Play	Controlled Playfulness
Self-directed Play	True Play	Play-Rich	Play-based Intervention
Functional Play	Purposeful Play	Appropriate Play	Play Patterns
Free Play	Goal-oriented Play	Play	

✦ How many of these play terms are you familiar with?
✦ Which terms most closely align with your everyday practice?
✦ Would you feel confident in defining these terms?
✦ Do you find any of the terms problematic? And why?

At the end of this chapter, you can explore some of the suggested definitions for the play terminologies.

Play is an expansive, enigmatic, and all-consuming aspect of human life, especially for children. In our efforts to understand it, play has often been deconstructed, reduced, and reshaped to fit specific agendas. For example, in early childhood education, we frequently view play as a means for learning or as a tool for developing skills and knowledge in preparation for formal education. It feels inconceivable to admit that sometimes play is utterly pointless yet still joyful, or that play is as much about processing displeasure as it is

DOI: 10.4324/9781003323211-6

pleasure. While the terminologies mentioned above aim to clarify the purpose and benefits of play, attempts to structure and define it have also resulted in a sanitised approach to play, and one which is driven by adult-agendas rather than children's intrinsic motivations. To understand these motivations, it is necessary to explore play that is self-directed and owned by the player. We will think more generally about play and then specifically about play in neurodivergent and disabled children.

INTRODUCTION

Play has become something that we all seem to be trying to catch and yet play cannot be caught. A fundamental aspect of play is that it is by its very nature about freedom and autonomy. Getting to choose how you play, who you play with and deciding for yourself its purpose, or pointlessness, is what makes it so necessary to human existence. For example, sometimes play is learning and sometimes play is lazy. Imagine a child lying down, staring at the sky and tracing her fingers around the shapes of clouds. Yes, she may be learning about shapes, or realising there are different types of clouds. Or she could simply be whiling away the time after a long day. Her tracing of the clouds is soothing and entertaining.

Play is also a form of resistance. There is no greater joy than seeing the rebellion of a child who through their refusal to conform to social norms actually shows us that the world does not always have to be approached logically, or functionally, and that sometimes the best things are gained by doing things in novel, messy, and nonsensical ways. Imagine the child who cares little for the function of Lego bricks and prefers pressing the fatty bits of their fingers onto the grooves to create circular imprints. Rather than counting the numbers by attaching the bricks, the child may develop number sense in running their fingers over each fatty groove. Or the child who has no interest in playing "calmly" but who wants to immerse themselves in their play from head to toe to get as many sensory delights as

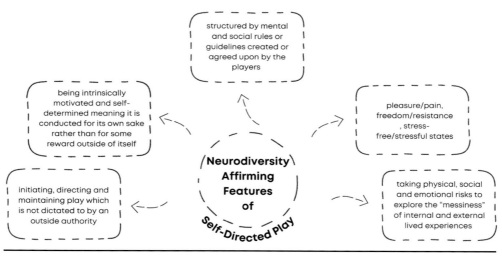

FIGURE 4.1 NEURODIVERSITY-AFFIRMING FEATURES OF SELF-DIRECTED PLAY

possible. When children have the choice to self-direct their play, it gives us the opportunity to see that play cannot be neatly packaged or defined but is infinite in its possibilities. To embrace this, it is important to understand the definition of self-directed play.

KEY TERM

Self-directed play is characterised by a number of features and may or may not result in learning or an outcome. Self-directed play serves many functions, including learning, developmental gains, rest, processing, self-regulation, seeking, and avoiding (not exhaustive).

Self-directed play is the experience of:

1. initiating, directing, and maintaining play which is not dictated to by an outside authority
2. being intrinsically motivated and self-determined, meaning it is conducted for its own sake rather than for some reward outside of itself
3. structured by mental and social rules or guidelines created or agreed upon by the players
4. pleasure/pain, freedom/resistance, stress-free/stressful states
5. taking physical, social, and emotional risks to explore the "messiness" of internal and external lived experiences

(adapted from Gray, 2013 and Trammell, 2023)

When early educators discuss, define, and describe play, there can be a tendency to think we need to have it all figured out. Afterall, play is constantly trivialised and undermined meaning much of our time is spent defending the affordance of play. To admit that we sometimes have no idea why children play the way they do is quite a vulnerable thing

Pardoxical   **amphibolous**   **rhizomatic**

FIGURE 4.2 DESCRIBING PLAY

to do. And yet, play researchers consistently recognise that play is intentionally ambiguous (Trawick-Smith, 2019). It has also been described as **paradoxical** in that it is and is not what it appears to be (Bateson, 1956). For example, think of the child who playfights yet means no harm to their playful opponent. Similarly, Spariosu (1989) refers to play as **amphibolous,** meaning play can have two meanings simultaneously. For example, play can be pleasurable and frustrating at once. Think of the child trying to find the right balance for their wooden blocks, deeply concentrated and immersed but with flashes of anger as the tower topples repeatedly. Deleuzian concepts are also used to describe play. Deleuze and Guattari (1987, as cited in Lester 2011) refer to the term **"rhizomatic thinking"**, which, translated to play, relates to playing having no beginning or end, just a "middle of things" with unlimited possible pathways. Play is mysterious.

This is especially true of self-directed play because we do not sit in the minds and bodies of our children, meaning their play-full motivations and determinations are not always immediately obvious. Additionally, we exist within a world where the adults' interpretation of play takes priority over children's sense-making. This usually leads to the adult getting to decide whether something is deemed as play or not. A child repeatedly kicking the side of some furniture may be, to us, misbehaviour, but to the child could be play for a whole heap of reasons. Simply, it is fun to kick stuff or they could be enjoying the sensory feedback in their legs (think of proprioception), or the repetitive action is assisting them in a daydream or helping them to process words they might want to utter later on.

The sanitisation of play has also led to the belief that there is a *right way to play*, meaning that children who are developing differently, or grappling with complex lived experiences have their play pathologised or stigmatised. Play researchers and advocates have shone a spotlight on play being pleasurable, stress-free, and the belief that play is an inherently positive act. However, this seems like a very one-sided description that does not account for the fact that play can also be harmful. For example, play can, at times, be harmful to others while still being play. Ultimately, if the child defines it as such, we can validate the play while recognising that the child may need support to understand the impact of their play on others. Think of the child who is getting clear enjoyment from teasing another child, and when asked to play nicely they respond with: "I was just playing". We can acknowledge it as play and also know that it is not okay to tease others. Similarly, play can be a stressful pursuit. Think of the frustration that can emerge when losing at a game, or the role play scenarios that help a child to process a real-world event such as being rejected by friends.

All this highlights that play is one of the messiest pursuits of childhood. Applying specific conditions, terminologies, or expectations can obscure its deeper complexities. This chapter will dive into this messiness by exploring self-directed play in neurodivergent and disabled children while considering the problems of play-based and adult-led intervention.

PLAY AND NEURODIVERSITY

There is a long-held belief that play does not come naturally to children with developmental differences and disabilities and that these children need to be taught how to play appropriately. However, growing evidence suggests that play is intrinsic to all children (see Pritchard-Rowe et al., 2023 and Harris, 2022), and it is up to educators to develop

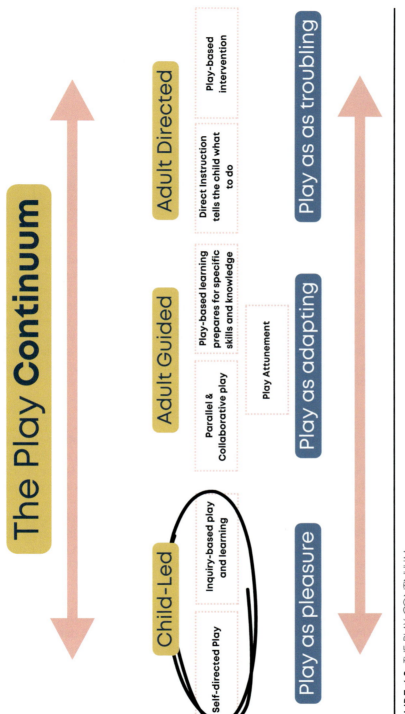

FIGURE 4.3 THE PLAY CONTINUUM

their understanding of the diversity and patterns of play – also referred to as play cultures. Historically, play in typically developing and non-disabled children has been prioritised and from this emerges typical definitions and descriptions of play that often exclude children who play differently (Goodley and Runswick-Cole, 2010). This exclusion results in the view that play needs to be deemed appropriate, functional, or purposeful to have value. However, embracing the messiness and ambiguity can be the gateway for inclusive experiences of play.

KEY TERM

Infinite refers to the limitless or endless in space, extent, or size; impossible to measure or calculate.

Messiness in play can also be translated in another way to mean infinite. If play has no beginnings or end, it also means that play has lots of possibilities, and this aligns well with the concept of neurodiversity. As educators, if we are open to the infinite possibilities of *all* children's play, we can honour and affirm the diversity of play rather than uphold the idea that there is a right way to play. For some, the idea that play cannot be reduced to a neatly packaged definition could be quite disorientating, but it could also be freeing. In previous chapters, you have begun to grapple with ableism and neuronormativity and both of these concepts extends to the way we perceive children's play. Let's think about this through the following provocations:

Provocation one: Hattie is typically developing. Her key person has noticed she loves to line things up. Her key person says this is one of her play schemas and intends to plan some activities and experiences to support and extend upon this. Her key person recognises that this is developmentally meaningful to Hattie, and she is keen to ensure this interest in lining things up is planned for.
Provocation two: The key person is also supporting Jamel. Jamel is autistic. He is obsessed with lining things up and shows a strong preference for repetition in his play. His key person says that it must be a symptom of his autism and when reading about autism, she has decided to use the advice to try and reduce and redirect this obsession.

When you read the two case studies, you might notice that Hattie who is typically developing is afforded a much greater understanding of her interest in lining things up. The key person is enthusiastic about this valuable play pattern, yet when it comes to Jamel who is autistic, his lining up is perceived differently. Just knowing that he is autistic shifts the perception of his play as problematic and in need of fixing or correcting. This is understood to be the pathologisation of play whereby children who engage in play that is associated with the traits of their neurotype become overlooked or misunderstood. There is so much unknown about the diversity of play because it has never received adequate attention in research which can then make it difficult to support it in practice. As educators, we are now presented with an opportunity to give life to all types of play in order to better understand and affirm it (Trammell, 2023). One of the best ways to do this is to enable time for children to engage in self-directed play where they can pursue their intrinsic motivations.

The Pathology Paradigm and Play

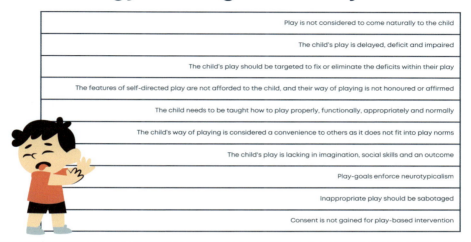

Play is not considered to come naturally to the child
The child's play is delayed, deficit and impaired
The child's play should be targeted to fix or eliminate the deficits within their play
The features of self-directed play are not afforded to the child, and their way of playing is not honoured or affirmed
The child needs to be taught how to play properly, functionally, appropriately and normally
The child's way of playing is considered a convenience to others as it does not fit into play norms
The child's play is lacking in imagination, social skills and an outcome
Play-goals enforce neurotypicalism
Inappropriate play should be sabotaged
Consent is not gained for play-based intervention

FIGURE 4.4 THE PATHOLOGY PARADIGM AND PLAY

The Neurodiversity Paradigm and Play

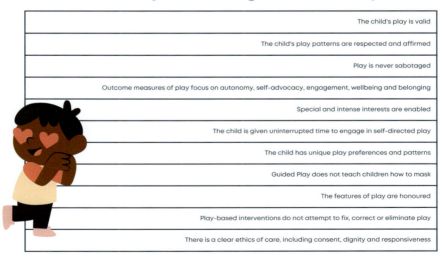

The child's play is valid
The child's play patterns are respected and affirmed
Play is never sabotaged
Outcome measures of play focus on autonomy, self-advocacy, engagement, wellbeing and belonging
Special and intense interests are enabled
The child is given uninterrupted time to engage in self-directed play
The child has unique play preferences and patterns
Guided Play does not teach children how to mask
The features of play are honoured
Play-based interventions do not attempt to fix, correct or eliminate play
There is a clear ethics of care, including consent, dignity and responsiveness

FIGURE 4.5 THE NEURODIVERSITY PARADIGM AND PLAY

FEATURES OF NEURODIVERSITY-AFFIRMATIVE SELF-DIRECTED PLAY

While previous descriptions of self-directed play lend themselves well to neurodivergence, the below features take into specific account ways of playing that include neurodivergent traits.

INITIATING, DIRECTING, AND MAINTAINING PLAY WHICH IS NOT DICTATED TO BY AN OUTSIDE AUTHORITY

Self-directed play is initiated and guided by the child, who decides how to proceed and when to stop. When an adult directs, demands, or instructs a child to play in a certain way, it ceases to be self-directed play. Educators or peers may influence, interact, or "meddle in the middle" (Fisher, 2016), but autonomy and choice are crucial to self-directed play. If you dictate what, how, and where the child should play, it is no longer self-directed.

For example, Rob makes his way over to the shoe storage and begins to take out each shoe, throws it and screams in delight.

NEURODIVERSITY-AFFIRMING ELEMENT

According to Naomi Fisher (2023), a significant benefit of self-directed play is its natural alignment with a diversity perspective. When children are encouraged and enabled to follow their own interests and curiosities, there is less competition and comparison among peers. Furthermore, it enables the adults in a child's life to meet them where they are at and is less focused on children falling behind. Instead, children's unique play patterns are understood in context as to what is meaningful to them. Advocating for self-directed play is also a clear resistance against standardisation and one-size-fits-all educational approaches.

KEY TERM

Self-determination is the process by which a person controls their own life, making choices and decisions based on their own preferences and interests.

BEING INTRINSICALLY MOTIVATED AND SELF-DETERMINED, MEANING IT IS CONDUCTED FOR ITS OWN SAKE RATHER THAN FOR SOME REWARD OUTSIDE OF ITSELF

Self-directed play is an intrinsically motivated and self-determined pursuit, prioritising the experience rather than seeking the shortest path or quickest outcome (Gray, 2013).

Trawick-Smith (2019) further emphasises the importance of immersing oneself in the play experience without external stressors or interruption.

For example, a child is fully immersed in outdoor play, and concentrating on a task. The key person suggests that her snack be made available a little later on while she is still playing but to let the key person know if she is hungry.

NEURODIVERSITY-AFFIRMING ELEMENT

Think of the child who is immersed in play or engaged in an activity that appears entirely process driven, such as painting or spinning. This experience is often referred to as a "flow state", a term coined by Mihaly Csikszentmihalyi to describe "the experience of complete absorption in the present moment" (Nakamura and Csikszentmihalyi, 2009). Csikszentmihalyi argued that these moments of complete absorption were akin to self-actualisation where one feels fulfilled by the realisation of their potential. It is a time and space in which there is no pressure to perform, rather it is the affordance being lost in the process.

From a neurodivergent perspective, flow also provides some insights into how we can support children who have special or intense interests, or are often seeking sensory highs and repetitive patterns of play. According to Edgar (2023),

> for many autistic people, their "special" or "strong" interests create flow states; this may be due to their interests being a source of safety, reliability, and predictability, which are all key factors to consider when reducing anxiety. Instead of learning being an effort, if you are in a flow state, it may feel like a joyful, fluid, meaningful, rejuvenating experience.
>
> *(n.p.)*

Entering a flow state is often driven by intrinsic rather than extrinsic motivation, and enables children to "wallow" in their play (Bruce, 1991). This in turn can have benefits to their creativity, involvement, concentration, energy levels, and persistence.

In autism studies, there is a growing body of research on monotropism. It proposes that some neurodivergent people tend to direct their attention towards specific interests and can, therefore, find themselves in a monotropic tunnel or state of "flow" (Murray, Lesser, and Lawson, 2005). Play and monotropism has not been extensively studied in early childhood, but it could be argued that self-directed play is compatible with monotropism and may offer insights into the importance of uninterrupted time spent engaging in interests

STRUCTURED BY MENTAL AND SOCIAL RULES OR GUIDELINES CREATED OR AGREED UPON BY THE PLAYERS

Gray (2013) highlights that although play is a voluntary choice, it has structure and rules, but these are often determined by the player. This feature of play may be misunderstood by educators who do not comprehend the self-directed rules created by the child.

NEURODIVERSITY-AFFIRMING ELEMENT

When adults think of rules, they may think of social or behavioural rules, but in play it spans much further than this, and refers to the internal mental rules that are part of a child's thinking process. For example, if you think back to the case study about Hattie and Jamel, Jamel liked to line things up and that was perceived as pointless or symptomatic of being autistic. However, if you were to think about the number of mental rules that could be at play when lining things up, including presenting, ordering, matching, sizing, counting, marshalling, parking, assembling, positioning, displaying, forming, ranging, arraying, controlling, commanding, visualising, grouping, sizing, precisions, aesthetics, making sense of things . . . the list could be endless.

Similarly, there are a number of neurotypes that are described as rigid, repetitive, or restrictive. For example, demand-avoidant children are sometimes accused of being rigid in their play, but there may be an argument that the so-called rigidity may indicate a structure or mental rule. For example, the rules of repeating actions or patterns. Similarly, we may find children who try to create new rules, for example going up rather than down a slide.

PLEASURE/PAIN, FREEDOM/RESISTANCE, STRESS-FREE/STRESSFUL STATES

Play is personal and will elicit a range of emotions and internal affective states (Murphy, 2022). Play is a way to process lots of different lived experiences, ideas, feelings, and emotions meaning that a child may use play as a means of making sense of the world. They may act out experiences in their play, or grapples with complex ideas. Furthermore, play can activate out stress systems making us determined or frustrated during the pursuit of play. Finally, play is not linear or compliant, and children will often use play to resist normative expectations.

For example, a child may make their toy figures fight because the child needs to express their anger in a safe way.

Play is also a process by which the chid can express their freedom and begin to establish their own boundaries.

For example, a child may enjoy the freedom of running off when being told to stay in a particular area. They are enjoying both the freedom and the autonomy to resist the rules

NEURODIVERSITY-AFFIRMING ELEMENT

Play cannot be narrowed down to one emotional state because it is much more complex and is critical to self-regulation and processing. The reason play is used therapeutically is because it offers the opportunity to support in healing which means figuring out more complex emotions, thoughts, and feelings.

Play therapists describe play as the child's "language" for understanding the world around them (Koukkourikos et al., 2021). We must therefore acknowledge that sometimes their play will be reflective of complex lived experiences. Simply stopping or re-directing play that feels uncomfortable also limits opportunities to understand it.

TAKING PHYSICAL, SOCIAL AND EMOTIONAL RISKS TO EXPLORE THE "MESSINESS" OF INTERNAL AND EXTERNAL LIVED EXPERIENCES

Play can naturally involve risks because it often steps outside social norms or reflects a child challenging expectations. For example, imagine a boy wearing a dress and role-playing outside his stereotyped gender role. This type of play carries emotional risks as it might lead to discouragement, teasing, or concern from others. However, we must create spaces in which children can play in ways that break normative trends and expectations and enable safe risks so that the child can benefit from the developmental gains.

NEURODIVERSITY-AFFIRMING ELEMENT

Neurodivergent play is often very self-determined in that the child will seek to play in ways that suit them regardless of the consequences.

WHAT IF SELF-DIRECTED PLAY IS NOT SUFFICIENT?

Educators may feel anxious about offering more uninterrupted and self-directed play to neurodivergent and disabled children, fearing it may seem neglectful. There are lots of pressures to be constantly interacting, teaching and intervening meaning we sometimes override our instincts about what is best for the child in the moment. However, it's important to remember that providing a broad range of play experiences is key. This includes playful moments, play-based activities, and some adult-directed activities. It's not about eliminating different types of play (refer back to the play continuum) but rather rethinking how we view play in neurodivergent children and ensuring a balanced variety of experiences.

There can be a tendency to think that we need to lead with one type of play. That can be unhelpful because it assumes that all children need the same things, which can differ from child to child and setting to setting. Instead of offering a dominant form of play, it is more beneficial to shift through different modes of play based on the context, needs, and motivations of the child. For example, one child in your setting might prefer solitary and repetitive play, engaging in it for sustained periods and resisting adult interference. This is child-led play and the child's engagement indicates that it is stimulating for them. Another child might enjoy the company of others but lack the confidence to suggest ways to play. In this case, an adult or peer can scaffold their play by providing gentle guidance and encouragement.

WHAT IF THE PLAY DOES NOT MAKE SENSE TO ME?

There are number of things you can do if the play does not yet make sense to you. You can access examples of each of the below tools at www.eyfs4me.com.

Play Dictionary	A Play Dictionary can be used to observe and make sense of patterns in play. It enables you to figure out the context of a play pattern over time.
Play Mapping	Play Mapping can be used when you want to map where and how a child plays so that you can identify key patterns.
Digital storytelling	Following a child's play journey through digital storytelling can be an amazing way to gain insights into a child's play over time, and to draw upon different sources to make sense of it. For example, through videos, photographs or soundbites.
Joint observation	We each come with different perspectives and experiences so drawing upon other observers can help you to build a clearer picture of what is happening.
Discovering diverse pathways of development	When we see play that does not neatly align with developmental expectations, we can have a tendency to consider it delayed, or problematic. Draw upon neurodiversity-affirming research so that you can expand your understanding of development diversity and play cultures. Remember, not all children have to be travelling down the same developmental pathway.

ACTIVITY - IS IT SELF-DIRECTED PLAY?

I frequently turn to social media for insights and discussions on various early childhood topics, especially related to inclusion. There's a vibrant community of educators who share ideas, thoughts, and engage in debates. When facing challenging reflections, I reach out online to seek others' views. This helps me broaden my perspectives and think beyond my own limitations. Recently, I asked the community about their experiences with child-led play in their settings and how it translates into practice. The responses varied, and one significant theme emerged: several educators were uncertain about what child-led play truly entails. The most common misconception was that setting up an activity and inviting a child to play constitutes child-led play. However, this is actually adult-initiated play, where the educator sets up the activity and children have some choice in how to engage with it. It is essential to clarify that adult-initiated play isn't wrong or bad; it just isn't the same as child-led play. In many responses, the challenge lay in the educator's struggle to distance themselves from the play and fully empower the child to direct it. Often, we may hesitate to admit that what children genuinely need is significant freedom in their play. I often refer to this approach as "backseat pedagogy", where the child truly owns their playtime, and educators give them the space to explore it on their terms.

Read the following examples. Would you define them as self-directed play? If so, what definition of play applies?

- A reception teacher sets up a play-based table-top activity for children to play with and identify 3D shapes. She sets a learning objective and calls the children up in small groups. She sits with them and encourages them to name the shapes. She then makes observations.
- A child with speech and language differences is placed into a play-based intervention group. Every day, he goes to the play room with a key person, and they play a range of games including what is in the box. The items consist of a range of toys and functional items.
- A child is building a tower and knocking it back down again. He repeats this several times. His key person sits beside him, and mirrors his play, and builds her own tower. Together in silence, they both continue to do this for a sustained period of time. The key person notices that the child is building a taller tower each time.
- A teaching assistant has noticed that the children are fascinated with digging in the outdoors. The next morning, she adds provocations to outdoor spaces including plant pots, soil, and a range of garden utensils. She lets the children knows she has added it to today's play activities.
- A key person tells a child that she is not playing with a toy in the way it is meant to be played with. She takes the toy, demonstrates its use, and hands it back. The child uses it in the demonstrated way a couple of times, and then abandons the toy.
- A key person tells the children that she has set up a number of activities to do that day. On each table, and in each area, there is a learning challenge and intention.

(Answers can be found at the end of this chapter)

PRESS PAUSE: WHO GETS TO DEFINE PLAY?

Another crucial point made by Lester and Russell (2010) is how adults often define play rather than letting children define it for themselves. This means that representations of play tend to create norms of what is considered play and what is not. This adult-centric view can lead to a misunderstanding of the true essence of the play. According to Lester and Russell, play always reflects children's subjective experiences and cannot be fully understood through adult interpretations. Children have a unique way of perceiving, feeling, and interacting with the world, which comes to life in their play. Take a moment to reflect on how frequently you ask children about their perspective on play or what meanings play might hold for them. Affording children time to share their personal meanings could lead to much deeper insights into the function of a child's self-directed play. It is useful to remember that the child is the teacher of play (Bondioli, 2002).

ACTIVITY

Using a floor book or scrapbook, agree on some play-based inquiries with children so you can begin to build a picture of how they define their own play. Simply start with "What is play?" or "What is your favourite thing to play with?". This gives you an insight into children's perceptions of play. Use visuals or alternative forms of communication to assist all children in contributing.

PATTERNS OF PLAY AND PLAY CULTURES

COMPANION RESOURCE

Play Radical is a website dedicated to Neurodivergent Play, Connection and Culture: https://playradical.com/

Due to the neurodiversity paradigm and subsequent movement of advocates, researchers and educators, we are now seeing an increase in research that attempts to flip old narratives and provide exciting insights into neurodivergent play. The neurodiversity movement spans a wide array of neurotypes, identities and ways of being, and, currently, there is a significant drive for autistic-led research, with other areas following suit. This means that lots of our understanding currently focuses on autism. Still, lots of the findings can be considered through the lens of other neurotypes or, at the very least, provoke our general thinking about differences and disabilities. Furthermore, many children in the early years are emergent neurodivergent, meaning we might still need to learn about their developmental pathway. There has been some important work on developing our understanding of neurodivergent play cultures and the importance of exploring our play patterns rather than pathologising them (see the work of Conn, 2015; Pritchard-Rowe et al., 2023; Elise Guthrie Stirling and Play Radical).

AUTISTIC PLAY PATTERNS

There is a significant body of research and advocacy exploring the patterns of autistic play. It is important that over time we develop an understanding of other neurotypes also, but what is refreshing is that we are increasingly seeing examples of how children play beyond conventional norms. One such study came from Carmel Conn (2015) who

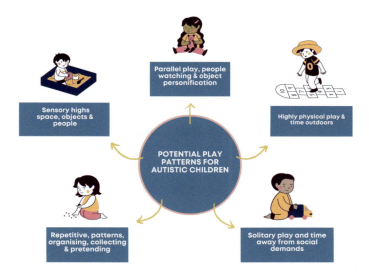

Conn, C., 2015. 'Sensory highs','vivid rememberings' and 'interactive stimming': children's play cultures and experiences of friendship in autistic autobiographies. Disability & Society, 30(8), pp.1192-1206.

FIGURE 4.6 AUTISTIC PLAY PATTERNS

interviewed autistic adults on the ways that they played as children. From this emerged rich and varied descriptions of the ways in which autistic adults were intrinsically motivated by their self-directed play. Below is an outline of some of the play patterns that emerged:

PLAY PATTERN	EXAMPLES
Sensory highs, space, objects, and people	✦ Heightened and pleasurable awareness to sensory stimuli ✦ Thrill they derived from running on the lines of tennis courts and being driven through the roundness of road tunnels (Prince-Hughes 2004) ✦ 'Ecstasy attack' of listening to flour-and-water paste being stirred (Birch 2003, 17) ✦ Watching each particle of sand pour through her fingers, "as though I was a scientist looking through a microscope" (Grandin and Scariano 1986, 18). ✦ Watching coins spin, "seeming never to get bored" ✦ Stared at the light reflected off the wet surface of bubbles, and listened as he tapped his mother's shoes repetitively on the floor.

Parallel play, people watching, and object personification	✦ Playing alongside each other on different tasks but enjoying the shared company ✦ Developing an attachment to objects or toys ✦ Being mesmerised by watching others
Highly physical and time outdoors	✦ Heavy work ✦ Using whole body to engage ✦ Taking risks
Repetition, patterns, organising, collecting, and pretending	✦ Lining things up ✦ Setting out and arranging of objects that are involved in their pretend play. ✦ Jeannie Davide-Rivera (2012) writes of how she enjoyed setting out a pretend school that was very close to its real-life equivalent. She describes how she collected real textbooks and equipment for her play since "pretend things would not do", and spent hours putting out tables and chairs, so much so that her friends would get tired of waiting and run off.
Solitary play and time away from social demands	✦ Wanting only one friend at a time, finding friendship easier with younger children who are happy to follow or with adults who could participate in high-level discussions of serious topics, having an imaginary friend, and feeling friends with characters in books and television programmes. ✦ An animal with which they experienced an intimate, emotionally satisfying, and enjoyable relationship was thought of as a close friend.

Adapted and expanded upon from: Conn, C. 2015. "Sensory highs", "vivid rememberings" and "interactive stimming": Children's play cultures and experiences of friendship in autistic autobiographies. *Disability & Society*, 30(8), 1192-1206

NEUROINSIGHTS

REFLECTIONS ON PLAY

How did you used to play? When you think about it – what did it look like? Did you build imaginary worlds? Did you crash, bang, jump, spin, scream, and shout? Did you find

(continued overleaf)

faces in the trees? Did you quietly make potions out of rainwater and leaves? Are your memories of play easy to describe with words, or are they more felt? A state of being?

Play is undefinable, because its possibilities are limitless. But, if we try to break it down, how about: play is the act of exploring and testing the ongoings of this world and how we as individuals perceive and process it. By doing this, we expand our understanding of what it is to be human, and what it is to be ourselves.

. . . Play is intuitive and creative. It can be done alone, with, or alongside others. It is never finished and should never end, though it may shift and look different over time.

When unmasked, a neurodivergent and/or disabled child may sometimes play in ways that we have been told to believe is "too noisy", "too chaotic", "too messy", "too rigid", or "too dangerous" even. When we used to take my son to soft play and he ran and spun, or dipped his hand in slush puppies, or climbed up the slide, or refused to wear socks, he was always made to feel he was "getting it wrong" by staff and other families. These are projections, and come from a place of fear around difference, and of those who can be themselves without compromise. Perhaps it's also envy that societal conditioning has not yet worn away at this innate curiosity, this pushing of limits, and at the experience of pure joy. Perhaps there is a fear that these children may never be tamed? And of what that will look like, and mean? I have too often heard the phrase "we do have rules" . . . but to live truly unmasked is to expose the fragility of society's most coveted rules and norms.

These attitudes towards difference are further socially reproduced in the many deficit-based describers for neurodivergence. It is critical that the language around ND play continues to be reframed in the broader culture in order to make meaningful change.

Neurodivergent play is sometimes a deep exploration of sensory experiences. With an often-elevated attunement to the senses, tweaking movements, objects, sound and light, changing the environment in playful ways can be beautifully experimental, sometimes subtly and other times not. The way a cymbal vibrates and rings out beyond the first clash depending on how hard you hit it, and with what; the cracking sound your mouth makes when you breathe out from the back of your throat; the way the background image blurs and light/dark contrasts in between the cracks in your fingers, especially when spinning, giving visual special effects at the same time as an intense bodily lightness. Try these things and you will understand them as play, and maybe see the "why?".

Playing with movement and the body, and the impacts and sensations of when it moves through space, crashes, spins, balances, and jumps is literally how we feel our physical presence - feel gravity's pull to earth - a somatic connection that can so easily be lost as we grow.

Play is freedom, and it is felt. It is a process that can bring unconscious thoughts and feelings into the material world. That's why making mess can be so important, because our unconscious is messy and we need to work through that! Likewise, testing at the boundaries of what risk is and how that feels - how can we know ours and others' limits without this investigation? I used to love repeatedly dipping my finger in the hot candle wax around a flame and pressing it against my lip. An experiment that was both a bit risky, and sensorily comforting.

Why is it that we, as adults, need to know the reason, the function, or the goal for a child's play, in order for us to believe it is valuable to them?

(continued overleaf)

(continued)

Adults too often have a desire to control and lead children, and, seemingly, to especially correct ND children's play. This is our first formative experience of this kind of top-down conditioning and the much-ingrained ableism of our society.

But our children and young people desperately need time, space, and safety in order to access the vital aspect of being, and of self, that is play. This is small but also a huge ask, when systems are so heavily burdened by their neuronormative criteria and outcomes.

We must and will keep carving them out though, because play is a fundamental act of liberation that cannot be stolen.

See Me Play is a self-directed playscheme for neurodivergent and disabled children, young people, and families, based in Margate. It was created because of the lack of safe feelings spaces available to my neurodivergent/disabled family. We desperately needed autonomy and freedom to be ourselves, and we needed community. See Me Play playworkers and carers can experience the pure joy (as well as many other feelings) of truly following an ND child's play; be it making volcanic mixtures that bubble and broil, creating new perspectives and worlds by climbing on anything that can be climbed on, or rolling yourself up tight in fabric until it spits you back the other way. See Me Play is committed to continuing to make change, and to sharing how important self-directed play spaces for ND/Disabled children are.

Last question: Do you still give yourself enough time to play, and how does that look and feel now?

Alice Davies
See Me Play Neurodivergent Play Space

NEUROMYTH: SOLITARY PLAY IS A PROBLEM

Developmental theories of childhood have long attempted to understand and define the sequential stages of play, and how these may link to learning and development. A common staged theory is the six types of social engagement in typically developing children (Parten, 1932). They suggest that children tend to transition from lower levels of peer engagement; they may seem uninterested in peers or show a preference for solitary play, and eventually will move into more social forms of play, for example through parallel and cooperative play. While stages or sequences of play can offer some usefulness in helping us to understand types of play, it can also lead us to believe that play takes us through a seamless developmental pathway, and deviation from this pathway must signify a problem. It is not uncommon for solitary play to be cited as a problem, especially among neurodivergent children. This preference can create a lot of worry, even if there is a positive effect on the child. While social play is important, it is not the only function of play. If you think of your hobbies or pursuits, there are likely many playful activities that you gain most enjoyment from because they are solitary. For example, imaging going for a swim and being told you must swim alongside someone or playing a computer game and being told to take turns with someone else because this indicates good social skills. Growing research suggests that solitary play is important for wellbeing among neurodivergent people (Simone and Haas, 2013). It is, therefore, important to remain critical of the automatic pathologisation of a desire for solitary play and risking play interference from adults or other peers. Some benefits of solitary play include:

- Time and space to become totally immersed in an area of interest.
- Opportunities for play as daydreaming, imagination, and thinking things through without interference.
- A break from social demands.
- Time for autonomy and pursuing one's own desires.
- Learning to enjoy one's own company and distinguishing between being alone and being lonely.

NEUROINSIGHTS

WHAT IS PLAY

When I asked educators how they would describe play, I got a range of answers, and something I noticed is that in answering, educators often talked about the value of play or why it is good, but very rarely did someone tell me what play actually is. When I thought about this, I couldn't say what it is. I am immediately enveloped by "learning through play" or "play and development" but very rarely do we let it exist as both something that exists on its own but also woven into everything else.

In talking to Daniela Tonazzolli from the university of Cambridge primary school, she explained that to her:

Play should not limited to early childhood; it's a fundamental aspect of human experience that continues throughout life. Regardless of age or developmental stage, individuals should be valued and respected for engaging in play in whatever form it takes for them. Recognising the importance of play across the lifespan promotes wellbeing, creativity, and social connection for people of all ages. It's about embracing the diversity of play experiences and honouring individuals' autonomy and preferences in how they choose to play.

From Tonazzolli's description, play is something that exists all around us, and is an inherent part of our experience, but what it is remains a mystery and maybe it is supposed to be that way.

Daniela Tonazzolli, Learning Coach EYFS, University of Cambridge Primary School

PRESS PAUSE

When considering the ways children play, it's important to focus on what brings them intrinsic joy and meaning. In a recent discussion with an area inclusion coordinator, they mentioned that a child was happiest when engaged in solitary play. However, they also believed that social interactions are an important aspect of play and should take priority.

We discussed how this approach might be harmful, as it deprioritises the child's happiness in favour of conforming to neurotypical ways of playing. While social interactions are important and can be encouraged in ways that are meaningful to the child, they should not replace other play preferences. Especially when a child is visibly happy with their choice.

DECOLONISING AND DIVERSIFYING PLAY

In 2017, Marianna Souto-Manning published an article emphasising that "play must be the right of every child, not a privilege. After all, when regarded as a privilege, it is granted to some and denied to others, creating further inequities" (p. 785). Souto-Manning observed that the increasing emphasis on standardisation and academic rigour erodes self-directed play opportunities. For example, educators tend to emphasise that learning must be occurring in play for it to be considered play, meaning only those interests that visibly offer learning opportunities will be followed, with little recognition that we, as educators, may not always be able to identify an interest because culture shapes and shifts the ways in which we play. Bettina Love (2014) illustrates this through an example where a Black child continually got into trouble for banging on the tables and asked to stop. However, on further exploration, the child was a big fan of hip-hop music, playing the drums, and building a rhythm. The denial or deprivation of self-directed play disproportionately affects non-dominant groups, including Black and Brown children and those from under-resourced communities, where developmental differences are also more prevalent.

Aaron Trammell (2023) extends this argument by stating that play has become overly sanitised by white European definitions, which view play as purely pleasurable and structured to facilitate learning. He advocates for recognising that play is complex and involves "diving into the messiness of life" (p. 3). Trammell argues that play can be haphazard and troubling, and we should avoid categorising these types of play as mere misbehaviours to be stopped. Instead, we should understand what is meaningful to the child in the broader context. For example, some children's play might be considered unruly or highly physical, resulting in greater surveillance or attempts to control their play. When we take into account intersectionality, it might be that children's play is judged on the basis of their identity and characteristics. For example, a girl may be discouraged from rough and tumble play with peers as it may be considered a masculine pursuit. Similarly, a Black neurodivergent child may be subject to harsher judgements than their white counterpart, who is showing similar play patterns.

Scholars suggest that play is often a risk as it is an attempt to cope with uncertainty, so how we attempt to control children's play can also disrupt how a child manages and maintains the risk to navigate that complexities in life. And so you can see from such examples that there is a difference between those who are afforded their rights to play and those who are denied.

PRESS PAUSE: WHY WE SHOULD REPLACE "ALLOW" WITH "EMPOWER"

I noticed that whenever I talked about play and anything child-related, I often used the term "allow". For example, "I allow the children to have free play in the mornings". I wondered whether the underlying message was that by allowing it, I was still situating myself as in control or in charge of children and their play. I made a simple shift in my language, and now I say "I enable . . ." or "I empower . . ." instead. This reminds me of my role in early childhood, which is to be a springboard for autonomy, wellbeing, engagement, and self-development.

HOW DID PLAY BECOME A VEHICLE FOR EARLY INTERVENTION?

When I began research for this book, I assumed that most studies on play focused on typical and non-disabled children's play. However, I discovered many philosophical and evolutionary discussions that appeared to embrace the diversity and complexity of play. This made me curious about how play, an activity all humans engage in, has come to be seen as only naturally occurring in those who conform to neuronormativity.

From an evolutionary perspective, play is older than culture, language, or even humanity. It is rooted in our biology as mammals and across species. Play is not something that we are waiting to be taught; it is just something that we all do in lots of different ways. Play is a primal experience, and for children especially, "play is interwoven into the fabric of their everyday lives" (Lester and Russell, 2010, p. 21). Yet, when applied to education, play has been narrowed somewhat to be intrinsically linked to learning, and has also been co-opted as way to correct, or normalise neurodivergent, disabled, and other marginalised groups through play-based intervention.

Educators can often feel limited in their early intervention strategies due to the strong emphasis on strictly following ableist evidence-based practices. For example, evidence suggests that good social skills include maintaining eye contact and yet this is not the preference for all children. This brings up an important question: whose evidence are we prioritising? Originally meant to guide interventions, evidence-based practice has sometimes become a tool for teaching conformity to neuronormativity, overshadowing the importance of real-life experiences. It is vital to remain curious about evidence while also critically evaluating its suitability to all children.

While evidence is crucial, we must avoid uncritically accepting overly prescribed practices that may inadvertently be impacting children's wellbeing, engagement and learning. Rigid adherence to neuronormativity can be harmful, potentially leading to interventions that do not consider the unique needs of the child or family involved. Interventions should prioritise providing children with a good quality of life that aligns with their unique learning differences and needs, rather than aiming for neuronormative outcomes.

The goal isn't to reject evidence but to approach it thoughtfully. Educators should engage in careful inquiry, evaluating how evidence applies to each child's and family's unique situation.

One of the most significant concerns related to intervention programmes is the risk that they teach children to mask or camouflage their inherent traits. Masking refers to the "conscious or unconscious suppression or projection of aspects of self and identity, and the use of non-native cognitive or social strategies" (Pearson and Rose, 2023, p.3). In other words, minimising your neurodivergent traits in social situations to fit in or assimilate. While this area of research has predominantly focused on adults and young people, one study has identified that masking can begin as early as ten years of age. Howe et al. (2023) found that children would conceal their autistic traits in pervasive and automatic ways. For example, they would suppress movement and stimming or hide aspects of themselves that others may reject. One of the themes in this study suggested that masking is a learned habit and that the children masked more within an educational context, implying that this environment implicitly and explicitly encourages suppression of the natural self. When we consider the role of early intervention and programmes, we do need to consider whether some of the modifications within these are training children to mask. The outcome measures of many intervention programmes are based on neuronormative and compliant behaviours; for example, the Nuffield Early Language Intervention (NELI) aims to improve children's language skills and behaviour but places significant emphasis on "listening rules" including sitting still, looking and being quiet (West et al., 2024). I am not suggesting we shouldn't have programmes that support children's language and behaviour. Rather, the programme does not account for individual differences and prescribes outdated ideas about how we listen, pay attention, and engage. This is a programme that also relies on external rewards such as "Best Listener" stickers and certificates. Behaviour modification often uses rewards to instil behaviours. In short, the desired behaviour is more important than how the child might actually feel internally. Furthermore, we do need to interrogate any programme that advocates for language while telling children they need to "keep quiet". Suppose you have a neurodivergent child who joins this group and stims as a way of communicating or prefers to look away when listening. In that case, they are gradually being taught that this is not an acceptable way of behaving or communicating and, eventually, this becomes modified. But at what cost? Masking is understood to have quite significant mental health costs, including burnout (Higgins et al., 2021), loss of identity, loss of self-identity (Radulski, 2022) and disconnection from authentic self (Miller, Rees, and Pearson, 2021). While the impact might not always be externally visible, there is increasing recognition that the internalised self is harmed, and to mask is energetically draining and stressful. Think of the times we hear a parent say that at the end of a school day the child suddenly collapses into a heap or brims with stressful energy because they have spent the day trying to fit in.

ACTIVITY

Consider the following questions:

1. How might early intervention programmes balance the need to support neurodivergent children's language and behaviour development with the potential risk of inadvertently promoting masking behaviours, considering the identified association between masking and mental health costs?

2. How can educators ensure that intervention programs consider individual differences, especially for neurodivergent children, and avoid reinforcing outdated notions of acceptable behaviour, thus fostering a more inclusive and supportive learning environment?

3. Reflecting on the potential long-term consequences of masking, how can intervention programmes be adapted to prioritise the authentic self-expression of neurodivergent children, recognising the mental health challenges associated with masking, such as burnout, loss of identity, and disconnection from one's authentic self?

PLANTING SEEDS FOR NEURODIVERSITY

When thinking about the combination of play and neurodiversity, it is useful to consider how you withhold judgements in defining children's play as right or wrong. Some other ways to embrace the diversity of play include:

Follow children's interests even if they don't make sense to you. Following children's interests seems quite obvious in an early childhood space, but we are often more likely to honour and welcome interests that make sense to us. For example, if a child expresses a love for a particular character or type of play, it can appear like a more accessible thing to accommodate. But children will also have less obvious interests, and they might be unable to describe or provide reasoning for why they are drawn to a particular way of playing. Children's play dispositions are intrinsically motivated and unique, and through playful provocations, novelty, and stimulations, they explore the world around them. Following interests should include:

✦ Noting down how children **choose** to spend their time (*The first place Mohammed heads to in the morning is the outdoor play area, and is often found to be on the climbing frame*)

✦ The **presence** of repetitive actions and behaviours (*Kiran really seems to enjoy piling the crates on top of the other time and time again*)

✦ **Embodiment** (how do they use their bodies to play) (*Hatty is less interested in painting with brushes and prefers to use her hands instead. She also likes to sprawl the paint on her arms*)

✦ Vocalisations and **language** used (*Mei screams in delight and babbles a lot when playing in the water*)

✦ **Flow** state (how immersed they become in play) (*Kenan likes to be left to his own devices when digging and foraging through the mud. He can do this for extended periods of time and often has a very concentrated face*)

✦ **Ownership** (taking control of an interest) (*When Zelos arrives in the morning, he will go around collecting his favourite toys and put them all in the same spot ready to play with*)

Engage in **parallel** as opposed to face-to-face play. For many children, the interference of an adult in play can be disruptive and sometimes quite overwhelming, especially for children who are regulating social, emotional, and physical demands. A way to be with children in their play is to play alongside, side-by-side, either mirroring the child's play or playing in your way. This communicates to the child that you respect their play patterns but you are also gently offering a shared play experience while gaining insights into their play and explorations.

Do it to know it. So frequently educators will say to me: "I don't see the point in the child's play" or "all they do is XYZ" and the educator can seem totally perplexed as to why anyone would be motivated to play in the way that they do. Although we might not be able to fully experience what another individual experiences, we can at least attempt to gain new insights by also playing in the same or similar ways. For example, an educator recently said to me: "all this child does is run up and down for ages". Rather than to be an outsider looking in, I advised that the practitioner try running up and down as a way to embody what the child might be experiencing. When they returned from their running adventures, they described the experience as "exhilarating", "freeing", and "risky".

Build upon children's interests by planning **simple to super** experiences. According to Stacey (2018), organising play opportunities to sustain attention (or to support flow states) can be useful by providing resources that can be manipulated differently. For example, sand would be considered a simple resource, but adding digging tools makes the play opportunity more complex. As the child immerses in the play, you may add super opportunities, such as mixing sand and water with the tools, meaning the child can engage in multiple ways based on their original interest in sand. Following this framework requires understanding the child's playful dispositions, and care should be given to providing play experiences that are compatible with a child's sensory prefer-ences. Another way in which we can use simple to super is to ensure that we are not incorporating too many elements to a child's play without first considering their prefer-ences. For example, you might find that for some children simple play experiences are more developmentally meaningful.

IS ALL PLAY OKAY?

As an early childhood educator, I have always been under the illusion that play in young children is inherently pleasurable and benevolent. For example, I regularly pro-mote the features of self-directed play that largely focus on the positive attributes of play-filled lives, which, despite their usefulness, situate play as a white, Eurocentric, and western endeavour (Trammel, 2023). When advocating for the de-pathologisation of play in neurodivergent and disabled children, I have attempted to reframe the often-rejected patterns of play, which are usually deemed symptomatic of their supposed wrongness (Goodley and Runswick-Cole, 2010). This also serves as a resistance to the notion of a universal "right way to play", which often privileges white, typical conforming minds and non-disabled bodies. However, there is a flaw in viewing play as only pleasurable, stress-free, and having positive affect.

While advocating for the de-pathologisation of play, I have also been met with cognitive dis-sonance when an educator informs me that a child enjoys invading another's personal space, destroys things, appears angry at play or reenacts distressing real-world events. Like many other play advocates, I have promoted the "all play is okay" mantra to attempt to usualise play that falls beyond neuronormativity. I wonder if this invalidates the troubling and marginalised play patterns we might also witness. I also wonder if this is illustrative of my own reluctance to sit with the discomfort that I ultimately do not believe that "all play is okay", but I do believe that we must "give life" to both the pleasurable and tortuous complexities of play and to move away from attempts to purify play to consider it appropriate (Trammel, 2023). Play gives us informa-tion about the child, and we should be able to interpret play without categorising it as wrong or right; rather we should validate it as a reflection of emotional states and internalised worlds coming to life. We are not just "learning through play" but playing to exist and to make sense of that existence. Let's consider some scenarios where the child's play might indicate that they are not okay.

WHAT IF A CHILD IS DISPLAYING AGGRESSIVE BEHAVIOURS?

The word "aggressive" can make people uneasy. It's usually used to describe play that's rowdy, unpredictable, very physical, and includes expressions of anger. Before we explore the reasons behind aggressive behaviour, let's break down what we mean by "aggressive" and how it can be understood in different ways. We'll take a closer look at a case study to illustrate these points.

Toby considers his key child, Tarek, to be very aggressive during play. He has noticed that he will often make lots of seemingly angry noises and is constantly bumping into, shoving, and pushing other children out the way in his pursuit for play. At the water tray, he can never just play nicely and there is always a tsunami of water and he splashes and smashes the toys into the water tray. Toby feels like he is always asking Tarek to "calm down" and to "be careful" and will often ask Tarek to say sorry to friends and peers who get caught up his aggressive play. Toby's colleague sees this differently and says that to describe him as aggressive suggests that he is intentionally causing harm. She also views his vocalisations as determination within the play. For a three-year-old who is also suspected to be neurodivergent, she considers the term aggressive to have potentially damaging implications on how his play is viewed.

From the above case study, you can see two key people who have interpreted Tarek's play differently. Whereas one sees the play as aggressive, the other sees it as a child whose play is highly physical and energetic.

PRESS PAUSE

✦ How might Tarek "intervene" to stop the "aggressive" behaviour?
✦ How might Shelley "intervene" to support the highly physical behaviour?

Toby:

I do not feel comfortable with Tarek's behaviours, and I think he needs to be calmer because it is disrupting the other children. Things can be played with nicely. My response with this has been to issue warnings using a "red card" and if he gets warned more than a few times, I take him away from the play. I have zero tolerance for aggression, regardless of his needs. I have let the parents know that he is aggressive, and asked if they can try to also address this at home. The red card seems to be working in that I can see that he will control himself better, but his parents have now commented that he is very upset and reluctant to come to nursery.

Shelley:

I decided to spend some time observing Tarek at play to establish what his intrinsic motivation is. He is definitely boisterous and still in that whole body phase of development. He will almost thrash himself at things, and be quite destructive, but he does not seem angry, and he certainly doesn't appear to want to hurt others. He just seems slightly unaware, and so immersed in his play that he no longer sees those around him. Much to other colleagues' concern, I decided that he needed more of this play, rather than less. I set up some obstacle courses outside, and I looked at his interest in water, and realised that a small square water tray in a tight corner was not enough space, and bound to cause concerns. I set up an outdoor water play area, and made sure there was lots of room. I also decided to put together a social story on "Watching where you go . . ." to bring his attention to safety in play. I also used some supportive visuals in the environment: for example, I added numbers to play areas so children understood how many could ideally fit round the water tray, and provided some partitioning and arrows so children could navigate safely. When I spoke with parents, I referred to his play as highly energetic and physical, and they seemed much more open to a discussion. They explained that they lived in a high-rise flat, and nursery is the place where he does feel less restricted. They also said that they will perhaps schedule in some more play time outside of the flat.

This initial case study aims to prompt reflection on the language we use to describe play and its potential implications. Now, let's focus on play driven by anger, a valid and expected emotional response in both young children and adults. Play provides a way to process, express, and work through the discomfort of anger. Understanding play through the lens of anger enables us to support children effectively:

1.   Acknowledge and Understand:

When anger manifests in a child's play, our goal isn't to simply stop the emotion but to support the child to process and resolve it. Self-directed play can be a means for the child to navigate and alleviate the feeling, leading to self-regulation.

2.   Address Feelings of Unsafe Environment:

Aggressive play may indicate a child feeling unsafe, resulting in chaotic play patterns. Providing predictable routines and rhythms can help re-establish safety. You might also provide rhythmic-based activities that link to the child's interests.

3.   Seek Grounding Experiences:

The child might be seeking experiences that help them feel grounded. Despite seeming counterproductive, empowering aggressive play through activities like heavy work or deep pressured play can be beneficial.

4.   Negotiate Play Continuation:

In heightened states of anger, a child may not be ready to talk or stop their activities. Acknowledge this and make environmental adjustments so that play can continue in a negotiated manner. For example, if a child is throwing items, perhaps take it outside, and offer alternative items to throw.

5.   Establish Non-negotiables:

Identify non-negotiable boundaries. For instance, if a child is breaking things, express, "I cannot let you throw and break toys, but I can find other things for you to throw". If hitting out at friends, say, "I cannot let you hit your friends, but we can go and let your frustrations out by running outside instead".

6.   Provide ongoing teaching for behaviours that you find challenging:

Some behaviours during play will require support and ongoing teaching. For instance, you might later engage in whole-group activities around keeping each other safe, addressing any challenges that arise during play collaboratively.

WHAT IF THE CHILD HAS EXPERIENCED ADVERSITY OR TRAUMA?

As early educators, we do not have specific qualifications in play therapy. In some cases, the child may benefit from someone with the expertise to help process and resolve traumatic experiences. However, given that we are increasingly the first line of support for children who have faced trauma and adversity, we must have some knowledge on how play can be used within co-regulation and self-regulation. Welter and Houck-Loomis (2018) recommends establishing consistent trauma-informed environments in early childhood education, for example, being aware of children's stress responses and reducing unpredictability or sudden changes.

Play can also serve as a means for children to express concerns, fears, and desires and to process life events, including traumatic ones. Early educators can draw upon the principles of play therapy because it intersects with the principles of many of our play-based frameworks, and emphasise the importance of relationships, interactions, and a child-centred approach. However, it's essential that we do not utilise practices that are reserved for play therapy, and avoid practices that could become unethical, such as probing a child with questions about their traumatic experiences. Instead, we use play as a tool for connection and understanding.

Axline (1947) was the one who saw the conceptual expression in the process of play and the one who introduced play as a form of therapy, as she believed that it was by itself a wound-healing process. Axline proposed eight key principles that she considered as necessary in play therapy:

✦   Development of good communication/relationship
✦   Acceptance of the child as they are in the moment
✦   Provision of opportunities for the child to express their feelings without shaming or judgement
✦   Awareness of the feelings expressed by the child and their reflection,
✦   Belief that the child has the capacity to process and work through difficult experiences,

✦ Non-directional play letting the child take the lead
✦ No rush to the child by providing an unhurried pedagogy
✦ Secure boundaries so that the child feels safe.

PARENT X CARER SOLIDARITY

As early educators, it can sometimes be challenging to know how to engage in a child's play or understand their motivations. The advantage for educators is the opportunity for professional development in this area, while parents and caregivers often learn as they go. For parents and caregivers of neurodivergent children, playing together may feel more challenging due to the pressures of playing "the right way" or finding meaningful connections. Here are a few ways to encourage parents and caregivers to embrace play with neurodivergent and disabled children:

Recognise Diverse Parent-Child Interaction Styles:

Most advice on parent-child interaction is designed with neurotypical children in mind. Parents might feel pressured to engage in ways that are uncomfortable for their neurodivergent child, such as making eye contact or being face-to-face. Instead, suggest alternative ways to join in their play, such as parallel play, providing commentary, or following interests even if they do not yet make sense to the parent.

Embrace All Forms of Play:

Children play in various ways, and so long as the play is not harmful or distressing, it is okay. Encourage parents to accept unconventional types of play, like repetitive or destructive play, recognising that these can be meaningful for the child.

Facilitate Playdates with Similar Peers:

For neurodivergent children, interacting with neurotypical peers might not always be beneficial and can sometimes lead to misunderstandings. Encourage playdates with children who have similar neurotypes or traits to foster connection and shared experiences.

By supporting parents and caregivers in these ways, we can help them create enriching play experiences that respect their child's unique needs and developmental path.

CHAPTER CONCLUSION

Play is a complex thing that often eludes precise definition. Scholars are increasingly moving away from defining it, and instead embracing its ambiguity. In this chapter, we have attempted to remove some of the boundaries that can be placed around play and reimagine more inclusive and intersectional play descriptions. What has become evident is that our current understanding of play is somewhat limited by the desire to promote play as something that is always joyful, pleasurable, stress-free, and inherently good. However, the essence of play extends far beyond these notions, encompassing a rich tapestry of experiences and expressions.

At its core, play is an innate aspect of childhood, woven into the very fabric of human development. As adults, it is incumbent upon us to cultivate an environment that nurtures and embraces all forms of play, even those that may initially confound or discomfort us. Rather than imposing preconceived notions of what play should entail, we must adopt a stance of openness and curiosity, recognising that every instance of play provides us with crucial information about the child's play patterns, processing, and motivations. Play serves as a window into the child's worldview, offering invaluable insights into their cognitive, emotional, and social processes. Observing and engaging with children during play gives us important glimpses into their inner workings, discerning how they perceive and interact with the world around them. As I have written about play, I have experienced a process of the more I learn about it, the less I know about it which reinforces the idea that play is designed to be ambiguous intentionally.

ACTIVITY – CHAPTER KEEPSAKES

Across this first chapter, think about what your keepsakes are, and note down the following:

- ✦ One thing you will start doing
- ✦ One thing you still stop doing
- ✦ One keepsake you will share with others
- ✦ One thinking knot that requires further exploration

EXPLANATION OF TERMS

Play-based learning includes a wide range of approaches across a range of environments, which includes staff-led activities and free play (EEF, 2023). The Early Years Foundation Stage Framework (DfE, 2021) is based on the premise that children should have a range of play-based experiences to support learning and development meaning. Play initiated by the child should then be structured around learning, progress and outcomes.

Child-led play involves play that is led by the child rather than the adult and is becoming an increasingly popular term and practice in specialist services such as speech, language, and communication therapy which traditionally relied on adult-directed playfulness.

Guided play is a shared experience between adults and children in which adults provide scaffolding toward a goal, outcome, or skill. It is considered a necessary component of extending play into learning.

Controlled playfulness refers to a child being able to self-regulate or control themselves during play.

Self-directed Play is the concept of allowing children to play without an imposed framework, on their own, without adult interference. It is defined by play that is:

Freely Chosen - by determining and controlling the content and intent of their play
Personally Directed - by following their own instincts, ideas, and interests
Intrinsically Motivated - playing in their own way for their own reasons (Gray, 2013)

You may find that the term **self-directed learning** is more commonly used.

Coined by Anji Play, **True Play** is deep and uninterrupted engagement in the activity of one's own choice. True Play is most frequently characterised by observable experiences of risk, joy, and deep engagement. This is the deepest manifestation of learning, growth, and development. True Play flourishes in places of love where the materials, environments, and decision-making attend to the needs and differences of the individual and the group.

When given space to reflect, those who experience True Play and those who take part in deep and engaged observation of True Play will create ecologies that prioritise the understanding of learning and development in their respective communities.

Play-rich recognises that play-based learning is insufficient. Rather, children should have abundant opportunities to engage in all types of play, not just those related to pre-determined learning outcomes. And children should have opportunities to play in ways that are meaningful to them (Murphy, 2022).

Play-based interventions are practices designed to improve socio-emotional, physical, language, and cognitive development through guided interactive play. They are play-based because they include components of playfulness and are designed with pre-determined goals or outcomes. Play-based interventions rarely reflect **play** itself.

Functional play refers to using toys, objects, and items designed for play in their intended function to participate in play as an occupation. However, it can sometimes be used to stigmatise children who do not play in normative ways, and can lead to the idea that play is dysfunctional.

Purposeful play refers to the idea that children should be taught to play in "developmentally appropriate" ways which includes an intended purpose or outcome. The issue with such a term is that it is the adult who gets to decide which play is deemed appropriate or not, which can result in the exclusion of diverse play patterns.

Appropriate play relates to age appropriateness, meaning to play in a way that is considered typical and expected for a particular age. Play is unique, and should not be restricted by age.

Play patterns is a term that has emerged from the research of Dr Carmel Conn in which the diverse ways of playing can be recognised by identifying new play patterns.

According to UNICEF, **Free play** is when children have full freedom to play in whatever way they want. Suzanne Axelsson issues a note of caution about this term, stating that "if freedom is the ability to act - or play without confinement or restraint, exempt from external control, unhampered, independently, with full right to make all of one's own decisions - are we able to provide this at preschools?" (2013).

Structured play, or **goal-oriented play**, generally involves using logic to solve problems.

Play is undefinable.

ANSWERS

✦ A reception teacher sets up a play-based table-top activity for children to play with and identify 3D shapes. She sets a learning objective and calls the children up in small groups. She sits with them, and encourages them to name the shapes. She then makes observations (adult-directed).

✦ A child with speech and language differences is placed into a play-based intervention group. Every day he goes to the play room with a key person, and they play a range of games including what is in the box. The items consist of a range of toys and functional items (adult-directed/playful).

✦ A child is building a tower and knocking it back down again. He repeats this several times. His key person sits beside him, and mirrors his play, and builds her own tower. Together in silence, they both continue to do this for a sustained period of time. The key person notices that the child is building a taller tower each time (self-directed with adult mirroring).

✦ A teaching assistant has noticed that the children are fascinated with digging in the outdoors. The next morning, she adds provocations to outdoor spaces, including plant pots, soil, and a range of garden utensils. She lets the children knows she has added it to today's play activities (self-directed, adult-initiated).

✦ A key person tells a child that she is not playing with a toy how it is meant to be played with. She takes the toy, demonstrates its use, and hands it back. The child uses it in the way demonstrates a couple of times, and then abandons the toy (adult-directed).

✦ A key person tells the children that she has set up a number of activities to do that day. On each table, and in each area, there is a learning challenge and intention (adult-initiated).

BIBLIOGRAPHY

Alexander, M. 2024. "Shut your face!"; Prioritising, valuing and enabling autistic children's autonomy. *Play Radical*. Available at: https://playradical.com/blog/.

Axelsson, S. 2013. Freedom, Free, Free Play. Interaction Imagination Blog. Available at: https://interactionimagination.blogspot.com/2013/01/freedom-free-free-play.html.

Axline, V.M. 1947. Play Therapy: The Inner Dynamics of Childhood. Houghton Mifflin.

Bakan, M.B. 2014. The musicality of stimming: Promoting neurodiversity in the ethnomusicology of autism. *MUSICultures*, 41(2).

Bateson, G. 1956. The message, "This is play." In B. Schaffner (ed.) *Group Processes*. Josiah Macy.

Birch, J. 2003. *Congratulations! It's Asperger Syndrome*. Jessica Kingsley Publishers.

Bondioli, A. 2002. *Gioco e educazione* [Play and education]. Franco Angeli.

Bruce, T. 1991. *Time to Play in Early Childhood Education*. Hodder Education.

Burghardt, G.M. 2005. *The Genesis of Animal Play: Testing the Limits*. MIT Press.

Cohen, C.P. 1989. United Nations: Convention on the rights of the child. *International Legal Materials*, 28(6), 1448–1476.

Conn, C. 2015. "Sensory highs", "vivid rememberings" and "interactive stimming": Children's play cultures and experiences of friendship in autistic autobiographies. *Disability & Society*, 30(8), 1192–1206.

Daly, A. 2016. A commentary on the United Nations Convention on the Rights of the Child, Article 15: The right to freedom of association and to freedom of peaceful assembly (Vol. 15). Brill.

Davide-Rivera, J. 2012. *Twirling Naked in the Streets – And No One Noticed: Growing Up with Undiagnosed Autism*. David and Goliath Publishing.

Department for Education. 2021. Early Years Foundation Stage. www.gov.uk/government/publications/early-years-foundation-stage-framework–2.

Education Endowment Foundation. 2023. Play-Based Learning. https://educationendowmentfoundation.org.uk/early-years/toolkit/play-based-learning.

Fisher, J. 2016. *Interacting or Interfering? Improving Interactions in the Early Years*. McGraw-Hill Education (UK).

Fisher, N., 2023. *A Different Way to Learn: Neurodiversity and Self-directed Education*. Jessica Kingsley Publishers. https://blog.jkp.com/2023/05/self-directed-education-neurodiversity/

Flattery, S. 2023. *Stim Joy: Using Multi-sensory Design to Foster Better Understanding of the Autistic Experience*. Doctoral dissertation, Iowa State University.

Friedman, S., Gibson, J., Jones, C., and Hughes, C. 2024. "A new adventure": A case study of autistic children at Forest School. *Journal of Adventure Education and Outdoor Learning*, 24(2), 202–218.

Goodley, D. and Runswick-Cole, K. 2010. Emancipating play: Dis/abled children, development and deconstruction. *Disability & Society*, 25(4), 499–512.

Grandin, T., and M.M. Scariano. 1986. *Emergence: Labeled Autistic*. Warner.

Gray, P. 2013. *Free to Learn: Why Unleashing the Instinct to Play Will Make Our Children Happier, More Self-reliant, and Better Students for Life*. Basic Books.

Guthrie Stirling, E. 2024. *My origami child*. [Blog] ND Connection, 7 March. https://ndconnection.co.uk/blog/my-origami-child.

Harris, G. 2022. Everyday playfulness: A new approach to children's play and adult responses to it, edited by Stuart Lester, Jeremy Lester and Wendy Russell. Jessica Kingsley Publishers.

Higgins, J.M., Arnold S.R., Weise, J., Pellicano, E., and Trollor. J.N. 2021. Defining autistic burnout through experts by lived experience: Grounded Delphi method investigating #AutisticBurnout. *Autism*. doi: 10.1177/13623613211019858.

Howe, S.J., Hull, L., Sedgewick, F., Hannon, B. and McMorris, C.A. 2023. Understanding camouflaging and identity in autistic children and adolescents using photo-elicitation. *Research in Autism Spectrum Disorders*, 108, p.102232.

Koukourikos, K. et al. 2021. An Overview of Play Therapy. *Mater Sociomed*, 33(4), 293-297.

Lester, S. 2011. The pedagogy of play, space and learning. In A. Pihlgren (ed.), *Fritidspedagogik*. Lund: Sutdentlitteratur, pp. 115-138.

Lester, S. 2013. 11 Playing in a Deleuzian playground. In E. Ryall, W. Russell, and MacLean, M. (eds) *The Philosophy of play*. Routledge, pp. 130-140.

Lester, S. and Russell, W. 2010. Children's right to play: An examination of the importance of play in the lives of children worldwide. Working Papers in Early Childhood Development, No. 57. Bernard van Leer Foundation.

Lott, N. n.d. Exploring children's right to play through the lens of Human Rights. www.socsci. ox.ac.uk/exploring-childrens-right-to-play-through-the-lens-of-human-rights.

Love, B. 2014. Hip Hop, Grit, and Academic Success: Bettina Love at TEDxUGA. www. youtube.com/watch?v=tkZqPMzgvzg.

Miller, D., Rees, J., and Pearson, A. 2021. "Masking is life": Experiences of masking in autistic and nonautistic adults. *Autism Adulthood*. 3(4), 330-338. doi: 10.1089/aut.2020.0083.

Murphy, K. 2022. *A Guide to SEND in the Early Years: Supporting Children with Special Educational Needs and Disabilities*. Bloomsbury Publishing.

Murray, D., Lesser, M., and Lawson, W. 2005. Attention, monotropism and the diagnostic criteria for autism. *Autism*, 9(2), 139-156.

Nakamura, J. and Csikszentmihalyi, M. 2009. Flow theory and research. In M.J. Furlong, R. Gilman, and E.S. Huebner (eds), *Handbook of Positive Psychology*. Routledge, p. 206.

Nutbrown, C. 2018. *Early Childhood Educational Research: International Perspectives*. SAGE Publications Ltd, pp.1-312. https://doi.org/10.4135/9781526451811.

Parten, M.B. 1932. Social participation among pre-school children. *The Journal of Abnormal and Social Psychology*, 27(3), 243-269.

Pearson, A. and Rose, K. 2023. Autistic Masking: Understanding Identity Management and the Role of Stigma. Pavilion Publishing and Media Ltd.

Play Radical. n.d. *Who is Max Alexander?* [Online] https://playradical.com/about/who-is-max-alexander/.

Pritchard-Rowe, E., de Lemos, C., Howard, K., and Gibson, J. 2023. Diversity in autistic play: Autistic adults; experiences. *Autism in Adulthood*, 6(2), 218-228.

Prince-Hughes, D. 2004. *Songs of the Gorilla Nation: My Journey through Autism*. Three Rivers Press.

Radulski, E.M. 2022. Conceptualising autistic masking, camouflaging, and neurotypical privilege: Towards a minority group model of neurodiversity. *Human Development*, 66(2), 113-127. https://doi.org/10.1159/000524122

Simone, P.M. and Haas, A.L. 2013. Frailty, leisure activity and functional status in older adults: Relationship with subjective well being. *Clinical Gerontologist*, 36(4), 275–293.

Souto-Manning, M. 2017. Is play a privilege or a right? And what's our responsibility? On the role of play for equity in early childhood education. *Early Child Development and Care*, 187(5-6), 785–787.

Spariosu, M. 1982. *Literature, Mimesis, Play*. Gunter Narr Verlag.

Spariosu, M. 1984. *Mimesis in Contemporary Theory*. John Benjamin.

Spariosu, M. 1989. *Dionysus Reborn*. Cornell University Press.

Spariosu, M. 1991. *God of Many Names*. Duke University Press.

Spencer, H. 1896 (1855). *Principles of Psychology*. Appleton.

Stacey, S. 2018. *Inquiry-based Early Learning Environments: Creating, Supporting, and Collaborating*. Redleaf Press.

Stenros, J. 2015. *Playfulness, Play, and Games: A Constructionist Ludology Approach*. Doctoral dissertation. University of Tampere.

Sutton-Smith, B. 2001. *The Ambiguity of Play*. Harvard University Press.

Trammell, A. 2023. *Repairing Play: A Black Phenomenology*. MIT Press.

Trawick-Smith, J. 2019. *Young Children's Play: Development, Disabilities, and Diversity*. Routledge.

Stenros, J. 2021. Why do humans play? Exploring the functions, benefits, and meanings of (dark) play. www.youtube.com/watch?v=F_w83–Z4Zg.

Walker, N. 2014. Neurodiversity: Some basic terms and definitions. *Neurocosmopolitanism*. https://neuroqueer.com/neurodiversity-terms-and-definitions/.

Welter, B.M. and Houck-Loomis, T. 2018. History through trauma. *Journal of Pastoral Care & Counseling*, 72(4), 285–286. https://doi.org/10.1177/1542305018813290

West, G., Lervåg, A., Birchenough, J.M., Korell, C., Rios Diaz, M., Duta, M., Cripps, D., Gardner, R., Fairhurst, C., and Hulme, C. 2024. Oral language enrichment in preschool improves children's language skills: a cluster randomised controlled trial. *Journal of Child Psychology and Psychiatry*, 65(8), 1087–1097.

PUT IT INTO PRACTICE
PLAY CHECKLIST

THE FREE-FROM PRINCIPLES

✦ Play needs to be free-from too much adult-interference

We must embrace that a back-seat approach to play can be beneficial at times. Taking a step back and tuning into opportunities for meaningful interaction are crucial but we should also be able to tune into play that is meaningfully self-directed and valid.

✦ Play needs to be free-from adult-driven outcomes

If play has a solely adult-driven outcome, it does not meet the features of self-directed play. This is okay so long as there is a balance, but if the first thing you are thinking is "what is the learning?" then you are forgoing being in the moment with the child and flourishing in the self-directed play.

✦ Play needs to be free-from interruption

Play needs time to unfold. Yes, the early years and especially the school system are subject to time constraints, but we need to think about ways of affording uninterrupted access to play, for example, adapting circle times, or snack times where everyone has to eat at the same time. Try rolling snack, or condense your circle times, and empower the benefits of uninterrupted play.

✦ Play needs to be free-from re-direction and sabotage

Play can be for play's sake. If we don't agree or like the type of play we are observing in a child, we should not re-direct it if it meets the features of self-directed play and the child is demonstrating a willingness and joy in their play.

DOI: 10.4324/9781003323211-7

✦   Play needs to be free-from compliance

So long as the play is safe, we should not focus on compliance during play: for example, "play quieter" or "only play in this way" otherwise we risk interfering with a child's divergent thinking, and we are taking away the freedoms that are meant to come with play and safe risk.

✦   Play needs to be free-from transaction

Play is often used as a luxury or reward both in early years settings and schools. The idea that the real learning happens when the adult is dictating what is permitted. Play is then used in a transactional manner. For example, "If you do XYZ, then you can play" or in more harmful practices, "You are no longer getting your golden time on Friday". For example, "If you do XYZ, then you can play". There is also the issue of Golden Time in school in which children are taught that they must earn play as a reward which undermines play as a developmental right. Play should not be reliant on a transaction, otherwise we are creating rules for play that lead to developmental deprivation.

CHECKING FOR NEURODIVERSITY-AFFIRMING PLAY-BASED INTERVENTION PROGRAMMES

Currently, early educators are expected to embrace and demonstrate their adoption of early intervention practices including intervention programmes. Regardless of whether educators fully subscribe to the principles of early intervention, including its terminology, it is essential for us as educators to scrutinise these strategies and recommendations. Our goal is to adapt them in a way that aligns with the principles of neurodiversity-affirming practice. Here are several ways to achieve this:

1.   Avoid teaching mimicry of neurotypical development

There's a growing body of evidence suggesting that interventions can often lead to masking, which carries a significant mental health toll. Masking involves children camouflaging or imitating neurotypical or desired behaviours to fit in socially, emotionally, academically, and physically. For example, being expected to give eye contact even if it feels uncomfortable.

2.   Focus on strengths, pleasure, and wellbeing

Interventions should respect and enhance aspects of the child's lived experiences that bring joy and happiness. For example, recognising and encouraging passionate interests can provide pleasure and relaxation through repeated or intense engagement in tasks, behaviours, or objects (Murray, Lesser, and Lawson, 2005). Predictable access to preferred activities and experiences not only reduces negative expressions but also fosters learning and genuine social bonding (Mottron, 2017; Grove et al., 2018; Wood, 2019).

3.   Prioritise autonomy and the right to say "no"

Reflecting on accounts from neurodivergent and disabled adults, early interventions should avoid overbearing physical prompting, ignoring communication attempts, or removing the right to say "no", as these practices can leave children passive, stressed, and vulnerable to abuse (Kirkham, 2017; McGill and Robinson, 2020). For example, if an intervention teaches a child to prioritise external demands over internal needs, they may begin to neglect these needs just to please others.

4.   Child-centered and child-led

Interventions must allow enough flexibility to become needs-led and personalised. While some interventions may focus on "fixing" traits, the primary goal should be meeting the child where they are at, rather than expecting them to conform to normative expectations (Aitken and Fletcher-Watson, 2022).

5.   Consider the child's whole mind and body perspectives

Measure the success of an intervention based on the child's whole mind and perspective, not just normative development measures such as speaking. You should develop self-reporting practices for children to provide feedback and consent through visuals. For example, "Would you like to take part?" with yes and no responses. Practitioners should also tune into signs of stress during intervention programmes as a potential sign of non-consent. For example, if a child is trying to return to their play, or getting upset, they should not be expected to continue in pursuit of an outcome.

6.   Be evidence curious and critical not just evidence-based

Educators are strongly encouraged to follow the evidence base of interventions but the evidence can be bias and ableist. Just because the evidence shows that children may have measurable outcomes, it does not mean those outcomes are always best suited to all children. Be curious and critical about evidence claims especially those that appear to be enforcing neurotypicalism.

7.   Prioritise play-full and exploratory approaches

Interventions should not sacrifice the features of play for structure and measurability. Children should have opportunities to lead, explore, and engage in ways that are meaningful to them. A play-full approach, following the child's lead and incorporating "teachable moments", is often much better suited that overly prescribed or instructive interventions that expect all children to meet the same expectations in the same way, for example, everyone must show listening skills in the same way.

8.   Consider everyday application and adaptability

It is important to consider how an intervention programme benefits and enhances a child's everyday experiences, including how some of the strategies or techniques can be applied outside of the programme to become meaningful. Educators should want to ensure that the skills learnt are sustainable and useful across different contexts. For example, teaching a child to name object words but not equipping them with functional or multimodal forms of communication may lead to minimal differences in reciprocal communication with peers.

PUT IT INTO PRACTICE: THE PLAY
PATTERN DICTIONARY

As you saw in Chapter 3, there is so much we still need to explore in terms of play patterns in neurodivergent and disabled children. Because there has been the outdated view that play does not come naturally to neurodivergent and disabled children, it can often be overlooked or we may not pay as much observational attention to it. The aim of this Put It into Practice is to help you to begin to build knowledge of particular play patterns. Included in this are some initial examples.

Not all play will make sense to you, and it may not "look" conventional. The key is to look beyond typical play, and to think about the diverse features of play:

- ✦   Are there any forms of repetition in their play, actions, or behaviours?
- ✦   Do they return to particular areas?
- ✦   Do they have a fascination with particular objects (remember that these can appear "quirky", for example, rotating door handles)?
- ✦   Have you mistaken a form of play for misbehaviour? For example, appearing to destroy or throw things?
- ✦   How do they react to the space, for example, sensory seeking or using a particular body part a lot?

Have a go at completing your own play dictionary . . .

Possible Play Pattern	Possible Provision	Role of the adult	Emerging interests & Extensions
"Freddy is fascinated by rotating the door handles, but not to escape. He also spins a lot especially in open spaces" Spinning with body and objects	Provide spinning toys such as spinning tops & oval/round items. Provide a rotation explorer basket Join in with whole body spinning for shared experiences. Incorporate rotation items such as a hula hoop	Parallel play – play alongside and repeat actions Provide some commentary and descriptive language such as: ✦ Rolling ✦ Round and round	Rotational Schema Sensory Regulation through stimming

REFERENCES

Aitken, D. and Fletcher-Watson, S. 2022. Neurodiversity-affirmative education: Why and how. *The Psychologist*. Retrieved from www.bps.org.uk/psychologist/neurodiversity-affirmative-education-why-and-how

Grove, R., Hoekstra, R.A., Wierda, M., and Begeer, S. 2018. Special interests and subjective wellbeing in autistic adults. *Autism Research*, 11, 766-775. https://doi.org/10.1002/aur.1931.

Kirkham, E. 2017. *The Effects of Early Life Stress on Affective Processing: Behavioural and Neural Correlates* (Doctoral dissertation, University of Sheffield).

McGill, O. and Robinson, A. 2020. "Recalling hidden harms": Autistic experiences of childhood applied behavioural analysis (ABA). *Advances in Autism*, 7(4), 269-282.

Mottron, L. 2017. Should we change targets and methods of early intervention in autism, in favor of a strengths-based education? *European Child and Adolescent Psychiatry*, 26, 815-825. https://doi.org/10.1007/s00787-017-0955-5.

Murray, D., Lesser, M., and Lawson, W. 2005. Attention, monotropism and the diagnostic criteria for autism. *Autism*, 9(2), 139-156.

Wood, R. 2019. Autism, intense interests, and support in school: From wasted efforts to shared understandings. *Educational Review*. https://doi.org/10.1080/00131911.2019.1566213

CHAPTER 5

PLAY-FULL, REST-FULL, AND STRESS-LESS ENVIRONMENTS

A NOTE ON THIS CHAPTER

When we think of early childhood environments, we might think of images of beautiful spaces that draw upon a particular international pedagogy or novel approach. Like others, I have spent time scrolling through Pinterest and other social media for inspiration while feeling that some of these spaces are beyond budget, design capacity, or match children's current preferences. Aesthetics have become a talking point in the early years, specifically caution about designing visually pleasing spaces that are incompatible with children's interests, needs, and motivations. For example, it worries me that there has become an aversion to plastic or commercial toys in favour of natural and heuristic materials. It does not need to be either/or and instead we should be aiming for balance across materials and resources which ultimately tune into individual differences, preferences, and needs. This chapter is not a mandate for how your environment should look. The focus is on widening accessibility and participation, particularly for neurodivergent and disabled children.

STARTING POINTS

Every day, you find yourself in various spaces and environments. You spend time at home, at work, and in community areas, both indoors and outdoors. Some environments are familiar, while others are new, and you navigate across the known and unknown regularly. Some people prefer predictability and structure, spending time in safe spaces, while others may be comfortable venturing beyond their daily routines. While most environments support your needs and wants, some may be incompatible. We don't just exist within

DOI: 10.4324/9781003323211-8

environments but constantly interact with them, significantly influencing our feelings of safety and wellbeing. Take a moment to think about the environments you spend time in:

+ Do you have an environment that you love to spend time in?
+ Why do you love to spend time in this environment?
+ In what ways does this environment meet your needs and wants (think mind and body)?
+ Are there any features or aspects that make this environment feel like a good space?

Now think of an environment you prefer less:

+ Do you have an environment you dislike?
+ What makes you dislike spending time in this environment?
+ How does this environment meet or fail to meet your needs and wants (think mind and body)?
+ Are there any features or aspects that make this environment feel less accommodating?

According to Steve Maslin (2021), research consistently shows that the design of environments can lead to stress responses. In other words, our environments impact our physical, social, cognitive, and emotional wellbeing. The purpose of this starting point task is to encourage you to think about the impact environments have on you so you can begin to explore environmental impacts on all children including those who are neurodivergent and disabled.

INTRODUCTION

Our responses to an environment can be deeply personal. How I feel in an environment will be different to yours. To illustrate, I recently said to my husband that I struggle to feel safe and comfortable if our house is not free of mess and clutter. If I sit in one room knowing there is a mess or clutter in another, I feel like my brain is stuffed with it, and I cannot focus. My husband, on the other hand, does not feel impacted by clutter or mess. He says it fades into the background when he needs to focus rather than being a distraction. We function differently around clutter. This example, though minor, underscores a larger point: environments should not be designed with a one-size-fits-all approach. Instead, they need to consider the varied wants, preferences, and needs of the individuals using them. While some universal elements can create a positive atmosphere, truly effective and supportive environments require specific consideration of the needs of the children in your care, meaning your environment will evolve over time based on the different groups of children in your care. It should also be a collaborative process in which children's views and behaviours actively shape the space. This means adapting and developing the environment over time to suit their needs better. In early childhood, continuous provision is a term often used to describe what is consistently available to children. Still, the environment is more multi-layered than this, and you might want to think about in terms of the following:

Play and Learning Base	Continuous Provision	Enhanced Provision
It s natural to want to create an ideal learning environment for children immediately, but it is important to understand their preferences, interests, and motivations first. While having a solid foundation is crucial, such as considering routines and familiarity, the environment should develop alongside the children. By deciding on key features, layout, and routines, you'll have the flexibility to adjust and improve the provision based on the children's needs and feedback. You might think of this as your play and learning base.	Continuous provision in EYFS refers to the resources and learning opportunities accessible to children all the time within a provision. When developed well, it will invite children to interact, explore, and learn. Having these resources available at all times enables children to choose what they would like to play and engage, leading them to discover new things about the world around them. It also enables them to develop their skills and interests in their own way and at their own pace.	Enhanced provision in EYFS refers to the changes, enhancements, provocations, and additions you make to a space based on children's interests, learning differences, and needs. For example, you might add construction materials to the block area based on a child's interest in building. Enhanced provision can take many forms, including the addition of new resources, changes to the layout of the environment, or the introduction of new activities or experiences. It is a flexible approach that enables educators to adapt to the changing needs and interests of the children in their care.

Across this chapter, you will explore how to develop a neuro-holistic environment that supports neurodivergent and disabled children. Four key themes will be covered:

1. Ableism and the Early Childhood Environment
2. Moving towards neuro-holistic environments which includes the following aspects:

  a. Physical and sensory including accessibility
  b. Social and emotional
  c. Temporal
  d. Outdoor and community access

ABLEISM AND EARLY CHILDHOOD ENVIRONMENTS

The design of our early childhood environments can reinforce certain social rules, cues, and norms. For example, desks may always have chairs around them because this is considered the "norm", even though some children may prefer to stand to play, and some may be physically disabled and not require a chair. Although neurodivergent and disabled children may be physically present in our spaces, there are often "hidden" aspects of these environments that can be exclusionary to them or imply certain messages about how that environment should be used. Our environment communicates a lot about the degree to which it is inclusive and so we must regularly consider what messages they convey.

THE FACADE OF INCLUSION

When we think of inclusive environments, we may focus on the physical aspects of that space. For example, we may consider accessibility or how we might make the space predictable so a child can easily navigate the space. Similarly, we might show that we are inclusive by the physical features and resources, such as visuals or displayed books that are considered representative. These things are vital and deserve attention, but how our environment looks on the surface can also sometimes conceal our lack of meaningful inclusion. There can be a tendency for educators to consider inclusion through place-based inclusion. For example, educators often equate inclusion with having neurodivergent and disabled children present in a shared space. However, this approach can overlook critical accessibility needs. If the physical environment is not adequately designed to support these children's needs, they may face barriers or stress, making meaningful inclusion unattainable. Consider the case study below:

Mohammed attends Little Stars three mornings a week. He loves his iPad and Paw Patrol, and his favourite things to play with are the small world characters and anything with wheels. He also likes to build towers and crash them back down. Mohammed has high support needs. He has cerebral palsy and some learning differences and difficulties. He has been allocated a 1:1 through some funding. Mohammed spends most of his time with his 1:1, and they go off and do individual activities so the 1:1 can work on his individual targets. He can also struggle physically, so he has less access to the environment in case he has an accident. While his peers will engage with him and ask questions, his parent has expressed concerns that he does not have much time to cultivate friendships.

PRESS PAUSE

1. How might the current approach to supporting Mohammed's individual needs impact his sense of belonging and social connections within the Little Stars community?
2. In what ways can the educational setting ensure a balance between addressing Mohammed's individual targets and fostering opportunities for him to build meaningful friendships with his peers?

The case study above shows that while Mohammed may be physically present in the setting, more is needed to ensure inclusive practices that support meaningful learning, participation, and belonging, including time for him to cultivate friendships (Kurth and Foley, 2014). The environmental support, including a 1:1 support worker designed to include him, can sometimes have an exclusionary effect because he spends time away from peers and is not included in everyday activities and experiences. Mohammed's experience is not unique and highlights a common challenge in early childhood education. Despite our best intentions, our environments and practices are not always designed with meaningful inclusion in mind. In many cases, early educators are under pressure to segregate, integrate, and in worst cases exclude those children who do not fit into the expected norms.

Meaningful inclusion: Actively tuning into the diversity of children and expanding, adapting and cultivating unique differences and needs while drawing upon collective practices that benefit all children.

Place-based inclusion: Children being physically present in an environment but not actively being included.

Exclusion: Removing or denying a child from participating in their education.

Segregation: Separating children based on their abilities or characteristics and separating them from typical developing peers.

Integration: Placing children with an educational space with the expectation that they must change their inherent traits and characteristics to participate.

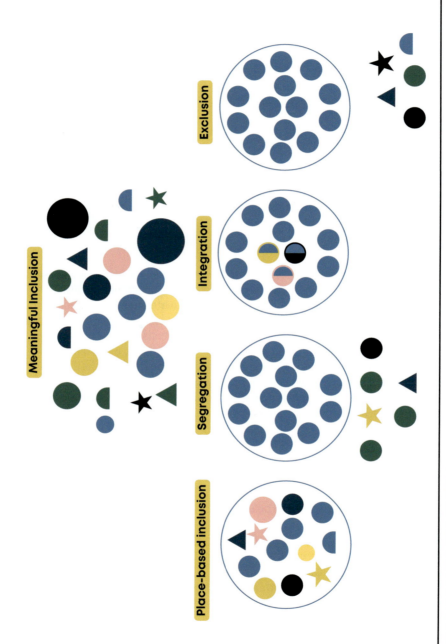

FIGURE 5.1 THE MYTHS OF INCLUSION

Since our curriculums, frameworks, and child development documents are designed primarily for typically developing and non-disabled children, this often influences how we design our environments. This approach generally categorises typically developing children as the norm, while those with *special educational needs and disabilities (SEND)* are viewed through a deficit lens. For example, it is not uncommon for early educators to express that a neurodivergent or disabled child is negatively impacting the experiences of typically developing children. This perspective emerges from the idea that it is the neurodivergent or disabled child who should ideally change to fit in, also known as integration. Consequently, inclusion becomes about how well a child can assimilate to fit existing norms. Martínez-Álvarez (2019) and Souto-Manning (2013) argue that this approach limits opportunities to innovate and rethink how we support children's participation, access, and experiences within our environments. In summary, if we are not actively adapting to the diverse needs and differences of children, meaningful change will not happen, and the same barriers to inclusion will persist.

NEUROINSIGHT

ENVIRONMENT

As an early years teacher trainee, I spoke to my university tutor about the messages my classroom design sends to neurodivergent children. I noticed visual reminders in every corner of every wall, and children constantly saw behavioural reminders that did not always match their developmental needs. For example, I do not think there is a classroom that does not have a set of visuals for whole-body listening, "golden rules", or how to sit and listen appropriately. So, while I may be a bit more laid back about fidgeting and movement, the child is still subjected to the norms of expected behaviour.

My tutor always reminds me that as children move into school, their developmental readiness often becomes overlooked in favour of academics, meaning our environments focus on encouraging sitting still for learning. I have removed lots of the visuals that dictate how children should behave and learn, and we have created some of our own class agreements and drawings. The children have taken ownership, and I've noticed empathy between peers. For example, I taught the children about stimming so they could better understand their neurodivergent peers and embracing stimming is now one of our agreements.

Early Years Trainee Teacher

It does not just fall to early educators to shift from place-based inclusion. We can only develop meaningfully inclusive environments by having an early education system that is committed to dismantling ableism in the physical design of spaces and in the "hidden" environment where norms become embedded.

ENVIRONMENTAL CONSIDERATIONS

Studies have demonstrated that the physical attributes of the environment can significantly influence children's perception of and engagement with both indoor and outdoor spaces (Sandseter, Storli, and Sando, 2022), as outlined below.

Shaping our emotions and how we feel in a particular space	✦ Spaces can elicit certain emotions and associations. For example, if we have been in a space that has positive experiences, we are likely to have better associations with that space and vice versa. ✦ If a child has continued negative experiences, it might be that you will need to consider how to build more positive associations over time so that the child doesn't development negative feelings about the space. ✦ Children may experience avoidance in spaces where that been stress or adversity. For example, coming into the entrance of the setting and realising that is where they must separate from a parent or carer.
Our sense of comfort and how well it meets our unique and individual needs	✦ We all have basic care needs within a space, and it is not just about meeting these but ensuring that a child knows the routines and rhythms of how these will be supported. For example, having consistent care routines, and clear but flexible social expectations. ✦ Children need to build up trust that their needs will be met. This does not just come naturally but through consistent routines and familiar environments.
Feelings of safety and capacity to go beyond comfort zones	✦ For a child to play freely, and in abundance, they need to first know that, fundamentally, they are safe. While there are basic safety principles, it is also knowing the individual child's tolerance for uncertain environments. ✦ The only way a child will go beyond comfort zones is to feel grounded within the play and learning zone they are in. It is about knowing that if you jump, you can land again.

Levels of engagement and motivation for involvement	✦ Ultimately, the way a child gets the most from an early childhood space is to know that they can pursue their interests, get lost within their play patterns in a flow state and to have their ways of playing respected, honoured, affirmed, and extended. ✦ Lots of disruptions and distractions can build negative associations and make children uncertain about who the space is actually designed for.

Children require environments with meaningful contexts for optimal learning and comfort for play, relationships, and care. This includes a variety of opportunities to explore and discover their interests and motivations while facing challenges through safe risk and critical thinking (Hirsh-Pasek, Golinkoff and Eyer, 2003). The environment encompasses more than just physical surroundings. It also includes emotional, temporal, social, and multi-sensorial components. To create a sustainable and healthy environment, we must consider all of these aspects, how they interact with one another, and how this impacts children with diverse differences and needs. For example, our environment may have many exciting features but may be inaccessible to some children. For example, a child who likes to move a lot may find contained nooks and crannies too restrictive. Likewise, a space may be visually pleasing but may only foster a sense of wellbeing if it is quiet and comfortable.

Your early years environment constantly communicates, reinforces, and upholds social rules and norms, and in some cases, this can be exclusionary to neurodivergent and disabled children. For example, a child may be encouraged to play and take safe risks but if they are then told to "be careful" constantly, they may develop confused understandings about that space. Therefore it is vital that we create spaces that support child health and happiness by taking a neuro-holistic approach to environmental design.

DEFINING NEURO-HOLISTIC ENVIRONMENTS

Early childhood spaces are dynamic and varied. Some may be in purpose-built environments, while others may be in converted homes, town halls, or community spaces. For childminders, the environment exists within their homes. The expectation is that early childhood spaces should also provide access to outdoor spaces, designated play areas, and opportunities to be within their communities. Early educators should think creatively about the layout and design, ensuring the space is inviting, safe, stimulating, and flexible to diverse differences and needs. Early childhood environments cannot be set up cookie-cutter-style because there is often much greater focus placed on the child-led components, and so educators must ensure the environment matches up to the cohort of children.

THE PHYSICAL AND SENSORY ENVIRONMENT

The **physical environment** is characterised by the objects, materials, and people that make up the learning environment and how it is laid out, set up, and maintained. As young children interact with the physical space and its elements, they actively shape their play, learning, and developmental experiences. Educators also provide a physical presence as a secure base, allowing children to feel safe and close while also encouraging exploration.

> **KEY TERM**
>
> A **secure base** is the physical presence of a familiar caregiver who provides a sense of safety and security for a child. This allows the child to confidently explore their environment and the world around them. The key aspect of a secure base is that the child can always return to the caregiver to regain a sense of safety and security.

The physical environment needs to account for both indoor and outdoor play along with rest, and routine spaces, such as snack and self-care areas. Architects recognise the profound influence that physical environments can have on human wellbeing and engagement, a principle particularly relevant in early childhood spaces. According to Smith et al. (2012), "environments that people inhabit and experience have the power to enhance the wellbeing of individuals and their communities" (p. 2). Therefore, it becomes imperative to design early childhood spaces with a keen understanding of the needs of children, and community.

The **sensory environment** is any aspect of the setting that can be heard, seen, touched, emotionally felt, or smelt. This includes the visual layout of the classroom, noise, sounds, or auditory input, sensory play materials such as sand and playdough, smell, classroom chaos, nature play, furnishings, and environment zones (Tamblyn et al., 2023).

Children interact with and interpret the physical environment through the senses, meaning every space is a sensory environment - not just designated sensory rooms. The eight sensory systems include: **visual, auditory, olfactory, gustatory, tactile, vestibular, proprioceptive**, and **interoception**. Sensory stimuli are a by-product of the physical environment, so educators need to consider how children process and make sense of their environments through their sensory systems.

Early childhood spaces are known for having a continuous flow of sensory information. In short, they can be busy and quickly become overwhelming, using up a child's energy. Educators need to consider not only the individual **sensory portraits** of children but also how they can provide multi-sensory equilibrium across the space.

A sensory spider can be a useful way to discuss the different sensory experiences of children with your setting.

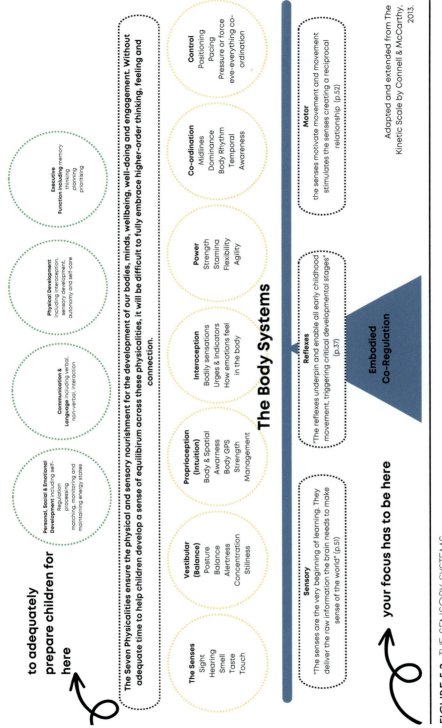

FIGURE 5.2 THE SENSORY SYSTEMS

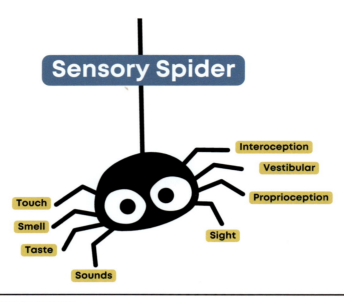

FIGURE 5.3 SENSORY SPIDERS

PUT IT INTO PRACTICE

LAYOUT THAT MAKES SENSE AND OFFERS PREDICTABILITY

✦ For example, the environment is organised into clearly defined areas such as a reading corner, art zone, and sensory play area.

✦ Each area is consistently arranged, and logical with visuals and signs that cultivate predictability. The environment is only changed around to meet the needs of the children, otherwise it should have a stable base layout.

✦ Too many changes to your space can overwhelm or confuse children, particularly if a child has executive function differences.

CLEAR AND FLEXIBLE PARTITIONING OFFERING OPPORTUNITIES FOR CONTAINMENT AND FREEDOMS IN PLAY

✦ For example, low shelves and dividers create distinct play zones within the environment. These partitions should be flexible and be easily adjusted to accommodate different play activities, allowing for containment when needed (e.g. quiet time or spaces for children to retreat).

✦ Equally, children should not feel "boxed in" so you will also need to consider spaces that offer freedom and afford space for energetic play.

CLUTTER-FREE WITH LOGICAL OPTIONS FOR STORAGE

✦ For example, storage areas and shelves are labelled with visuals and words, ensuring that toys and materials are logically organised.

✦ A clutter-free environment makes it easier for neurodivergent children to focus on specific activities, and the logical storage options facilitate easy access to desired materials. You may also have Special Interest (SpIN) Boxes for individual children who have specific play preferences and patterns.

SEQUENCED MATERIALS

✦ For example, play and learning materials are arranged sequentially, supporting neurodivergent children in understanding and following a logical progression. For instance, a photo sequence may be used to show examples of how a toy or resource could be used, or an environment is set up similarly each day where a child is developing increasing confidence in playing freely.

✦ It can be particularly beneficial to enable play creations to remain in place or set up so that children can return to play, or to take photos of play that can be shown the next day. Children can benefit from returning to familiar environments where they can pick up where they left off the day before.

FURNITURE AND LAYOUTS THAT SUPPORT PLAYING AT DIFFERENT HEIGHTS

✦ For example, the environment includes a variety of seating options such as floor cushions, child-sized chairs, and bean bags.

✦ You may also add sensory soothers to seating such as elastic bands around chair legs. There are also raised platforms such as tables without chairs for standing play and cosy corners with soft pillows for lying down. This accommodates the diverse sensory needs and preferences of neurodivergent children.

✦ Sedentary and "sitting still" behaviours are de-prioritised in spaces where children need to move freely to be able to think and play.

A GOOD RANGE OF TOYS, INCLUDING THOSE RELATED TO INTERESTS

✦ For example, the toy selection includes a mix of sensory toys, puzzles, building blocks, and items related to specific interests like animals or vehicles. This variety ensures that neurodivergent children can engage in activities that align with their preferences and developmental needs.

✦ Non-toys are also included within the environment including heuristic play, loose parts, and bric-a-brac.

✦ There has been a tendency in recent years to de-prioritise commercial toys, or plastic materials in early childhood settings, but this can be unhelpful when thinking about the diverse play patterns of children and for example, removing small world figures related to children's interests can result in the removal of potential special interests or particular fascinations.

CLEAR CONSIDERATION OF REASONABLE ADJUSTMENTS AND ACCESSIBILITY

✦ For example, environments are equipped with sensory-friendly lighting, noise-cancelling headphones, and adjustable tables and chairs.

✦ Visual schedules are prominently displayed to assist with transitions, and the physical layout is designed to accommodate mobility devices, ensuring that the space is inclusive and accessible for all. The planning for these things should not only happen when a child has developmental differences or disabilities but should be part of the overall consideration of inclusive spaces.

CLEAR, CONSISTENT, AND MODERATE LABELLING OF RESOURCES WITH OBJECTS OF REFERENCE, VISUALS, AND WORDS

✦ For example, each area and storage container is labelled with a combination of words, symbols, pictures, braille, and tactile objects of reference.

✦ This helps neurodivergent children understand the purpose of each space and locate materials independently. Labels are consistent throughout the classroom for added predictability. Avoid excessive labelling that can become equally confusing. Look around your everyday environment and think of a balanced use of labels and signposting that doesn't result in confusion.

THE SOCIAL AND EMOTIONAL ENVIRONMENT

Young children's **social environments** consist of the people and relationships important to them. Caregiving and personalised co-regulation from familiar and trusted adults provide the conditions for the child to figure out their own emotions, feelings, and behaviours (self-regulation). In essence, social interactions can help children's minds and bodies to find safety.

The **emotional environment** refers to "felt safety" in which children are nurtured to embrace joy, happiness, and connection. They are also free to express uncomfortable emotions and feelings without fear, shame, or judgement. The experience of emotions is unique to each child. Educators understand that emotions and how children feel them can be complex and disorientating, and they afford children the time, space, and support to figure out their emotional diversity. Children feel safe to "give life" to their emotional experiences and can draw upon various experiences to make sense of their emotional worlds through expression, connection, play, literacy, and representation.

Educators recognise the close connection between the emotional environment and the eight sensory systems particularly sensory overwhelm or underwhelm activating a child's stress levels. They know that sensory responses and reactions can disrupt children's emotional equilibrium. Therefore, they ensure the environment is flexible and adjusts to accommodate individual differences and needs.

This social and emotional environment provides an early blueprint through which children can relate to their peers and begin to make preferences in friendships and how they like to be with others. The social environment should provide opportunities for children to become autonomous, for example, knowing how to ask for help, self-advocate, and express needs and preferences. The social environment should also cultivate unique competencies in interactions and negotiating, for example, taking turns and helping children relate to each other, including how they might do things differently or be different from each other in how they socially and emotionally connect (see the Double Empathy Problem in Milton, 2012). Social and emotional environments should not be about enforcing compliance, such as neglecting emotional needs to fit into the rules and routines.

Social and emotional spaces must also account for bias. The anti-bias principles (identity, diversity, justice and activism) should drive the social environment:

✦ Educators will help children to understand their personal and social **identities**, such as racialised identity, gender, and social class.
✦ Educators will cultivate children's comfort and joy towards human diversity, use socially conscious language for human differences and form deep, caring connections across all dimensions of human **diversity**.
✦ Educators will support children's capacity to identify and understand bias and nurture each child's empathy and solidarity against **injustice**.
✦ Educators will welcome early forms of **activism** and cultivate each child's ability and confidence to advocate for themselves and others in the face of bias.

(Adapted from Derman-Sparks, L., LeeKeenan, D., and Nimmo, J. 2015.
Leading Anti-bias Early Childhood Programs: A Guide for Change.
Teachers College Press.)

COMPANION RESOURCE

You can read and watch about anti-bias education via the companion website: www.antibiasleadersece.com/the-film-reflecting-on-anti-bias-education-in-action/

PRESS PAUSE

While early childhood spaces are generally understood to promote "home-from-home" spaces that prioritise comfort and safety, the same cannot always be said for school environments where there has been a drastic increase in emotional school-based avoidance, and this disproportionately affects neurodivergent and disabled children (Connolly, Constable, and Mullally, 2023). The reality is that children are experiencing such heightened states of anxiety by being in hostile environments, that they cannot be themselves in these spaces. As early educators, we can learn from this crisis to provide spaces that help children to thrive. There can sometimes be a tendency to want to set up your early childhood environment to mimic a school-based classroom under the guise that this will ensure children are school ready. This is ill-advised and exposes children to environments that are now considered quite outdated, and uniformed. Your environment must be developmentally meaningful which ensures that children are gaining experiences that are compatible with what is needed in that moment as opposed to what they might (or might not) benefit from in the future. Furthermore, schools could potentially take inspiration from the approaches to high-quality early years environments.

POLYVAGAL THEORY AND THE EMOTIONAL CLIMATE

According to Desautels; "Our nervous systems are as unique as our thumbprints. Each of us carries around an individualised backpack that holds our distinctive maps of the world. Those maps have been unconsciously created to help us interpret and survive, as we are constantly detecting the "temperature" of a safe or threatening environment, relationship of experience" (2023, p.19). The environment is crucial in supporting emotional development and social engagement. Your early years environment will never be completely stress-free. Stress is a natural part of life that helps us recognise when something is wrong, such as sensing a threat or motivating us to address our unmet needs. The environment can reduce stress for young children or contribute to or worsen it. Stress affects us both physiologically – like sweating and a racing heartbeat – and through our behaviours. For example, I sometimes switch off to manage the sensory input in loud and busy spaces, which can sometimes be mistaken for rudeness when my social interactions decrease. Similarly, a child may appear to ignore instructions, but this might be down to stress or overwhelm instead of defiance. Furthermore, we do not always have a choice about which environment to be in. Children do not get to choose their environment during their early years and have little control over how that environment might work. Parents and carers will often spend lots of time trying to find a setting that they know will be sensitive to their child's preferences. Humans continually manage stressors in their surroundings while attempting to stay socially, emotionally, physically, and sensorily balanced within a space. We can understand the role of stress through polyvagal theory.

Polyvagal theory has been described as the "science of feeling safe" (Dana, 2018) and has been developed by Dr Stephen Porges (2011). The theory focuses on what is happening within our bodies and nervous system and how we respond to safety, danger and threats. You may already be familiar with the fact that when we as humans detect threats, or danger, we can enter different stress states, and the most referred to ones are flight or fight response. Polyvagal theory provides us with a bit more explanation as to how those stress responses are activated (think of it like an alarm clock):

PARASYMPATHETIC/VENTRAL VAGAL STATE (SOCIAL ENGAGEMENT SYSTEM)

When we feel safe, the ventral vagal pathway is activated and is linked to social engagement. Our bodies feel relaxed and grounded and we can tune into social, environmental and other emotional cues. We will feel present, tuned-in and responsive. Bombèr suggests that it can be useful to think about how you might describe this state to children, for example, "Are you in your happy place" or being in the "What colour do you feel?".

SYMPATHETIC STATE (FIGHT/FLIGHT SYSTEM)

When the body senses a threat, another part of the ventral vagal pathway is activated. It is useful to remember that our nervous system uses sensory information and past experiences to make predictions about whether there is a threat, and this can be quite unique to the individual. For example, I have a fear of flying and enter sympathetic state (flight) when I am confronted with stepping onto a plane, whereas my husband finds flying exhilarating and exciting so enters ventral vagal state (socially engaged).

You might notice bodily changes in a child entering fight or flight, for example they may be breathing in huffs or puffs or be red faced. Or they may hold parts of their body that may be reacting such as a churning stomach. The child may seem hypervigilant or jumpy and may become overwhelmed by demands or instructions. We sometimes might notice that their energy levels are bordering on hyperactive, or that they appear to be retreating or hiding away. Do note that being energetic or nesting can also be a sign of social engagement and relaxation and in deciding upon a child's emotional state, you need to think of the bigger picture.

Consider, again, what you might refer to this state as and how you can help a child to know that they are experiencing fight or flight. This could also be accompanied by visual representations for children of different communication profiles.

This state is also associated with neurodivergent meltdown in which the child has become flooded with sensory input and is unable to process what is happening leading to heightened emotional and physical reactions.

DORSAL VAGAL STATE (FREEZE SYSTEM)

For some children, the third state will be activated and is often associated with children who are experiencing toxic stress, or trauma. Unfortunately, this means that neurodivergent and disabled children who have been exposed to consistently ableist practices will likely be vulnerable to toxic stress. This system immobilises children into freeze states, of which the following can occur:

✦ Hyper-freeze which creates the feeling of being outside of your body, leading to masking, or risk taking.
✦ Hypo-freeze or flop when we simply surrender to the threat and may feel unable to move or function. This experience is commonly associated with neurodivergent shutdowns in which the child is unable to speak, move or function.

(adopted from Bombèr, 2020)

The child may not appear to hear what we are saying, and may appear vacant or blank. They almost act in unusual ways, for example, using vocalisations. There may be the presence of self-stimulatory behaviours such as rocking, or the child may appear floppy, and restless.

This state is also associated with neurodivergent shutdown in which the child has become too flooded with input and they have shutdown. It is important to remember that children are not choosing to enter freeze, rather it is the brain and bodies protection system.

The important thing to remember with these states is that the environment can engage each of these responses and the child is not necessarily making a conscious choice about their reactions.

SNAKES AND LADDERS

Porges often discusses the hierarchy of states within polyvagal theory. As explained before, at the top of this hierarchy, a child experiences a sense of connection, safety, and readiness for engagement (mobilised). However, they are continually and subconsciously monitoring for threats or dangers, which could cause them to descend the ladder. In many cases, the child may not have immediate control over their response (this develops over time), and they may drop down to either the fight or flight response, or into a freeze state, where they become immobilised. I visualise this process akin to the game "Snakes and Ladders". Positive, calming, and connecting experiences enable the child to climb the ladder, while threats and dangers act as slippery snakes, causing them to slide back down. Over time, as we develop self-awareness through learning about our brains, bodies, emotions and behaviours, there are less slippery snakes, and more autonomous control of going up and down the hierarchy.

For neurodivergent and disabled children, polyvagal theory still applies as our nervous system is based on the same principles as neurotypical populations. However, there may be increased sensitivity to stress, and oftentimes, the presence of trauma due to existing in an ableist world. It is important to point that out that Porges focused on neurotypical pro-social skills as evidence of safety and connection, and as educators we must be flexible in understanding that what is pro-social to one child may be different to another. Stress can be unpredictable at the best of times, but unpredictability is often a significant trigger for children with developmental differences who rely on familiarity and predictability as a safety strategy. Much of the support can come through stress prevention and increasing a child's window of stress tolerance through social engagement experiences that are unique and intrinsically motivating to them. We must never expose children to stressful experiences so that they get "used to it" as this can lead to masking.

RESPONDING TO STRESS STATES

The reality is that the way you respond to a child who is experiencing one of the stress states will vary dependent on your holistic knowledge of the child. However, it is also important to draw upon some general "felt safety" strategies.

PLANTING SEEDS FOR NEURODIVERSITY

USE WHOLE-BODY COMMUNICATION TO SUPPORT SAFETY

Children look to us for signs that they are safe. Using whole-body communication, we can help them feel secure in various ways (see Figure 5.4 on whole-body communication). Each child may react differently, so it's important to use a variety of actions and behaviours to connect with them effectively.

Using gestures, facial expressions, tone of voice, and body language can create a reassuring environment that promotes co-regulation. This means we help children balance their emotions and stress by staying well-regulated while supporting ourselves. The more we show safety, the better we can support their emotional wellbeing.

DO ENVIRONMENTAL SCANS AS A PREVENTATIVE AND RESPONSE

The environment can often trigger stress in children. Noise, distractions, or busy spaces can make them feel disoriented. By scanning the environment and making small changes, we can create a safer, more soothing space.

Simple adjustments like dimming bright lights, opening a window for fresh air, or clearing away distractions can make a big difference in helping a child feel more at ease. These changes can significantly reduce stress and promote a sense of safety.

PROVIDE SENSORY COMFORT

Each child has their own unique sensory preferences, so it's important to consider what makes them feel safe and comfortable. For instance, a child may have a transition object, comforter, or favourite toy that helps ground their feelings and emotions. Recognising and incorporating these individual needs can significantly enhance their sense of security and wellbeing.

PROVIDE AN EXIT STRATEGY

When children are experiencing stress, it is important to give them an exit strategy so they have the choice to remove themselves from a situation. Using visuals or talking to them about their options can be helpful in the moment and as preparation, ensuring they do not feel trapped by stressful situations. This empowers children to feel more in control and reduces their worry.

Provide plenty of gateways for social engagement. As educators, we should be centring joy and social engagement wherever possible, offering children lots of ways to develop the feel-good factor (see Gateways for Social Engagement below for some ideas).

Whole-Body Communication as Co-Regulation

Limit your language
When a child is distressed, they are using all their energy to regulate and so may not process lots of language. Avoid phrases such as "use your words" and offer physical reassurance instead.

Pace and Space
Engage in a relaxed rather than urgent pace. Slow down your pace of speech and movements to minimise the sense of urgency

Intonation
Use a non-threatening tone. Children will pick up on your intonation for cues of safety. You can be clear yet compassionate

Proximity
a child may feel impulsive or vulnerable, so be mindful of personal space. Personal space should be respected and side-by-side co-regulation can feel less pressured

Cues and gestures
Use your body as a communication tool with reassuring gestures and actions. For example, model your own self-regulation such as deep breathing or narrating your own self-regulation.

FIGURE 5.4 WHOLE-BODY COMMUNICATION

GATEWAYS FOR SOCIAL ENGAGEMENT					
Below are some ideas for cultivating social engagement:					
Find time for laugher, humour and silliness	Model breathing techniques, such as belly breathing, dragon breathing and weighted breathing prompts to bring awareness to the body	Get outside, and embrace space, freedom and fresh air	Provide activities that are sensory soothing, rhythmic and repetitive	Blow and catch bubbles	Sing and Dance together
Set up a playlist of the children's favourite songs	Stim together	Provide self-hugs and massages	Watch funny videos	Squish and squeeze your bodies to release tension	Turn off the bright lights and embrace natural hues
Blow raspberries, gurgle and hum	Cuddle plushies	Stretch your body parts and reach for the skies	Nest under blanket	Do some heavy work	Stretch, knead and squash sensory materials

Play sound affects	Reduce noise and embrace natural sounds	Tell children you hold them in mind, and provide affirmations	Parallel play with special and intense interests	Read multi-sensory books	Explore the environment barefoot
Chant	Provide a sound bath	Rock, swing, swaddle and sway	Shake off the stress residue	Have a cuddle	Sit back to back and take deep breaths
Sitting in positions that feel comfortable	Lying down, or hanging upside down	Lying under a weighted blanket	Walking	Eating yummy foods including "safe foods"	Uninterrupted Play

GLIMMERS AND TRIGGERS

In neurodivergent and disabled children's development, there is often a tendency to focus solely on what challenges they face or what negatively impacts their participation and engagement. While it is crucial to ensure they receive adequate support, this approach can sometimes cause us to overlook the moments of joy, pleasure, and positivity within their experiences.

The concept of "glimmers", as discussed in polyvagal theory (Porges, 1995), offers a contrasting perspective to triggers. For instance, while a child might be triggered by harsh strip lighting, they might experience glimmers of comfort and delight in natural surroundings, feeling the warmth of the sun on their skin. Glimmers are essential for soothing our often-overwhelmed nervous systems, providing feelings of safety, happiness, and relaxation.

A research paper by Conn (2023) captured the glimmers experienced by autistic adults reflecting on their childhood play. The title referenced "sensory highs," "vivid rememberings," and "interactive stimming"–moments of joy and connection sparked by engaging freely in autistic play. Exploring both triggers and glimmers in neurodivergent and disabled children can help create environments that minimize triggers and foster glimmers.

PRESS PAUSE

✦ In what ways can an understanding of "glimmers" from polyvagal theory reshape our approach to supporting neurodivergent and disabled children?

✦ Reflecting on your own experiences, can you recall a time when you witnessed a neurodivergent or disabled child experiencing a "glimmer" of joy or comfort? What factors contributed to this moment?

✦ What strategies could be implemented to intentionally create environments that evoke moments of "glimmers" for neurodivergent and disabled children?

PUT IT INTO PRACTICE

DEVELOPING AND SECURE ATTACHMENTS BUILT ON UNCONDITIONAL REGARD, ATTUNEMENT, AND UNDERSTANDING:

✦ For example, educators in the classroom consistently demonstrate warmth, empathy, and understanding toward each child. They also remain vigilant to emotion and compassion fatigue and actively prioritise self-regulation for co-regulation.

✦ They see the best in each child and reflect this through their practices. For example, questioning quickly made judgements and reframing.

✦ They engage in activities that foster a sense of belonging and trust, such as daily greetings in preferred forms of communication, shared stories, and individualised attention, creating a secure attachment between the children and adults.

✦ There is an understanding that healthy attachments take time, and where there is developmental diversity, attachments might "look" different. For example, some children may not show affection via hugs but by playing alongside a familiar adult.

CHILDREN KNOW THEY CAN SEEK OUT COMFORT, HELP, GUIDANCE, AND REASSURANCE FROM FAMILIAR PEOPLE

✦ For example, a designated "comfort corner" is established where children can find familiar soft items, such as plush toys or blankets, along with a trusted caregiver.

✦ This space serves as a "safe haven" for children to seek comfort, guidance, or a listening ear when needed. Similarly, educators identify the different ways in which children feel comforted and how to connect with them. For example, going outdoors and running around in the fresh air, or stimming together.

ENVIRONMENT ENABLES CO-REGULATION THROUGH A RANGE OF WAYS

✦ For example, the classroom provides sensory tools like fidget toys, calming music, and cosy corners equipped with weighted blankets.

✦ These resources support co-regulation by helping children maintain their sensory needs and emotional states with the assistance of educators or peers.

✦ Co-regulation is understood as a process of matching energies to tasks as opposed to expecting children to be calm at all times.

CHILDREN HAVE TIME AND SPACE TO "GIVE LIFE" TO FEELINGS AND EMOTIONS

✦ For example, children are not told to stop expressing emotions such as "don't cry" or "don't be silly" but instead reminded that it is okay to express and feel emotions.

✦ The routines include designated "rest time" after certain activities or transitions. During this period, children have the freedom to engage in quiet activities, like drawing or journaling, allowing them time and space to process and express their feelings in a supportive environment.

✦ A diverse range of literacy opportunities are made available to make sense of feelings and emotions.

THE ENVIRONMENT CONTAINS EMOTIONAL LITERACY RESOURCES AND PROPS

✦ For example, the classroom includes emotional literacy, including a feelings/energy chart, emotion cards, and books that explore a range of emotions.

✦ These resources actively promote emotional literacy, providing children with tools to identify, express, and understand their feelings and the feelings of others. Emotional literacy is adapted to suit a range of needs, for example, the use of neuroinclusive, or social stories or the use of symbols and signs to further understanding.

AROUSAL AND RELAXATION CYCLES ARE CONSISTENT

✦ For example, the daily routine incorporates periods of high-energy activities, like outdoor play, followed by calming activities, such as storytime or gentle music.

✦ This consistent rhythm supports neurodivergent children in maintaining their arousal levels and transitioning smoothly between different emotional states. Needs are met consistently, with recognition of stress responses (fight, flight, freeze, and fawn).

✦ These elements collectively create an emotionally supportive and regulated environment where children feel secure, understood, and equipped with the tools to navigate their emotional experiences.

✦ Needs are met in a timely manner.

REVISITING THE DOUBLE EMPATHY PROBLEM

In Chapter 4, you were introduced to the Double Empathy Problem (Milton, 2012, 2014) as part of developmental diversity. We will touch upon this again here when thinking about the social environment for all children.

When considering early childhood spaces, it's important to also think about the social skills, interactions, and communication preferences of children. Varied communication styles among children can sometimes create challenges in understanding each other, especially between neurodivergent and neurotypical conforming children. Often, when difficulties arise, there's a presumption that the neurodivergent child is failing in their communication and needs to be taught to conform to neurotypical norms. This expectation can place a significant emotional and social burden on the child, forcing them to adapt their communication style to fit others. For example, a child may find eye contact difficult but be taught this is a polite way to interact.

As a reminder, Dr Damien Milton's research (2012) presents an insightful perspective that influences social interactions. Milton focused on interactions between autistic and non-autistic individuals and the research revealed that both individuals struggled to comprehend each other, leading to what he termed as an "empathy gap". Contrary to popular belief, Milton found that it wasn't solely autistic individuals who faced challenges in communication. Instead, both autistic and non-autistic individuals grappled with understanding each other's communication preferences, contributing to the empathy gap. This observation gave rise to his theory of the Double Empathy Problem, advocating for the recognition and support of diverse communication preferences rather than assuming autistic individuals are deficient communicators. While this research focuses on autistic people, the findings could be translated to other neurotypes and disabilities to recognise various empathy gaps.

EXAMPLES OF EMPATHY GAP TRAITS

NEUROTYPICAL COMMUNICATION	NEURODIVERGENT COMMUNICATION
Provides eye contact	Has sporadic eye contact
Talks about a range of topics	Prefers to talk in-depth about a specific topic or interest
Prefers chatty cooperative play	Prefers quiet solitary or parallel play
Neutral intonation	Variable intonation
Likes face to face communication	Likes side by side communication
Likes touch	Does not like touch
Likes to remain still or sedentary during interactions	Likes to move or stim during interactions

Please note: these are examples. Communication preferences vary and are very unique. It is crucial to understand the child's unique communication identity, and then to help children to understand each other's preferences.

The Double Empathy Problem has significant implications for the way we plan for our social and emotional environments. We need to consider how to close the empathy gap for children rather than develop environmental practices that require neurodivergent children to change who they are to fit in. Some ways in which we can support social and emotional spaces include:

EARLY EDUCATORS DEVELOP AN UNDERSTANDING OF EACH CHILD'S COMMUNICATION IDENTITY AND SOCIAL PREFERENCES

- ✦ For example, children's preferred communication methods such as mouth words, signs, visuals, body language
- ✦ Different social customs such as greetings, conversing, playing, and initiating are observed to look for preferences. Then support is given to all children to understand each other's similarities and differences.

SOCIAL AUTONOMY IS RESPECTED, AND THE ENVIRONMENT REFLECTS OPPORTUNITIES FOR DIFFERENT LEVELS OF SOCIABILITY

- ✦ For example, the classroom layout includes designated areas for group activities, paired interactions, and solitary play.
- ✦ Children are encouraged to choose the social setting that aligns with their preferences, allowing for diverse social experiences that respect individual autonomy.
- ✦ Children's "space bubbles" or personal space are considered and the environment reflects different types of proximity so children can make choices about how far or near they wish to be to others.

CHILDREN ARE SUPPORTED WHEN SOCIAL BATTERIES ARE LOW, AND SCRIPTS ARE USED TO HELP CHILDREN UNDERSTAND EACH OTHER'S TOLERANCE TO SOCIAL INPUT

- ✦ For example, a "quiet zone" with soft lighting and comfortable seating is available for children to retreat to when they need a break. Social scripts, visual cues, or a designated buddy system are utilised to help children communicate their social needs and understand each other's boundaries.

CHILDREN CAN OPT IN AND OPT OUT OF SOCIAL EXPERIENCES THROUGH THE USE OF VISUALS

- ✦ For example, a visual schedule includes symbols or images representing social activities. Children can use a designated "opt-out" symbol to signal when they prefer not to participate in a particular social experience, fostering a sense of control and agency over their interactions.

CHILDREN ARE NOT FORCED TO SHARE OR TAKE TURNS. INSTEAD, PRO-SOCIAL SKILLS ARE ENCOURAGED WITH BALANCED WITH CHOICE

- For example, the classroom has multiple sets of popular toys, reducing the need for immediate sharing.
- Educators facilitate discussions on taking turns and sharing, emphasising the importance of respecting others' choices and providing alternatives for cooperation, ensuring a balance between pro-social skills and individual choice.

SPECIAL INTEREST GROUPS ARE SET UP FOR SHARED EXPERIENCES

- For example, regular sessions are dedicated to "Special Interest Groups" where children with common interests gather to engage in activities related to their passions.
- This provides a platform for shared experiences, fostering a sense of community and connection among children with similar interests.

NEUROINCLUSIVE STORIES ARE USED TO SUPPORT ALL CHILDREN'S UNDERSTANDING OF SOCIAL AUTONOMY

- For example, Storytime includes books that feature diverse characters and scenarios, highlighting different communication styles and social preferences. These neuroinclusive stories help children understand and appreciate the varied ways individuals may engage socially, promoting empathy, and understanding.

SPACES ACCOMMODATE SOLITARY, OBSERVER, PARALLEL, AND COOPERATIVE PLAY:

- For example, the classroom offers various play areas, including cosy corners for solitary play, observation zones for those who prefer watching before participating, and spaces for both parallel and cooperative play.
- This ensures that the environment caters to different social engagement levels and preferences.

EDUCATORS LEARN ABOUT CHILDREN'S INITIATIONS FOR PLAY AND INTERACTIONS

- For example, non-speaking signs of play initiation such as moving closer to a peer or indicating a desire to play by offering an object or toy, also referred to as "penguin pebbling" (Stimpunks, n.d.).

NEUROFACT: THE ENVIRONMENT CAN CONTRIBUTE TOWARDS PHOBIAS

It takes a lot of emotional, physical, and social energy for some children to feel safe in particular environments. Once a child establishes safety, they may become quite attached to the environment and benefit from familiarity and predictability. However, it is important to be aware that fear or phobias of certain spaces can emerge if children develop negative associations with a space. For example, I supported a neurodivergent child who became very distressed when taken to the nappy change area, which was in a separate room. This environment requires children to be in a state of undress, which can be a confusing and disorientating experience. The act of undressing and changing the child's nappy presented with a set of sensory challenges, plus it was carried out in a separate space. It was decided that the child needed support to feel comfortable with the transition to the nappy change room. We also decided that it made sense to change the child in a familiar environment and so we set up a nappy change corner also within the room, and laid it out so there was still privacy. The child responded well to this and then had some voluntary opportunities to head to the separate nappy change area, and was given time to make sense of the space before being expected to use it. Over time, the child could choose where to have their nappy changed and eventually chose to go to the separate area once the fear of the unknown became less intense. However, toilet trauma and phobias can happen at any age, and often continue to be a fear for children of school age. The self-care spaces are as important in terms of environmental considerations as are the main spaces.

THE TEMPORAL ENVIRONMENT

The concept of the **temporal environment** encompasses the timing, sequence, and duration of routines and activities occurring within the day. This includes routine transitions, ranging from arrival to playtime, meals, rest periods, and both small – and large-group activities. The various transitions between these activities are integral to maintaining consistency and harmony. Below are some temporal considerations.

SOUND, ACOUSTICS, AND NOISE

KEY TERM

Sound generally refers to volume, pitch, or patterns related to speech, music, or some other code, such as nature sounds.

Noise is unique to the hearer but refers to distracting, annoying or unpleasant sounds. Noise largely refers to auditory input can you can also have visual noise which refers to busy environments.

Sounds, noise levels, acoustics, and music all need to be well managed in an early childhood environment. However, you won't always get it right because preferences vary. Some children can filter background noise and distractions, while others may feel quite disoriented. Sound is challenging to manage because we cannot close our ears to it like we can close our eyes to sights. Children may indicate aversion to sounds by covering their ears or hiding away. Conversely, they might seek sound by turning up music or placing their ears next to objects. Certain sounds can also be emotionally triggering; for example a child might show an aversion to certain music because it may be associated with an undesirable routine such as tidy up. Equally music can activate and bring joy to the senses.

When considering sound and acoustics, start by reducing obviously unpleasant noises. For example, if you are setting up a cosy corner, avoid placing it near a window with outdoor traffic noise, as this could distract a child trying to relax. While these might seem like obvious considerations, it's important to remember that sound and noise aversion are very personal. For instance, I supported one child who enjoyed the sound of water pouring, while another found it distracting. It is vital that you co-design the environment with children checking in on their preferences and ideas.

Think carefully about the areas you set up indoors and outdoors, and consider where you impose noise. For example, if outdoors, is it beneficial to play the radio, which drowns out soothing and calming environmental noises that are rhythmic and soothing such as bird song.

NEUROINSIGHT

FEEL-GOOD FACTORS

My group of children love music. It gives us such a feel-good factor across the day. When a child starts at my setting, I ask the parents and carers for their child's favourite songs, and it doesn't have to be a nursery rhyme. I get all kinds. However, I ask for songs that are calming but also energising and I have playlists for different moods. I was caring for a child with complex needs, and his mum said they did a lot of meditation at home, and he loved the rhythm of a meditation bell, so I added that to the playlist and it was so lovely for all the children.

Childminder

LIGHTING

Light illuminates what we see and helps regulate our circadian rhythm, so we have a sense of time and what we should be doing. Although neurodivergent individuals often report time being quite distorted, we generally know when it is time to be awake or sleep. In an early childhood setting, lighting can be a good indicator of routines and rhythms. For example, lower lighting can be beneficial during nap time, and natural lighting over strip lighting can help with mood and focus. We also know that lack of access to direct sunlight can greatly impact our mood. For example, some of us experience seasonal stress or depression.

Visually calm environments support children's moods and regulation. Natural lighting is often idealised in early childhood settings as optimal for learning and development, but it is not always clear why or whether it is always optimal. However, natural lighting influences our moods and behaviours; for example, a gloomy day might make us feel lethargic, while a bright sunny day can lift our spirits. However, this response is personal and does not always follow a seemingly logical pattern, especially for neurodivergent children. For instance, one child might prefer to stay indoors and play video games on a sunny day, while another might want to go outside and play.

Good use of lighting is crucial for designing an early childhood environment, with variation and moderation being key. Access to natural light is beneficial, but accessibility needs consideration. Direct sunlight can be distracting and affect temperature regulation, so shaded areas and cool-down spaces are important. Artificial lighting also has its uses, but constant exposure to strip lighting can cause headaches and fatigue, and various types of artificial lighting can negatively affect those with disabilities. There are intolerances to different light frequencies, colours, and intensities, so it is best to avoid environments lit solely by lamps or fairy lights, as they can be visually intolerable to some.

When using artificial lighting, focus on its purpose. For instance, a lamp with a spotlight placed directly above a mark-making corner might cause glare. Or the light from an unused interactive whiteboard may be distracting. A range of lighting options can support different learning and play behaviours but settings should also be mindful of sufficient lighting for different communication modes. For example, when speaking, we need to be in environments that are well noise-controlled but you will also have children who are using sign and visuals. Can these be seen clearly? Can spaces still be navigated safely with the range of lighting used? I recently visited a setting that had lots of vintage-style lamps which looked lovely yet the room felt too gloomy and appeared to disrupt communication.

SMELLS, TASTE, AND AIR QUALITY

Have you ever been mid-conversation with someone and suddenly a horrible smell emerges? Our first panic is usually: "I hope that person does not think that is coming from me", and second, you might find the unpleasant smell has distracted you. Similarly, have you ever been around someone and they have a delightful but sickly perfume that gives you a headache?

Early childhood environments can be smelly places. Early educators often become accustomed and less offended by the range of smells that occupy the space and from a dignity perspective, they do not draw attention to smells which naturally come from humans. I had a meaningful conversation with a colleague who emphasised that our role as caregivers is to uphold a child's dignity, which includes accepting the smells they may produce due to toileting, growth, or self-care. In other words, we grow used to these smells because our primary focus is on providing sensitive and respectful caregiving. With that being said, smells can influence the mood and wellbeing of an environment. For example, we might find smells unpleasant but we also might have memories evoked by smells. Think of the comfort blanket that comes in with a child that is full of homely smells. Similarly, we might find one smell unfamiliar and unpleasant but to another person, it is the most delightful smell around. For example, people often talk about smelling their dogs' paws which smell like popcorn but evoke the most joyous sensory highs.

Smell cannot be switched on and off but maintaining good air quality is useful such as opening windows for a fresh breeze. Humans are generally better adjusted to natural aromas than artificial ones. For example, if we use lots of cleaning material in our setting, how is this ventilated by natural air flow? Do we open windows during or after cleaning? Aim to neutralise smells and maintaining good air quality, but also ask children about favourite smells and least favourite smells so you have an indication of their sensory preferences.

TEMPERATURE

If we are not comfortable with temperature, we will feel distracted. Have you ever been in a hot space and felt overwhelmed by the physiological and psychological impact of being hot and sweaty? It can disrupt our focus and wellbeing. Children will have different interoceptive needs, meaning their experiences of being hot, warm, cool, or cold may vary regardless of the actual temperature. According to Fischer et al. (2024), people are not only influenced by actual body temperature but also environment and context. For example, if a child is sat playing, and there is a draft coming from under the door, this might feel uncomfortable, whereas a breeze from outside may be refreshing. Temperature tolerance is also influenced by movement. For example, we can be outdoors in the cold but not feel uncomfortable because we are active and engaged and our temperature is being regulated by movement.

PUT IT INTO PRACTICE

THE PLAY AREA IS THOUGHTFULLY ORGANISED WITH CLEAR PATHWAYS AND DEFINED ZONES

- ✦ For example, the playspace is set up with distinct areas for different activities and experiences, making it easy for young children to move around autonomously.
- ✦ This organised space allows children to explore without feeling overwhelmed or confused by the space.

CHILDREN CAN FREELY EXPLORE AND MAKE CHOICES ABOUT WHERE TO PLAY OR TAKE A BREAK

✦ For example, visual cues and simple signs indicate different play areas. Children are encouraged to choose where they want to play, and there are cosy provisions for those who may need a break from sensory stimulation, for instance, a blackout sensory tent.

CONSIDERATION FOR SENSORY TRIGGERS AND EFFORTS TO PROVIDE A BALANCED ENVIRONMENT

✦ For example, the play environment is designed to minimise bright lights, loud noises, and crowded spaces, with dimmable lights, soft background sounds, and quiet corners available for children seeking a more soothing experience.

✦ Access to outdoors is well managed, and where possible, free flow opportunities are offered.

MINIMAL CLUTTER TO REDUCE SENSORY DISTRACTIONS

✦ Visual noise is kept to a minimum and clutter removed

✦ For example, toys and materials are stored in labelled storage and cabinets to keep the environment tidy.

✦ Distractions are minimised, with clear and simple visuals to help children focus on play activities.

THOUGHTFUL USE OF SCENTS AND SMELLS TO CREATE A COMFORTABLE ENVIRONMENT

✦ For example, scented playdough or natural aromas are used sparingly to avoid overwhelming young senses.

✦ The scents chosen are neutral or based on individual preferences to ensure a pleasant olfactory experience for children.

COMFORTABLE CLOTHING IS ENCOURAGED, PRIORITISING SENSORY PREFERENCES

✦ For example, children are encouraged to wear soft and comfortable clothing, avoiding items with irritating seams whenever possible.

✦ The emphasis is on both safety and sensory comfort in their wardrobe choices.

A VARIETY OF SEATING OPTIONS CATER TO SENSORY NEEDS

✦ For example, the play area includes cushions, rocking chairs, and soft mats for children to sit on or move around.

✦ This variety accommodates different sensory preferences and supports the development of sensory-motor skills.

INDIVIDUALISED APPROACH CONSIDERING SENSORY PREFERENCES, USING SIMPLE SENSORY CUES

✦ For example, before children start attending, caregivers create simple sensory profiles for each child, noting their likes, dislikes, and preferences.

✦ This information helps shape the play environment to suit individual sensory needs, ensuring a positive and enjoyable experience.

MINIMISATION OF COMPETING SENSORY INPUT

✦ For example, play zones are arranged strategically to avoid overwhelming sensory experiences. For example, calmer spaces such as reading and relaxion are close together.

✦ High-energy activities are placed away from quieter areas, and caregivers plan activities with consideration for managing sensory input effectively.

OFFERING EXPERIENCE-SENSITIVE ALERTING AND CALMING ACTIVITIES

✦ For example, a cosy corner in the play area includes soft textures, calming visuals, and a few soothing toys.

✦ Additionally, there are areas for more active play to provide toddlers with a range of sensory experiences, promoting self-regulation and exploration.

OUTDOOR SPACE, INCLUDING COMMUNITY

The indoor early years environment is just one of many places where children can play, learn, and develop. Equal attention should be given to outdoor spaces and the local community. One of the arguments for empowering outdoor experiences for neurodivergent and disabled children is that they place less neuronormative demands on children (Conn, 2016). When early educators take play and learning outside, the social rules and norms of everyday life become more relaxed, and educators seem more open to children pursuing their own play interests. For example, expecting children to be sedentary or still outdoors appears to be less of a focus, and embracing movement more welcomed.

It's important to acknowledge that each setting may offer different types of outdoor space and every space has potential. For example, you might have a smaller area with little green space but you could set up a planting space, or have a minimalist design so that the space can be opened up. Additionally, it's crucial to consider the community and how children engage with, navigate, and participate in their local surroundings. Our communities reflect our identities and our lived experiences and so it is important to think about how these connections are made within the setting.

THE IMPORTANCE OF REST-FULL ENVIRONMENTS

How do you feel after a busy day at work? You might sometimes find that the constant demands, processing, expectations, and social interactions overwhelmingly affect your sense of wellbeing, engagement, and tolerance. Moments of kicking off shoes, peeling off uncomfortable clothing, or trying to find time to decompress are important. And even at work, we likely look for those micro-moments to rest. As humans, we are constantly seeking that moment of recovery and repair to maintain ourselves. The same applies to the children we care for and educate. A revelation for me was learning that there are seven types of rest, and this has become a significant part of my planning when thinking about environments and supports for all children. Let's unpick the seven types of rest:

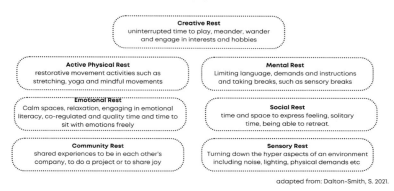

adapted from: Dalton-Smith, S. 2021.

FIGURE 5.5 THE SEVEN TYPES OF REST

REST TYPE	DESCRIPTION	AUDIT
Physical	Physical rest comes in two primary forms: passive and active. Passive rest refers to activities like sleeping and napping, while active rest includes more restorative actions such as stretching, deep massages, or heavy work.	✦ There are spaces where children can wallow in rest through napping, chilling out, retreating and hiding. ✦ The environment affords different rest positions, for example, places to lie down, sprawl out, curl up and snuggle. ✦ There is access to resources for active physical rest such as a sensory soothing basket, or visuals to encourage different restorative movements. ✦ Rest "playlists" are available for children to listen to as they chill out.

191

Mental	Our world is always "on", and taking a break from the constant mental stimulation is crucial. Giving our brains a chance to recharge and process information enables us to stay focused, alert, and productive.	✦ There are spaces that are quieter where children can escape to. ✦ Adult- child interactions strike a good balance, with educators being able to read cues that a child might need some mental rest, for example reducing instructions. ✦ Solitary and parallel play is nurtured with an understanding that some children need time to "zone out" from the mental stimulation. ✦ Repetitive and rhythmic activities are provided for children who need to switch off. ✦ Noise-cancelling resources can be used such as headphones or ear muffs. ✦ Different volume levels are encouraged for different activities with explanations provided to children why the volume matches the mood.
Emotional	Allowing ourselves to rest emotionally is critical as it provides time to process our feelings and maintain emotional balance, avoiding burnout. Remember that these types of rest are crucial for educators too. While it can be difficult to prioritise emotional rest, as we often feel guilty for taking time for ourselves, it's imperative to remember that self-care is not selfish.	✦ Children are offered choices as to whether they want quality time, or time alone. ✦ Mindfulness and bodyfulness is nurtured so children can take time to process emotions and also figure things out through movement such as painting, dancing and stretching. ✦ Journaling and artful expression are encouraged. ✦ Educators can reduce stressors in the environment when emotions are high. ✦ Self-care is accessible such as massaging tools, or being able to spend time outdoors. ✦ Neuroinclusive stories are used to help children process emotional scenarios. ✦ A range of emotional literacy opportunities are available, for example books, music, art and spending quality time with trusted educators or friends.

Sensory	Sensory rest is a practice that involves taking a break from the constant barrage of sensory stimuli we face every day. From noise to light to other external factors, our senses are frequently overwhelmed.	✦ Sensory scans are part and parcel of everyday practice, and where possible sensory input is reduced, for example, switching off strip lighting, or providing fresh air. ✦ Movement is encouraged and welcomed, including heavy work, stretching, and experiencing freedom to express yourself through bodily actions.
Creative	Focusing on creative relaxation can prompt children to enter flow states or to pause on everyday demands. Creative rest is driven by process over product and offers children time to wallow in their worlds.	✦ Children have access to a range of creative materials that might prompt creative relaxation. For example, art supplies and sensory materials. ✦ Children are provided with time to enter flow states and have uninterrupted time to play and just "be". ✦ Children can pursue their own interests and are provided with provocations and invitations to engage in things that interest them and provide sensory and cognitive highs.
Social	As social beings, we interact with others on a daily basis. However, it's essential to take a break from these social interactions. Socialising can be draining, including for children. This is why social rest is crucial – it allows us to recharge and feel refreshed.	✦ Children can choose who to spend time with, and are not expected to constantly be socially "switched on". They can also choose not to spend time with others. ✦ Solitary and parallel play is encouraged as a way of providing social rest. ✦ Social demands are reduced when a child is clearly out of energy, for example, sharing and taking turns expectations adjusted. ✦ Children can opt-in/out of social routines. ✦ Auditory information is reduced as well as instructions and expectations for conversational turn taking. ✦ Demands are reduced. ✦ There are spaces where children can escape to, to get away from other children and adults.

Spiritual	This form of rest aids in giving us meaning and purpose. Spiritual rest serves as an anchor particularly in times of stress or uncertainty. If a child appears withdrawn, disengaged, or isolated, spiritual replenishment can be useful. It's important to note that spiritual rest will be unique to the child. Anything that fosters a connection with purpose, inner self-awareness, or instils a sense of tranquillity and stability can be spiritually revitalising.	✦ Educators understand children's personal and social identities and provides opportunities for them to interact and engage with things that are meaningful to them, for example, listening to music that matters, or engaging in rituals that are grounding. ✦ Children can pursue and get lost in their interests with plenty of time to play. ✦ Children can engage with art, music, expression, poetry, and other forms of literacy that are relevant and representative of their experiences.
	Adapted from Saundra Dalton-Smith (2021.	

PARENT X CARER SOLIDARITY

Parents and carers of neurodivergent or disabled children often worry about how their child will be welcomed and supported in a new environment. It's crucial to reassure them by clearly explaining how their child's needs will be met.

Talking to parents and carers about their recommendations and ideas for making the environment more accessible and accommodating can be very helpful. This collaboration ensures that the space is better suited to their child's unique needs and helps build trust and confidence in your setting.

Some practical ideas are outlined below:

VIDEO AND IN-PERSON TOURS

✦ **Video Tours**: Creating video tours of the setting can be a great way to show parents and carers the play and learning areas. Filming when the environment is not in use allows them to observe the space and consider how it may suit their child's unique needs.

✦ **In-Person Show Rounds**: Following up with an in-person tour demonstrates how the space comes to life. Videos can also introduce parents and carers to staff members.

GATHERING FEEDBACK FROM PARENTS AND CARERS

✦ **Tailored Feedback**: Instead of generic questions, ask specific ones to get more useful feedback. For example:

　✦ How can our space be more autistic-friendly?
　✦ How might we support children with physical disabilities?
　✦ What features of the environment would make dads feel more welcome?

✦ **Inclusive Approach**: Ask all parents for feedback, not just those with lived experience of neurodivergent and disability, to build a network of diverse perspectives.

BUILDING COMMUNITY

✦ **Reflecting Home Life**: The early childhood setting should reflect the community and the diverse home lives of the children. Engage families in discussions about what could be included in the setting. For example:

　✦ Create a family music playlist.
　✦ Display photographs of important people.
　✦ Incorporate home routines and rhythms into the setting.

By using these strategies, we can create a welcoming, inclusive environment that meets the needs of all children and their families.

CHAPTER CONCLUSION

The environment plays a crucial role in influencing children's experiences in your setting. However, it's not just about how we set up, organise, or design a space. We need to carefully consider various design elements to ensure that children can access and engage in ways that are meaningful and comfortable. While there are core principles for designing environments, it's also essential to consider the diverse needs and preferences of each child. Every environment is unique.

This chapter provides a range of ideas and prompts to help you create a space that caters to your unique group of children, enabling them to take ownership and feel autonomous. Reflecting on these ideas can help you enhance your environment.

Think about the following questions:

✦ What actions can you take to foster a love for the environment among the children?
✦ How can you meet the specific needs and wants of your children?
✦ What features of your environment make it a feel-good space?
✦ Are there any aspects that might cause discomfort, and how can you address them?

Regularly reflecting on and exploring how your environment is working allows you to be responsive and flexible to the changing needs of the children.

ACTIVITY - CHAPTER KEEPSAKES

Across this first chapter, think about what your keepsakes are, and note down the following:

✦ One thing you will start doing
✦ One thing you still stop doing
✦ One keepsake you will share with others
✦ One thinking knot that requires further exploration

BIBLIOGRAPHY

ASI Wise Sensory Project. (11 November) 2022. Build your own sensory spider with our easy DIY guide [Video]. YouTube. https://sensoryladders.org/sensory-spiders/.

Barrett, L.F. 2020. *Seven and a Half Lessons About the Brain*. Houghton Mifflin Harcourt.

Bombèr, L.M. 2020. *Know Me to Teach Me: Differentiated Discipline for Those Recovering from Adverse Childhood Experiences*. Worth Publishing Limited.

Bowlby, J. 1979. The Bowlby-Ainsworth attachment theory. *Behavioral and Brain Sciences*, 2(4), 637–638.

Conn, C. 2015. "Sensory highs", "vivid rememberings" and "interactive stimming": Children's play cultures and experiences of friendship in autistic autobiographies". *Disability & Society*, 30(8), 1192–1206.

Conn, C. 2016. *Play and Friendship in Inclusive Autism Education: Supporting Learning and Development*. Routledge.

Connell, G. and McCarthy, C. 2013. *A Moving Child Is a Learning Child: How the Body Teaches the Brain to Think (Birth to Age 7)*. Free Spirit Publishing.

Connolly, S.E., Constable, H.L., and Mullally, S.L. 2023. School distress and the school attendance crisis: a story dominated by neurodivergence and unmet need. *Frontiers in Psychiatry*, 14, 1237052.

Dalton-Smith, S. 2021. The seven types of rest. TEDx Talk. www.ted.com/talks/saundra_dalton_smith_the_real_reason_why_we_are_tired_and_what_to_do_about_it?subtitle=en.

Dana, D. 2018. *The Polyvagal Theory in Therapy: Engaging the Rhythm of Regulation* (Norton series on interpersonal neurobiology). WW Norton & Company.

Derman-Sparks, L., LeeKeenan, D., and Nimmo, J. 2015. *Leading Anti-bias Early Childhood Programs: A Guide for Change* (Early Childhood Education Series). Teachers College Press.

Edgar, H. 2024. Embracing autistic children's monotropic flow states. [Online] https://ndconnection.co.uk/blog/embracing-autistic-childrens-monotropic-flow-states.

Fischer, S., Naegeli, K., Cardone, D., Filippini, C., Merla, A., Hanusch, K.-U., and Ehlert, U. 2024. Emerging effects of temperature on human cognition, affect, and behaviour. [Online] www.sciencedirect.com/science/article/pii/S0301051124000504.

Hirsh-Pasek, K., Golinkoff, R.M., and Eyer, D. 2003. *Einstein Never Used Flash Cards: How Our Children Really Learn – and Why They Need to Play More and Memorize Less*. Rodale.

Kurth, J. and Foley, J.A. 2014. Reframing teacher education: Preparing teachers for inclusive education. *Inclusion*, 2(4), 286-300.

Love, H.R. 2021. Administrators as heterotopia architects: Supporting expansive possibilities of inclusive early childhood education. *Young Exceptional Children*, 24(3), 138-153.

Martínez-Álvarez, P. 2019. Dis/ability labels and emergent bilingual children: Current research and new possibilities to grow as bilingual and biliterate learners. *Race Ethnicity and Education*, 22(2), 174-193.

Maslin, S. 2021. *Designing Mind-Friendly Environments: Architecture and Design for Everyone*. Jessica Kingsley Publishers.

McCarthy, S., Connolly, M., and McCarthy, C. 2023. *Making Space for Autism: Strategies for Assessing and Modifying Environments to Meet the Needs of Autistic People*. Pavilion Publishing and Media Ltd.

Milton, D.E. 2012. On the ontological status of autism: The "double empathy problem". *Disability & Society*, 27(6), 883-887.

Milton, D.E. 2014. Autistic expertise: A critical reflection on the production of knowledge in autism studies. *Autism*, 18(7), 794-802.

Miserandino, C. 2003. The spoon theory. But you don't look sick. https://butyoudontlooksick.com/articles/written-by-christine/the-spoon-theory/

Nakamura, J. and Csikszentmihalyi, M. 2009. Flow theory and research. In M.J. Furlong, R. Gilman, and E.S. Huebner (eds), *Handbook of Positive Psychology*. Routledge, p. 206.

Porges, S.W. 1995. Orienting in a defensive world: Mammalian modifications of our evolutionary heritage. A Polyvagal Theory. *Psychophysiology*, 32(4), 301-318. https://doi.org/10.1111/j.1469-8986.1995.tb01213.x.

Porges, S.W. 2011. *The Polyvagal Theory: Neurophysiological Foundations of Emotions, Attachment, Communication, and Self-regulation* (Norton series on interpersonal neurobiology). WW Norton & Company.

Porges, S.W. and Buczynski, R. (15 June) 2011. The polyvagal theory for treating trauma. Webinar, p. 2012.

Pound, L. 2019. *How Children Learn* (New Edition) (Vol. 1). Andrews UK Limited.

Sandseter, E.B.H., Storli, R., and Sando, O.J. 2022. The dynamic relationship between outdoor environments and children's play. *Education*, 50(1), 97–110.

Sandseter, E.B.H., Sando, O.J., Lorås, H., Kleppe, R. et al. 2023. Virtual risk management – Exploring effects of childhood risk experiences through innovative methods (ViRMa) for primary school children in Norway: Study protocol for the ViRMa project. *JMIR Research Protocols*, 12(1): e45857.

Souto-Manning, M. 2013. On children as syncretic natives: Disrupting and moving beyond normative binaries. *Journal of Early Childhood Literacy*, 13(3), 371–394.

Stimpunks Foundation. n.d. Penguin Pebbling. Stimpunks Glossary. https://stimpunks.org/glossary/penguin-pebbling/.

Tamblyn, A., Sun, Y., May, T., Evangelou, M. et al. 2023. How do physical or sensory early childhood education and care environment factors affect children's social and emotional development? A systematic scoping review. *Educational Research Review*, 41, 100555.

Wilson, L.L. 2022. *Applied Educational Neuroscience and Trauma: Teachers' Perceptions and Practices after Professional Development*. Ball State University.

PUT IT INTO PRACTICE
ENVIRONMENTAL FOUNDATIONS

Foundation	Description
Rooted in connection	An environment is an intricate network of relationships and connections that form the invisible architecture underlying our experiences and interactions. Just as tending to a garden ensures its growth, so does time spent building connections. These connections can foster an emotionally vibrant and dynamic environment where growth and understanding of each other can flourish.
Safety and risky	An atmosphere of safety lays the groundwork for children's emotional and cognitive wellbeing. Providing stability and a nurturing environment ensures that children can explore, inquire, and play without the weight of fear or apprehension. They can take risks, secure in the knowledge that they are safe. Children should be supported to take emotional, social and physical risks in safe spaces.
Affirming	The environment must affirm, rather than deny the essence of who children are and the contributions they bring to our spaces. An affirming environment provides the necessary conditions for children to flourish emotionally, intellectually, and socially by embracing their unique identities and qualities. Such an environment acknowledges that each child's story is valuable and that their presence enriches the space.

DOI: 10.4324/9781003323211-9

Creating community	The environment must mirror the rich tapestry of the community by embracing the diversity of children and families it serves. A truly inclusive environment celebrates the unique backgrounds, cultures, and perspectives that each individual brings. This reflection of the community fosters a sense of belonging and recognition, paving the way for an authentic and holistic learning experience.
Unhurried	An environment should respect children as they are now and who they will become. Doing so captures their uniqueness while providing the space and support for them learn at their own pace. As we continue to uphold this principle, we nurture children who believe in themselves, their capacity to learn, and their power to fully embrace the here and now.
Play-full	An environment should prioritise child-led experiences and advocate for play agency, interest-led experiences and inquiry-based learning. It invites children to be self-directed in their learning journey, fostering a sense of empowerment and intrinsic motivation. As we continue to embrace this approach, we cultivate learning that thrives on curiosity, adaptability, and a lifelong love of play.
Autonomy building	Environments should prioritise self-expression, self-advocacy, and decision-making which become the scaffolding upon which children construct their identities and build life competencies. By nurturing these skills, we equip children with the tools to navigate a world that values their voices and empowers them to contribute meaningfully to their communities and beyond.
Belief in belonging	Environments that actively support belonging become spaces of acceptance and growth. They communicate the message that each child and family is an integral part of the larger tapestry, enriching it with their unique threads. As we nurture these environments, we foster a generation that values diversity, understands the importance of empathy, and contributes to building a world that thrives on community.

CHAPTER 6

AFFIRMING CURRICULUM, DOCUMENTATION, AND GOAL SETTING

STARTING POINTS

A common theme in this chapter is the concern from educators that, despite their positive attitudes towards inclusive and neurodiversity-affirming practices, they are often hindered by systemic issues in educational and health services that limit this potential. For example, the early education system is increasingly being driven by an agenda from Ofsted and the Department for Education to standardise the early years curriculum into a one-size-fits-all *progression model* (Ofsted, 2022) where all children are expected to meet the same outcomes. Similarly, the health service is still largely dominated by a pathology paradigm that focuses on normalisation and correction through early intervention. Although there is strong resistance to these issues, together they pose a significant threat to anti-ableist practice and meaningful inclusion. Throughout this chapter, we will examine key issues related to rigid curriculum and the problems with corrective early intervention, while exploring how neurodiversity-affirming practices can serve as a form of resistance to both of these. Both within education and health, you are required to document the process of learning, development, progress, and the identification of any need. Each of these will be considered across this chapter. Let's start with the early years curriculum and aim of early education. Consider the following:

- ✦ What do you consider the aim of early education to be?
- ✦ How do you envisage children will develop and learn at your setting?
- ✦ Do you believe that all children will develop and learn in the same way?
- ✦ Do you believe that all children will acquire the same skills and knowledge and demonstrate these in the same way?
- ✦ Should all children be subject to the same outcomes or expectations?

The purpose of asking these questions as a starting point is to help you reflect on your own ethos regarding the aims of early education. It also encourages you to consider your beliefs about how children learn and what they should learn. As we progress through this

DOI: 10.4324/9781003323211-10

chapter, you will explore how to navigate the requirements in education and health while also considering how you can resist ableist elements within both areas.

This chapter will be broken up into Part One where we explore the early years curriculum (education) and Part Two where we will explore corrective early intervention (education + health).

INTRODUCTION

Part One – Curriculum (Universal)

According to Ofsted (2022), their working definition of curriculum is:

✦ a framework for setting out the aims of a programme of education, including the knowledge and skills to be gained at each stage (intent)
✦ for translating that framework over time into a structure and narrative, within an institutional context (implementation)
✦ for evaluating what knowledge and understanding children have gained against expectations (impact).

Applying the principles of neurodiversity-affirming practice to this definition highlights a key limitation in the current early years curriculum. It fails to fully acknowledge that there are variations in learning and development because it is built on the premise that all children's "knowledge and skills" must ultimately be measurable and standardised according to Ofsted and the DfE's socially constructed expectations. Although the principle of the Unique Child (DfE, n.d) acknowledges that children develop at their own pace, this individuality is undermined when children are required to conform to standardised measures of progress and school readiness. It creates a contradictory approach to early childhood education. For example, children are currently assessed against a set of Early Learning Goals (ELGs) that only describe neurotypical and non-disabled development meaning by their inherent existence, some neurodivergent and disabled children will have failed before they have even started their early childhood educational experience. By way of illustration, an aspect of the Early Learning Goal for Physical Development is that a child is expected to be able to "move energetically, such as running, jumping, dancing, hopping, skipping and climbing" (p.13). If a child has a physical disability, or complex need meaning they will not demonstrate these particular physicalities but show energetics in another way, even with accommodations to the goal, the message remains that this is the favoured way of moving energetically. Ironically, energetic movement is then frowned upon at school for not meeting the conditions of "whole body listening". Additionally, the education system still segregates children who are not deemed to be making neuronormative progress into a *special* category, operating on the notion that these children can only be deemed successful by achieving neuronormative and non-disabled outcomes, even if they are neurodivergent or disabled. None of this is to say that there should be no goals or moments of pause on a child's developmental journey but these must be flexible rather than fixed in terms of expectation.

PRESS PAUSE

✦ How would you or do you define an early years curriculum?

✦ How would you or do you ensure it is inclusive of children's lived experiences?

✦ What are the most important features of an early years curriculum?

✦ What are your non-negotiables in delivering high-quality early childhood education?

FOUNDATIONS - AN INCLUSIVE CURRICULUM

As outlined in previous chapters, place-based inclusion is not meaningful inclusion. While there is no general consensus on what makes an early years curriculum inclusive, there are a number of principles that should be explored when considering neurodivergent and disabled children. An early years curriculum must also acknowledge that:

✦ **Diversity of learning and development is inevitable and should be embraced.**

This means recognising that each child is unique, with their own pace of development, learning preferences, strengths, and needs. An inclusive curriculum values these differences and provides varied learning opportunities that cater to diverse needs, ensuring all children feel capable and supported.

✦ **How children learn is as important as what they will learn because this provides the springboard for lifelong learning engagement**

Understanding and respecting the different ways children learn helps build a dynamic environment where children can flourish. By focusing on the process of learning, educators can create experiences that are engaging, meaningful, and can lead to a variety of teaching methods that support all children. For example, you may have children who are acquiring spoken language and others who are acquiring sign language **(how)** and you want to introduce new vocabulary **(what)**. You would then offer this through spoken language and sign language and assess progress as per each child's communication preference.

✦ **Observation, assessment, and planning should affirm strengths, differences, and skills, using these as building blocks to support needs**

Effective assessment involves observing children in various contexts to understand their unique interests, strengths, traits, differences, and needs. By exploring the child's holistic profile, you can then make sense of what is developmentally meaningful to them, and plan activities and experiences that are compatible with their developmental pathway. Children's lived experiences should be documented in ways that affirm and honour their holistic profile as opposed to pointing out their deficits of failings to fit in. Documentation practices should promote a sense of competence and confidence in their unique knowledge and skills. For example, a child may have a particular fascination or interest, and you may draw on this when deciding your learning intentions.

✦ **Meeting a child where they are at and engaging in self-directed play is the starting point for relational and guided play**

Self-directed play is the starting point in early childhood. That is not to say that other types of play and guidance are absent, rather they branch out from meeting the child where they are at. Educators should connect with children with their current skills, knowledge, and interests. This approach fosters trust and creates opportunities for guided play, where children can explore new concepts and skills in a supportive and interactive environment. For example, a child with situational mutism may find indoor environments too demanding, and is much more open to adult-child interactions in outdoor spaces where there is more freedom. In this case, they may be more responsive to adult input and interactions.

✦ **A curriculum should not lead to stigma, othering, or exclusion. If it does, it is not inclusive by its very nature**

An inclusive curriculum should be designed to prevent any form of bias and marginalisation of children. It should promote both equality and equity where it is underatood that children may different support in order to participate and engage. All children feel a sense of belonging and acceptance. If a curriculum results in some children feeling excluded or "othered", or incapable of learning, it fails in its fundamental purpose of being inclusive.

PRESS PAUSE

High-quality early years education is thought to be advantageous for children's longer-term outcomes, particularly those who would be considered disadvantaged or under-resourced. It is important to remain critical to such evidence, namely what outcomes are considered valuable? For example, outcomes might suggest that children are likely to go onto achieve good GCSEs suggesting that academic outcomes are important, but has this also been considered alongside mental health and wellbeing outcomes? Furthermore, outcomes and quality of life on the journey to those outcomes must be equally valued.

Similarly, physical access to early education must not be confused with access to high-quality early education and experiences. Settings must not overlook that these high-quality is dependent on a well-funded, well-trained, accessible and sustainable sector. If a setting is underfunded, this results in disadvantaged children going to under-resourced settings, and then expecting success.

UNIVERSAL, TARGETED, AND SPECIALIST

Additionally, inclusion should be underpinned by the recognition that not every child has the same starting point or exists within the same context, making equitable decisions integral to your practice. While all children should benefit from an inclusive curriculum, they may need different types of support both within and beyond that curriculum to access, engage, and learn effectively. Within educational inclusion, this support is often categorised into a hierarchy of universal, targeted, and specialist input. However, it is important to understand this as an interconnected process where each loop of support interacts with the others, creating an ecology of inclusion.

FIGURE 6.1 LOOPS OF INCLUSION

These terms are defined as:

Universal Practice can be defined as the interest and needs-led curriculum that is available to all children and should provide the foundations for supporting learning and development. It also encompasses relationships, routines, wellbeing, and adjustments.

Targeted practice can be defined as the adaptations you make to your pedagogy and practice to ensure it remains accessible to a child who has developmental differences, disabilities, or difficulties. It exists within your universal curriculum but with adjusted expectations based on your knowledge of the child.

> **Specialist practice** can be defined as the adaptations made to your curriculum and practice with the input of specialist knowledge from within or beyond the setting such as from a speech and language therapist (SaLT). Specialist practice should be informed by an understanding of the child's differences and needs, and practices should honour, affirm, and support differences that may be lifelong.
>
> Targeted and specialist practice does not replace your universal but loops into it to strengthen children's learning and development experiences.

As stated in the starting points, educators are not only ensuring that the early years curriculum is accessible but will also be navigating the bridge between early education and health through the process of early intervention which is where targeted and specialist practice becomes relevant.

Part Two – Early Intervention (Targeted and Specialist)

Every Early Years Educator is taught about the importance of early intervention and their accountability in responding to children's needs in a timely manner. Early intervention is an umbrella term for "identifying and providing effective early support to children and young people who are at risk of poor outcomes" (Early Intervention Foundation n.d.). Neurodivergence and/or disability are often viewed as risk factors for poor outcomes, while the role of ableism in amplifying these risks is frequently overlooked.

Therefore, early intervention is considered crucial in the work of an Early Years Educator. Through observations and assessments, educators, alongside parents or carers will typically determine whether a child requires further support, and they have a duty to intervene in a timely manner. However, early intervention can only be effective if when initiated it leads to:

✦ **Timely access**

The very premise of early intervention is that a child is given support within a timely manner to ensure the right support is put in place at the right time as opposed to spending excessive amounts of time on waiting lists in which their differences and needs go unmet or change over time.

✦ **Appropriate thresholds**

Early intervention should not be afforded only to those in crisis nor should a child have to reach crisis point to be considered for support. Thresholds for those with emerging or low support needs are as vital because they can prevent exacerbation of difficulties and can potentially lead to a child, parent, carer, or educator developing an understanding of the child.

✦ **Multi-agency working**

Multi-agency working is a collaborative process where each and every contribution is valid. It should not be an authoritarian process but one in which a network of perspectives is formed to ensure well-matched support. Too often, however, early educators, parents, and carers can feel disempowered by the underlying power balances that can occur amongst different roles and responsibilities. For example, following advice from a specialist because they are considered the "expert" even if the advice seems poorly matched to the child's needs.

✦ **An "experience-sensitive" approach that accounts for differences as well as difficulties**

Early intervention addresses a wide range of risk factors, including abuse and poverty, which are inherently negative experiences that need to be eliminated or reduced. However, being neurodivergent or disabled is not itself inherently negative, yet it is often treated the same as other risk factors that are vastly different in nature. This can lead to mismatched approaches that focus on making someone less neurodivergent and/or disabled. For example, if a child is referred to a SaLT because they have a stammer, the focus might be on reducing or eliminating the stammer without recognising that this might be a part of a person's lifelong communication identity.

The "experience-sensitive approach" emphasises doing what is in the best interests of the child, rather than focusing solely on elimination or reduction. According to McGreevy et al. (2024), "it promotes a sense of agency, identifies strengths, barriers, and needs, and supports wellbeing to create opportunities for the child to flourish authentically, living their best life **according to their own norms**" (p. 7).

✦ **A strength's led and capacity building mode**

Early intervention should work on the basis that it should build upon strengths to scaffold needs. While strength-led approaches are not new to educators, they can be tokenistic or not consistently applied because the deficit-approach appears to get more results. The reality is that education and health are underpinned by a pathology paradigm when considering neurodivergent and disabled children, meaning that strength-led practice is hard to make a reality. Treating neurodivergent and disabled children as risk factors is not effective for helping to build their capacity which requires self-belief and self-esteem.

BOTTLENECK INTERVENTION

In the current climate, early intervention is like a constrained bottleneck. There is too much demand, and not enough capacity. When this happens, it is inevitable that procedures for accessing support become about those who are most in crisis. A deficit approach then becomes the dominant way to quickly identify and respond to that crisis. In order for any level of efficiency to be achieved, a setting has to be able to prove that the child's problems are bad enough that they must then be squeezed through that bottleneck. One of the ways in which services (who are also victims within this system) manage the demand of this is to try to address needs categorically. For example, all children with speech delays receive the same intervention programme irrespective of the variations and differences that occur between each child, family and context. Over time,

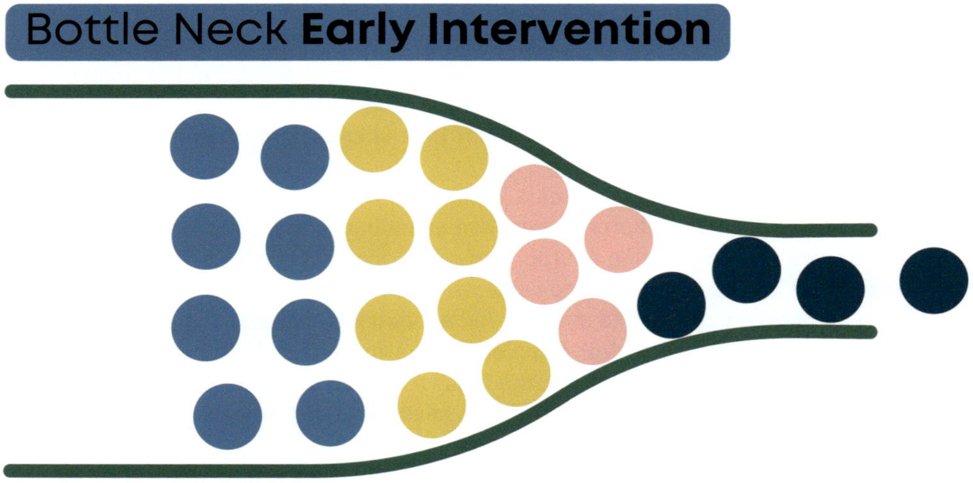

Bottle Neck **Early Intervention**

FIGURE 6.2 BOTTLENECK EARLY INTERVENTION

early intervention has become less timely and too much emphasis is placed on meeting all needs through a universal model. The way to reduce this bottleneck is to have the right services matched up to the children's differences and needs, and ensuring the programmes and approaches account for neurodiversity

EARLY INTERVENTION: FIT FOR PURPOSE?

Numerous early educators have said to me "if we could fix early intervention, then it could be really effective". I disagree with this because it suggests that early intervention as a blanket approach is or has previously been sufficient for the specific needs of neurodivergent and disabled children. More broadly, there are issues that do require prevention, reduction, and elimination of issues that could threaten a child's later outcomes. For example, reducing poverty is an undeniable risk to a child's outcomes and we should work towards eradicating that level of deprivation.

Similarly, a lack of access to healthcare services including assessment, diagnosis, and support is also a risk to children's outcomes. It becomes more complicated, however, when being neurodivergent and/or disabled is assumed a risk. For example, imagine a parent believes their child to be autistic. Good early intervention may increase access to healthcare including a diagnosis thus reducing the risk of their autistic needs going unmet. However, once that child is diagnosed, they are usually then exposed to another type of early intervention that prioritises normalisation. For example, intervention programmes may then be utilised to attempt to reduce and eliminate autistic traits. In short, early intervention has helped identify someone's healthcare needs, but there are also attempts to reduce and eliminate it through early intervention strategies and programmes. A parent explained this to me as being "the very services designed to support my child have become the services that have caused most harm to my child". They went onto explain:

> I wanted my child to access diagnosis so he could make sense of his traits and learn to accept himself. However, the diagnostic process for my child was one of the most traumatic experiences I have had as a parent. I was so relieved to get an appointment after fighting for it for well over a year but felt endlessly uncomfortable by the information I had to provide.
>
> The assessment felt cruel. Things were said in front of my child that I fear he will have internalised for the rest of his life. There was no recognition that he was at the receiving end of this assessment, and upon diagnosis, the discussion immediately turned to all the intervention programmes I could use or invest in to make him less autistic. I asked if any support groups existed to help him "lean in" to his autism and the doctor looked puzzled by the question. Neurodevelopmental diagnosis is a confusing process. Imagine the moment of everything making sense, but then being told to go against everything that makes sense. I wanted to rip up the report when I got it and rewrite it.

This brings me back to the issue with early intervention. As a broad brushstroke to risk reduction, it lacks the nuance needed for meaningful educational inclusion and has too much ableism embedded within it to make sense to neurodiversity-informed and -affirming practice.

IF NOT JUST EARLY INTERVENTION? THEN WHAT?

To be clear, early intervention may be necessary but not always sufficient for neurodivergent and disabled children. As a setting, you have a duty to follow local and national procedures and you must always act with the best interests of the child. However, we also need a more accurate way of describing early support that does not just focus on reduction and elimination but also provides neurodiversity-affirming practices.

When speaking with early educators about the support they provide, they will often refer to the idea that they are "tuning in" to a child's differences and needs and then making decisions based on what is developmentally meaningful to the child. This is relevant to all children, not just those who are neurodivergent or disabled. Attunement can be defined as: "our ability to be aware of and respond to a child's needs" (Child Development Institute, n.d.) and to do this in ways that bring harmony to the child. For educators already exploring neurodiversity-affirming practice, they found that the term "intervention" seemed like a synonym for interference. Given that the majority of early intervention programmes or approaches targeted at neurodivergent children do attempt to normalise the child, it is not a stretch to say that this does, in fact, interfere with their divergent pathways. The process of early attunement, on the other hand, is about tuning in to the child's individual differences and needs and responding in ways that bring harmony to the child. When we take

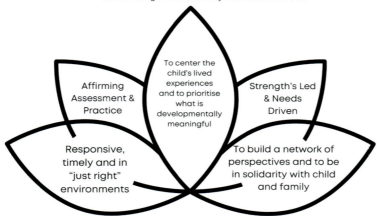

Early **Attunement**

Our capacity to be aware of and respond to a child's differences needs and to do this in ways that bring harmony to the child. Early attunement embraces what is developmentally meaningful to the child as opposed to intervening and interfering in order to correct through traditional early intervention methods.

- To center the child's lived experiences and to prioritise what is developmentally meaningful
- Affirming Assessment & Practice
- Strength's Led & Needs Driven
- Responsive, timely and in "just right" environments
- To build a network of perspectives and to be in solidarity with child and family

FIGURE 6.3 EARLY ATTUNEMENT

into account this way of describing the way children are supported, it ensures again that children's lived experiences are protected from unnecessary harm.

Early attunement can therefore be an appropriate way to describe the practices beyond early intervention that are focused on understanding and affirming different ways of developing, learning, and being. It is important for educators to be able to capture this process of attunement through affirming documentation, which includes:

- ✦ A commitment to the whole child through the holistic profile
- ✦ Strength's-led observations
- ✦ Affirming assessment and sense-making
- ✦ Attuned goal setting

Before we unpick this practically, it is useful to consider our role in documentation.

STORYTELLERS, BIOGRAPHERS, AND ADVOCATES

As an educator, you have the privileged role of being a storyteller. In a child's earliest years, as they begin to discover their own voices and narratives, you facilitate this process through various forms of documentation and advocacy. Whether it involves noting observations, writing detailed descriptions of their learning and development, or seeking external support through referrals, the way you document a child's experiences becomes part of their personal biography. These records may be something they look back on in the future to better understand who they were and who they have become. For many of us, old school reports and educational paperwork reflect whether we were viewed positively or negatively and so we know the weight words can carry. However, for educators documenting in the moment, these tasks can often be reduced to mere policy and procedure, which can de-personalise the child, and their lived experience. There has become such an emphasis on paperwork reduction in early childhood education that it overshadows important reflections and interrogations on how we can ensure that paperwork is seen as more than a to-do task, rather it contributes to the child's life story.

And so to begin, we have to ask what story is it that we want to tell for a child? And what emotions do we want to elicit if they were to look back on how we described them. Inspired by the Divergent Perspectives blog by Elaine McGreevy and Emily Price (2022), consider the following questions:

1. How would I feel about the language used in this documentation if it was describing myself or a loved one?
2. Would I be comfortable with how I described the child and their needs if they were to read this in the future?
3. Does the documentation accurately describe the supports the child's differences and needs?
4. Does the language used in the documentation involve judgement, shaming, pathologising, or dehumanising?
5. Does the report adequately describe the child's strengths and needs? Have their strengths been given sufficient attention alongside their needs?

It is of particular importance to consider the ways in which we document the lives of neurodivergent and disabled children who are more frequently subject to descriptions that focus solely on their delays and deficits. It has become normalised that we would think of such children on their "worst days" because this is the only way to meet the thresholds for support from overstretched and underfunded services. It is safe to say that some children are written about in terms of their potential whereas others are only positioned as problems. You will now think about how you can disrupt current systems and process for more affirming documentation.

Neurodiversity-informed and -affirming practice cannot happen if it does not translate into the way we document children's lives across education, health, and social care. However, it is the area that is met with most resistance because educators are often balancing incompatible demands. Before we can get to the heart of affirming documentation processes, it is useful to consider why it has become entrenched in education to write about, and document neurodivergent and disabled children's lives in deficit ways.

Clinical Psychologist Hanna Venton-Platz who works for autistic advocacy organisation Spectrum Gaming, stated that when writing about children and young people, she always imagines she is writing *to* the child, not about them. The documentation we produce is ultimately about the child, so it is essential to remain child-centred, always considering their thoughts, feelings, and perceptions. For children who are neurotypical conforming, strength's-led documentation is often assumed, and such children are written about in ways that capture all their golden threads of learning, their interests, joys, and the ways in which they have demonstrated their learning and development. However, this is not always afforded to those with lifelong differences. To this, however, we have to always think of the whole child.

THE WHOLE CHILD

In 2018, Pen Green Centre for Children and Families & Charnwood Nursery School working group "acknowledged that some children's progress cannot easily be demonstrated or celebrated when using the current development matters" (p. 4). As a result, they produced a *Celebratory Approach to SEND assessment in the Early Years* for the Department for Education. This guidance advised educators to be mindful of a "norm-referenced" approach that did not acknowledge the whole child. It is clear from their work that Penn Green recognises that a failure to understand the child holistically can lead to a limited perspective of their potential, and the possible pathways of learning and development.

KEY TERM

Norm-referenced means that the child development statements focus on what is considered normal or typical for a child of a particular age or phase, and does not refer to diverse profiles.

Since this time, the Development Matters has undergone a re-write that has unfortunately resulted in narrower descriptions of development. The DfE has increased its agenda on normalisation of all children for school readiness. Irrespective of this agenda, educators should resist by adopting a commitment to understanding holistic development and that which is developmentally meaningful to the child. Applying a holistic profile to all children ensures that greater observational attention is paid to the child across their developmental experiences.

NEUROINSIGHT - STAGES AND AGES

INFANTALISING CHILDREN VIA AGES AND STAGES

During a conversation with Parent and Carer advocate Sarah Doyle, she explained that ages and stages can be ableist for many reasons. As a parent to an autistic child, she often felt that her child's developmental differences were infantilised. For example, her key person once explained that although Robin was chronologically three years of age, he was only performing in the stage band 8–20 months. Therefore, his next steps would focus on cultivating milestones within this area. Admittedly, this is something I did as an Area SENCO. Still, Sarah pushed back to clarify that neurodivergent children often do not fit into the narrowness of the EYFS framework. So, by focusing on normative milestones, her child was being taught to mimic neurotypical behaviours. Only when they discussed her child beyond these milestones could more meaningful discussions be had and next steps became more child-centred. One of the most important changes we can make in our language is to stop asking: "How is this child delayed?" but instead: "How does this child do it differently?". We can then use a framework to support rather than fix the child. I am often asked what to do if we are not relying so much on tracking and staging of development. My answer is to focus on being able to describe the child via their strengths, interests, differences, and needs. Being able to do this allows us an insight into a child's holistic development, and the emphasis from any professional or specialist should be to focus on helping a child to thrive by supporting their areas of need, rather than trying to align their tick boxes so that they appear to be meeting age-related expectations.

Sarah Doyle

APPLYING EARLY ATTUNEMENT

The Holistic Profile

Below is an outline of the holistic profile with prompting questions:

Element	Possible Questions
Interests All humans have unique preferences and interests. It might not always be immediately obvious or have a visible purpose, but that doesn't mean, intrinsically, it doesn't hold meaning.	✦ What is the child interested in? Do they have any particular fascinations, passions, or motivations? ✦ Where do they like to spend time? ✦ Do they have any particular preferences for people or objects? ✦ In what ways do they play? And in what locations? ✦ Do they have an affinity with the indoors or outdoors? ✦ Do they have any special objects or comforters? ✦ Do they engage in any repetitive behaviours or actions?

Strengths All children have unique strengths that should be acknowledged and celebrated. Compliance to neuronormative expectations is not a strength.	✦ What actions or behaviours appear to provide intrinsic motivation? ✦ What would they "say" they are good at? ✦ What would you say they are good at? What would those close to them say they are good at? ✦ Do they show pride in any particular areas? ✦ Is there anything they do that shows skill, determination or autonomy?
Traits There is often a focus on symptoms but neurotypes also have traits.	✦ What are they good at? ✦ What do they like to do? ✦ Who or what do they like to play with (people or objects)? ✦ Do they return to a particular area of experience? ✦ What physical skills do they use? ✦ What can they do autonomously? ✦ Who are their favourite people? ✦ How do they self-advocate?
Differences We should be careful not to assume delays in different neurotypes. In some situations, a delay could be a gateway to a lifelong difference.	✦ How do they do things differently? ✦ What communication preferences do they have? ✦ What social preferences do they have? ✦ What physical preferences do they have? ✦ Do they use alternative learning methods, for example, visuals or Makaton? ✦ How they emotionally regulate?
Needs All children have individual needs that will need supports, scaffolding and adaptive practices.	What are their primary and secondary areas of need: ✦ Communication and interaction ✦ Social, emotional, and/or mental health ✦ Cognition and learning ✦ Physical and/or sensory Of these areas, consider if the child has: ✦ High support needs ✦ Medium support needs ✦ Low support needs Also consider whether these support needs can be met: ✦ Within setting and home at a universal level ✦ With targeted support ✦ With specialist input

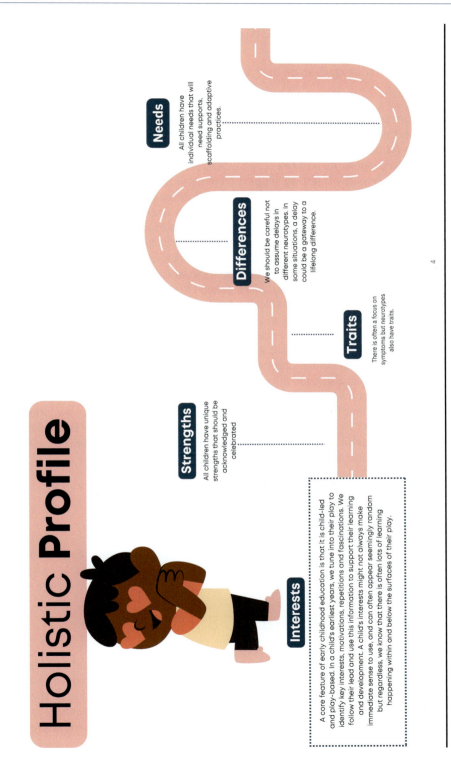

Holistic Profile

Interests

A core feature of early childhood education is that it is child-led and play-based. In a child's earliest years, we tune into their play to identify key interests, motivations, repetitions and fascinations. We follow their lead and use this information to support their learning and development. A child's interests might not always make immediate sense to use, and can often appear seemingly random but regardless, we know that there is often lots of learning happening within and below the surfaces of their play.

Strengths

All children have unique strengths that should be acknowledged and celebrated

Traits

There is often a focus on symptoms but neurotypes also have traits.

Differences

We should be careful not to assume delays in different neurotypes. In some situations, a delay could be a gateway to a lifelong difference.

Needs

All children have individual needs that will need supports, scaffolding and adaptive practices.

FIGURE 6.4 THE HOLISTIC PROFILE OF LEARNING AND DEVELOPMENT

NEUROMYTH

"You should describe children on their worst days to secure support"
(Murphy and Benham, 2023)

I have written about this concept elsewhere and in other books, including 50 Fantastic Ideas for supporting neurodiversity (Murphy and Benham, 2023) but it is worth bringing it up again here as it has been a powerful way of provoking conversations about the current systems for SEND support. As an Area SENCO, describing children on their worst days had become a customary part of getting support from services. To think of children at crisis point or writing only about their most significant difficulties as evidence that they needed support. There is something very wrong with the system when we are asking "how bad is it and does it justify supporting this child". To me, it indicates a broken system, not broken children. I have encountered resistance against this approach on a few occasions, and it has largely come from parents who do not see their children as simply having bad days, but who see the good days, the wonderful moments in which they get an insight into their child's meaningful developmental experiences. When I first introduced the idea of "my way to a good day", I was met with a lot of reluctance from the sector, including educators who felt that it wasn't realistic to switch because it would just mean they would not get accepted referrals. I truly hear this, and I would also venture that however neurodiversity-affirming we intend to become, the constraints of a broken system will also always need to be navigated. I have used the term before, and I will use it again, and it is compromise. We need to think about how we are engaging in microactivism amongst navigation such systems. And so I have pushed through with this, and since delivered training to many local authorities where I have been candid that we need to be prepared to try something new, otherwise the status quo will never be changed. The premise of my way to a good day is simply about reframing so we build upon the positive experiences the child is having, while still acknowledging that there are risks in finding our way to good days.

COMPANION RESOURCE

My way to a good day (Murphy and Benham, 2023): https://fantasticneurodiversity.com/

STRENGTH'S-LED OBSERVATIONS

For several years, I worked as a local area inclusion coordinator for a local authority. My primary role involved visiting early years settings to observe children with developmental differences and needs, and to determine the support they required. Reflecting on this time, I recognise that I often reinforced a deficit-based approach. My focus was primarily on identifying the problems or concerns with each child, rather than paying sufficient attention to their strengths, traits, and evidence of diverse learning.

As a specialist, I was trained in early intervention, prevention, and reduction and I never thought to question a system that was designed to help. With the best intentions, my goal was to identify issues quickly and resolve them so that children fit back into what was neuronormatively expected. However, I now realise that this was a very surface-level approach, which failed to understand the diversity of learning and development. This approach overlooked the unique qualities and potential of each child, and resulted in my poor observational attention.

OBSERVING AGAINST DEVELOPMENTAL MILESTONES

As educators, we have duties under the Early Years Foundation Stage (EYFS) Framework statutory requirements (DfE, 2023) and the 0–25 SEND Code of Practice (DfE, 2023), which rightfully require us to be alert to emerging difficulties and to act upon concerns. Our concerns are usually determined by observing children in alignment with child development documents and progression tools. In short, we are instructed what to expect developmentally, and when, in terms of a child's chronological age. If a child does not demonstrate what is expected, it could indicate the presence of a special educational need or disability. We would then document this in some way via handwritten or digital observations, and through early discussions. This then becomes evidence that we have been alert to those concerns.

The process of identifying developmental difficulties in children is often effective for those who generally will conform to neuronormativity. However, it does not adequately account for children who are on a divergent developmental pathway. Consider this scenario: you observe a four-year-old child who engages in solitary and repetitive play for extended periods. Additionally, this child appears withdrawn and sometimes distressed. They do not seem to experience enjoyment from their play and show signs of anxiety when other children attempt to join in. In this context, identifying solitary play as a concern is appropriate because the child's overall behaviour indicates potential difficulties.

The problem arises when we generalise that solitary play is inherently problematic for all children above a certain age, regardless of the broader context. For instance, consider another four-year-old child who also engages in solitary and repetitive play, however this child appears immersed and engaged, displaying signs of enjoyment such as making sing-song sounds, smiling, and focusing intently. They may be protective of the play they are creating and so prefer other children not to join in. They are, however, content with others playing nearby in parallel.

Traditional child development theories suggest that by the age of four, children should be engaging in cooperative social play rather than associative or parallel play. Solitary play is typically considered normal only up to the age of two. Beyond this, it may be considered a "red flag" in development. The influence of these staged developmental theories often leads educators to overlook the unique context in favour of confirming concerns. Consequently, behaviours that may indicate a developmental difference are instead viewed and documented as problems.

This approach fails to recognise and value developmental diversity and divergent pathways. It is crucial to understand that while some behaviours might be concerning in one context, they can be developmentally meaningful in another. Educators need to move beyond a one-size-fits-all framework and consider the unique context of each child's development. By doing so, we can better support children who do not fit neatly into traditional developmental milestones, recognising their individual strengths and needs rather than merely categorising their behaviours as problematic.

Additionally, we must recognise that the term 'milestones' implies a race from point A to point B, suggesting that faster progress is better (Bloem and Evans, 2024). This perspective conflicts with the principle of the Unique Child. Instead, we should adopt more inclusive language that highlights developmentally meaningful experiences for all children, regardless of their pace.

EXPANDING OBSERVATIONAL ATTENTION

In 2021, the Froebel Trust published a guidance document on how to appropriately capture children's learning and development using digital documentation. Concerns have been raised that reliance on digital tools can lead to standardised and de-personalised practices, failing to capture the unique aspects of each child's learning and development. The study also explored whether certain characteristics or play behaviours influenced the frequency of observations a child received. Researchers aimed to determine if learning was being overlooked due to a lack of proportionate observational attention. The findings were insightful, confirming that some children did receive less observation, as highlighted in the table below:

Children with fewer observations	Children with more observations
Quiet or less talkative	Highly "verbal" or talkative
Shy	Outgoing
Not confident in communicating English	Speak English fluently
Spend lots of time outdoors	Mainly plays inside
Runs a lot/highly physical	Likes quiet/still activities
Do not join in group activities	Joins in group activities

Does not produce "work" such as drawings	Produces lots of "work" such as drawing and crafts
Independent or does not come to adults often	Dependent on adult/seeks attention
Many absences	Few absences

While the study did not explicitly state that the presence of a special educational need or disability influenced observational attention, you can likely see from the list that children with developmental differences or disabilities are perhaps more likely to fall under that list. For example:

+ A disabled child may have more absences due to medical or therapeutic appointments.
+ Children who do not conform to neurotypicality may be less inclined to join in group activities because they are incompatible with the child's preferences.
+ Quiet children may have different communication identities such as being non-speaking, minimally speaking, non-verbal, or be acquiring language in a different way to what is considered typical.
+ Some children may prefer time spent outdoors because there are fewer social demands compared to indoors.

Of equal concern in these findings is that children whose language is different from English have their learning overlooked, potentially leading to greater stigma towards those who will eventually speak more than one language.

This results in two implications for children with developmental differences:

1. Learning is being overlooked in children who do not conform to neuronormative expectations
2. When observations do occur, the focus is often less on learning, and more on the ways the child might be presenting as a problem.

To move towards neurodiversity-affirming practice, educators must therefore shift from less observational attention, to holistic and strengths-led observational attention valuing all the diverse ways in which children learn, develop, and engage with their early childhood experiences.

PLANTING SEEDS FOR NEURODIVERSITY

All observational techniques listed here should be done with the child's consent and comfort in mind. Observations that involve photography or video should be done sensitively, and should not be invasive.

Most settings, including childminders, have access to digital technology and are likely already using platforms that allow photos and videos. Across a busy day, there are lots of things that we can miss. If you would like to be more in-tune with a child or group of children, **video observations** can be vital. Short videos that can be watched back allow us the headspace and time to really focus on what is happening in a child's play. This is a practice I have used a lot in recent years and it is amazing how many things I pick up the more I watch. This type of observation can also be great for shared discussions with parents, the child, or colleagues. I always suggest "bite-size" observations as opposed to longer videos which can be difficult to watch back. Over time, these bitesize videos can build up a much clearer picture of learning and engagement. If you choose this option, it is important to ensure that consent and the right to say no is used with young children. Simple visuals can be used, and children can indicate if they want the observation to stop. It can also be nice to watch the videos back with children.

I struggle at times to write about what I am observing. While it might have looked a little strange, I relied heavily on a dictaphone for observations back in my setting. I found that narrating what I observed with the dictaphone led to more detailed descriptions of children at play. Listening back also sparked lots of other thoughts and reflections, and even better, I could capture children vocalisations and "voice".

Short joint observations can expand our understanding of children and build a network of perspectives. Sometimes, we can spend so much time interpreting or making sense of what we see when we would benefit from a fresh pair of eyes and ears.

Another important way of gathering insight into children's play and learning is to speak with parents about capturing learning at home. Everyone uses technology nowadays, and often parents have photos, videos, and snapshots that focus on their child's interests and fascinations. Watching back together also gives us an opportunity as educators to affirm the child's identity. It is important to remember that when a child is identified as "SEN", parents and carers are often subject to many discussions based on problems or concerns.

Draw out a basic bird's-eye view of the space. Observe the child's movements across the day and map it out. At the end of the day or session, use this to inform your thinking about the child's play interests and behaviours.

Part of an educator's role is to figure out children's play interests and motivations. It can often be the case that it takes longer to figure out what neurodivergent and disabled children's play means because it can often be pathologised as a symptom of their neurotype or condition. When I was a practitioner, we would always use play mapping to determine which areas of provision a child was drawn to, and we would map out any repetitions or fascinations. Looking at your play map at the end of the day can reveal many things that may have otherwise been defined as fleeting behaviours.

Children's play can be highly variable, and may not always make immediate sense. For example, a child may be quite physical or energetic, or the play may appear somewhat random. Taking a **sequence of photographs** in close succession can give you insights into a child's play, learning, and development. You might notice a particular pattern, skill, or interest or identify a specific need. For example:

A practitioner notices her key child enjoys spinning. This can be seen as disruptive and a colleague says the child needs to learn how to move appropriately. The practitioner takes a sequence of pictures and they lay the images out together. She is then able to talk though the complex process of spinning, noting down that the child is learning to

✦ coordinate both side of their body
✦ balance and remain steady footed
✦ orientate and navigate space

All of which contributes towards vestibular development that controls balance, posture, gaze stabilisation, and spatial orientation. In short, spinning is an appropriate movement.

Another example:

The children all eat snacks together, and a key person sometimes takes a sequence of images to observe self-care and motor skills. When she looks back at the sequence of photographs, she is able to identify that a child seems to struggle to grasp particular items which would explain why they drop cutlery and spill drinks a lot. This child has been told that they are moving their arms too much but on closer inspection, it is fine motor skills including grasping hands that requires support.

When you are short of time or when capacity is limited, key word observations can be useful (and fun). From your observations of a particular child, use key words to describe what you are observing across a time period or over the day, and then look for themes across the key words. This can be really useful when more than one key person is also taking part. For example:

Running
Climbing high
Rolling
Laughing
Pushing
Looking closely
Shouting
Rejecting
Red-faced

Summary: Lots of large movements and seeking freedom to move. Energetic and using up lots of energy. Said no or was resistant to quieter activities or coming in from outside.

Action: Set some challenges for tomorrow such as obstacles and incorporate different movements that require slowing down/speeding up.

> Lining up
> Stacking
> Back and forth
> Organising
> Solitary

Summary: Appears to be creating patterns and order and repeating the same sequences.

Action: Took photo of some of the set-ups and laid them out as a provocation the next day.

Jigsaw observations require different individuals to capture observations and then you put them together to form a picture of what is happening. You can either state a specific focus, make them random, or allocate different tasks, for example: "I will focus on strengths, you focus on interests" or "you focus on communication, I will focus on physical". The aim of this is to build a network of perspectives recognising that observations are subjective, and different interpretations can help you to a) build a bigger picture and b) identify any bias or hidden spots within the knowledge base of different individuals.

AFFIRMING ASSESSMENT

When we commit to observing through a holistic profile followed by affirming assessment, it ensures that we provide adequate attention to all aspects of who they are. I see this as a foundation for understanding children and this speaks to the premise that we should meet children where they are at. Once you have observed a child through the holistic profile, you should then consider;:

Is the child on a typically developing pathway, or a divergent pathway of development? The answer to this question will depend on the focus for support. For example, if a child is largely conforming to typical development, you will rely upon curriculum documents that best describe them. If they have diverged in their development, the focus will be on understanding the diversity or variation within their development.

What unique milestones are they demonstrating and how can you build upon these development meaningful experiences while meeting the areas of need? This will be decided in solidarity with parents and carers.

What would be developmentally meaningful for this child? And what framework should be used for planning next steps or goals?

Are there any low, medium, or high levels of support that need to be accounted for when planning forward for this child?

GOAL SETTING

Whether you are supporting children at the universal, targeted, or specialist level, one of your key tasks is setting goals or deciding on next steps based on each child's current developmental pathway. When supporting children at a universal level, you will use everyday curriculum documents, such as Development Matters (DfE, 2023) or other child development guidelines, to observe where the child is currently. You will then decide what you would like them to learn next and plan the appropriate steps. Ideally this will be child-led and child-centred and will involve collaboration from parents or carers. This ongoing process also enables you to identify any differences or difficulties and to adapt your practice accordingly. Some children may encounter minor difficulties or delays, with some adapted practice, and continue to develop in the way that is expected for them.

Some children, however, may be on a different developmental pathway. Their difficulties may be the result of a lifelong difference, for which they require an educator who has an understanding of these differences and what they mean for the child's learning and development. For these children, you will need to think about targeted and specialist goals or next steps. Health services will have the intention of reducing barriers and increasing participation but as they are also still dominated by a pathology paradigm, the goals, or advice you may receive, may be ableist, and the focus may be also be on:

✦ encouraging neuronormativity
✦ reducing or eliminating undesirable traits

Goals may set unrealistic expectations, with an emphasis on expecting the child to change who they are to fit in. Whether you are writing universal, targeted, or specialist goals, a neurodiversity-affirming approach should be taken to ensure that they are developmentally meaningful and avoid ableism.

ACTIVITY

Take a look at the following SMART-ish goals for a range of developmental differences and needs: do you believe that these goals are affirming or not?

Goal	Suitable	Not Suitable
Key person will encourage sustained eye contact or provide appropriate gaze up to 30 seconds by holding a novel object near eyes during social interactions up to three times a day.		
Will be able to answer what and how questions with 80% accuracy during play, for example, what colour, what shape, how many, where is it etc.		
To speak in an appropriate tone of voice (quiet) during circle time interactions 3 out of 5 times during the week.		
To increase tolerance to textures by incorporating into play experiences such as sensory play.		
To accept the invitation to play with a different toy or game when initiated by another child.		
To use whole-body listening during circle time with a focus sitting still for 80% of circle time Maintaining eyes looking forward for 80% Keeping hands in lap when reminded of "quiet hands".		
Encouraging use of appropriate language in various contexts over echolalia or familiar phrases. Ignore echolalia but respond to appropriate responses.		
Moves and walks like other children of the same age, understanding how to navigate space.		

Greets peers by smiling, and providing eye contact.		
Engages in conversational turn-taking by waiting for a pause before responding.		
Through prompting, the child asks for verbal permission to access a toy that has been intentionally placed out of reach (sabotage).		
Child will use their words when upset to explain why they are upset rather than having a tantrum.		
*Answers and explanations can be found at the end of this chapter.		

NOT SO SMART

It's ironic that goals for children with developmental differences are often framed using the acronym SMART, which stands for Specific, Measurable, Achievable, Relevant, and Time-bound. The word smart is synonymous with intelligence, a concept that is widely debated as ableist, socially constructed, and standardised in measuring someone's mental worth and perceived ability. However, the issue with SMART goals extends further. SMART is commonly used to develop measurable goals, particularly for children who are not progressing according to neuronormative standards. If you were to search for SMART goals via a search engine, you would likely encounter goals similar to those that were outlined in the activity, all of which are potentially unsuitable for neurodivergent and disabled children. One of the key issues that has been identified by Emily Hammon a.k.a. Neurowild (2023) is that they rely on the idea of neuronormative consistency. Many neurodivergent children are existing in spaces that are not well designed with them in mind, and according to Hammond, it can be difficult for neurodivergent children to reach this consistency with so many ableist barriers. For a child to meet a SMART target, the emphasis is placed on the child to change who they are to fit in, rather than acknowledging the broader context of which they exist. Furthermore, SMART targets often set measures that are unsuitable for children with developmental differences. This is not to say that SMART targets could not be re-worked to be more neurodiversity-affirming, but it is also useful to explore whether alternatives could be sought, some of which are outlined below.

S.H.A.R.E. GOALS

Component	Description
Strengths-led	Goals should meet children where they are and will be unique to their developmental profile. Remember that normative milestone documents don't necessarily reflect neurodivergent or disabled children which can lead us down the wrong developmental pathway. Focus on what is meaningful and needed for that particular child. Strengths should not be based on how a child conforms or is compliant to rules and expectations but that which is meaningful to them individually.
Ableist Goal: To reduce special interest in diggers by removing diggers, and replacing them with other wheeled vehicles. Child (A) should engage with an alternative toy for up to 60 seconds once per day.	
S.H.A.R.E. Goal: To build upon interest in diggers by adding additional provocations and invitations. For example, books on diggers (Learning intention: introducing new vocabulary), and providing different materials such as sand, mud, and stones for the child to collect with the digger (Learning intention: using a range of descriptive words and sounds during play).	
Honours and affirms differences	When deciding on what you want to work towards, consider how this relates to all domains of development. Goals rarely benefit one aspect of learning, and too much specificity can actually narrow opportunities to learn.
Ableist Goal: To show effortful control (Personal, Social, and Emotional Development) during circle time by sitting still, and not shouting out.	
S.H.A.R.E. Goal: To provide motivating experiences during a circle time that enable movement (sitting, standing, and stretching), and freedom to contribute in a range of ways (hands up, shout out, whisper to a friend) which will later support effortful control across different contexts (Personal, Social and Emotional Development).	
Autonomy building	Goals should never be about enforcing compliance or making children "fit in" so that they become more convenient to teach. Goals should focus on choice, consent, and the child developing a growing capacity to express their needs in their preferred way.

Ableist Goal: Child (A) to accept invitations to play from adult or peer without resistance.	
S.H.A.R.E. Goal: Child (A) to be supported with ways to either accept or decline invitations to play from peer or adult in prosocial ways. Alternatives to hitting out or shouting "no" will be given.	
Recognises and affirms intersectional identity	Goals must not focus on training a child to behave or learn neurotypically. Explore the different traits and consider how you might affirm the child's ways of being.
Ableist Goal: To encourage face-to-face eye contact for up to 30 seconds during interactions.	
S.H.A.R.E. Goal: To acknowledge main ways of communicating, and to mirror this during interactions and play.	
Engagement and wellbeing focused	A sense of wellbeing, belonging, and engagement are critical for our lifelong learning. Goals should promote enjoyment, pleasure, fun, and joy. They should be rooted in what the child is motivated to do, rather than what they have to.
Ableist Goal: Child must communicate play visual to gain access choice of play.	
S.H.A.R.E. Goal: To follow child's lead in play, and to enable uninterrupted opportunities for play, with sensitive scaffolding.	

SPECIALIST DESCRIPTIONS AND GOALS

A concern that is regularly raised by early educators is that in many cases where a child is under specialist support, descriptions and goals are written by someone other than the key person. It cannot be guaranteed that the person writing this information takes a neurodiversity-affirming stance, and they might not be aware of the settings commitment to this either. As educators, solidarity with parents, carers, and specialists is integral to effective and consistent support, therefore the way discussions may be approached need to be done sensitively and with compassion. The reality is that the majority of those working towards inclusion are doing so with the best of intentions, and are often constrained by the same processes that settings might also be facing. There are a number of things to do to ensure that neurodiversity-affirming practice becomes the collective aim:

✦ Develop a working policy for neurodiversity-affirming practice;
✦ Always provide a cover letter or email to outline your approach;
✦ Use advocacy scripting to help guide some of the discussions around ableist descriptions and goals;
✦ Examples of each of these can be found at www.eyfs4me.com.

ADVOCACY SCRIPTING

While specialists may have expertise in their field, early years practitioners also have valuable expertise in understanding the needs and nuances of individual children in their care.

(Dani, Early Years Educator and parent of an autistic child)

An important reminder for any educator who feels that their "voice" does not matter in neurodiversity-affirming practice is that everyone comes with their own unique perspective and expertise, and all voices are valid. Specialists rely and value your contributions, but they might also have different priorities and agendas. They will be grateful for opportunities to discuss their support, and getting it right for the child.

NEUROINSIGHTS

NAVIGATING TRICKY CONVERSATIONS

I have access to a support worker who works with myself as the childminder and the family, and they essentially coordinate referrals and ensure we are clear on the local authority processes. I get on really well with this person, and I have been grateful for their support but some of what they ask me to do, including how I write about the child, is just not sitting right. I got myself very worked up because I don't want to offend a specialist but in team around the child (TAC) meetings, the support worker talks in ways that do not mirror our approach in the setting.

I have a tendency to undermine my own expertise, and to consider myself as "just a childminder" but I have had to push through that and have an honest conversation that we will need to compromise on our approaches, and this needs to be in partnership with the parent. However, I also did not want to call this out in front of the parent potentially fragmenting the partnership and so I arranged a chat with the support worker, and explained that there is a slight mismatch in our views towards children with SEN. Rather than bombarding the specialist with lots of views, I just spoke about some non-negotiables, for example:

✦ That to say the child is suffering from a developmental delay is not accurate, and the child is generally very settled and happy. To assume suffering could cause worry and distress.
✦ That I will not score the child's level of SEN as this is not a realistic reflection of their development. For example, the support worker has told parents that the child is 3 years of age but acts more like a 1-year-old and is scoring 45 out of 72.
✦ That we need to avoid some of the goals that are forcing the child to behave in more typical ways. For example, the support worker has advised that the child should sit still for 60 seconds at a time but they engage by moving around.

To highlight three things made the situation more manageable, and the support worker apologised and said that perhaps they need to rethink some of their language. Naturally there was a little bit of defensive, for example, the support worker said "well you know, this is how we ensure support" and I emphasised that this is why we could work together to find middle ground.

I have realised that going too firm on my views could alienate the support worker and I really do think there was something there where we could learn from each other alongside the family. Things have shifted, not as quickly as I would like but there is a noted difference in how language is used, and I can see that she is thinking things through and I was delighted when she said during a meeting "what language are we all comfortable with here?"

Childminder

Below are just some examples that either yourself or the parent could ask when navigating the conversation through the use of advocacy scripts.

Component	Potential advocacy-based questions	Example scripts
Strengths-based	✦ Are my child's strengths documented in any written evidence? ✦ Is there a good balance of strengths and needs? ✦ Are strengths meaningful, personalised, and specific to my child?	✦ This goal does not reflect my child's unique strengths. Can you provide some examples based on your knowledge? And I can also provide some based on my parental expertise.

	✦ Do the strengths reflect divergent pathways or enforce neurotypicalism/masking? ✦ Can the strengths be built upon? ✦ Does written evidence reflect my child's perceptions of their strengths and my "voice" as the parent?	✦ Maintaining eye contact when asked to use "looking eyes" is not a strength or preference for my child, and may teach them to mask. Can this goal be changed to reflect that they can look where feels comfortable please?
Honours differences and needs	✦ In what ways are you adapting practice and provision to ensure my child's differences are supported? ✦ How are other children taught about my child's differences to address the Double Empathy Problem? ✦ How will you gather information about my child's communication identity?	✦ Can you explain how my child will have access to their communication tools during the day? ✦ The focus of this goal appears to be based on my child changing their communication style to fit in with his peers. How will the goal incorporate children learning about my child's communication style?
Autonomy building	✦ In what ways will my child be given choices? ✦ In what ways can my child express their needs, and is it aligned to their communication identity?	✦ I am not comfortable with my child being taken out of the classroom for that intervention programme. Can you please use her visual symbols so she can consent.
Recognises multiple identities	✦ What other aspects of the child's identity are important in how you will formulate descriptions and goals? ✦ What privileges and marginalisations may we need to be aware of?	It is important to me that you consider my child's religion in thinking about goals, and how you will provide resources for this. Would it be possible to provide visuals for prayer time? Symbols characters are white, and we are a Black family. Can you update this please. My child's language and dialect mean that the words he is using hold personal meaning. Please do not ask him to say this another way.

Engage- ment and wellbeing focused	✦ How are my child's play patterns and preferences planned for? ✦ What co-regulation and self-regulation strategies have been included for my child, and how have these been personalised?	The goals seem to be very adult-directed. Can you include goals that focus on self-directed and un-interrupted play.

NEUROINSIGHT - COMPASSION OVER SHAMING

COMPASSIONATE MODELLING VERSUS SHAME RESPONDING

Another conversation I had with speech and language therapist Alice Hill was about our impulsive or instant reactions to deficit approaches. If you are moving towards neurodiversity-affirming practice, you may find yourself triggered by the use outdated, or harmful language or approaches used. In Alice's reflection, she explained:

I read a referral to our service that was written in a really deficit focused way and it made me cross. I went to write an email to the referrer to tell them as much, but took a breath and remembered what you said in your training about modelling more ND affirming language rather than shaming and challenging. So instead I accepted the referral and in my acceptance letter used the language that could be used.

For Alice, she could see that the reality is that the child needed support from adults in solidarity, not in conflict, and so by modelling neurodiversity-affirming language, they could build a collaboration over time in which some of these things could be addressed.

Some ways of modelling include:

Statement: "The child is ASD"
Response: "Yes, he is autistic"

Statement: "Play does not come naturally to the child"
Response: "Neurotypical ways of playing might not, but let's think about their unique play patterns"

Statement: "The child won't share"
Response: "I wonder if this is a way for the child to express their self-advocacy that they had not yet finished with what they were playing with"

Statement: "The child won't sit still during circle time because they poor attention skills"
Response: "Maybe movement could be a way to supporting their attention skills"

(continued overleaf)

(continued)

Statement: "We need to describe the child on their worst day"
Response: "No worries. I think to find this out, it would be useful to first begin thinking about what a good day looks like"

Alice Hill
Speech and Language Therapist
Destination Communication

CONCLUSION

The way in which we collaborate to document the lived experiences of children in their earliest years goes far beyond mere administrative tasks. An early years curriculum should embrace diversity and be flexible to the variety of ways children learn. Delivered sensitively, it can become a springboard for imparting knowledge and skills along with a lifelong love of play and learning. There must, however, be a commitment to understanding how children learn, not just what they learn especially given that current expectations are neuronormative.

As children progress through their earliest years, it may be that they require a type of attunement that recognises a need for adapted, targeted, or specialist support. While early intervention more broadly is important, its aims of reduction and elimination may not always be compatible with lifelong differences. As an educator, you may draw upon neurodiversity-affirming practice including early attunement to ensure that a child accesses what is developmentally meaningful to them.

Enveloping all of the processes and approaches in education and health is the documentation that helps to build a better understanding of the child, and what they need to thrive. As storytellers, educators have the privilege of helping to capture this information in ways that support rather than hinder the child. The process of documentation is not an isolated activity, but one which is collaborative and should centre the child's voice and lived experiences. In the present moment, it's crucial that we approach every child's story sensitively and in ways that are meaningful to them with an understanding that our words will speak to the child in a number of ways. Whether they internalise our descriptions or look back in the future to understand how they became who they are, we want to positively contribute to that biography. Recognising and amplifying their strengths while addressing their areas of need is essential for fostering a supportive learning experience, and often provides us with more tools to support in appropriate ways.

We exist within a time where we must navigate systems and processes that remain dominated by a deficit-approach. While some negotiation and compromise is needed to ensure children can access education and health, it is also worth remembering that if we do not push back now, who will? The longer we choose compliance to harmful systems, the longer they are maintained. Drawing upon the words of Wolfe-Rocca: "it can be overwhelming to witness/experience/take in all the injustices of the moment; the good news is that they're all connected. **So if your little corner of work involves pulling at one of the threads,**

you're helping to unravel the whole damn cloth" (Ursula Wolfe-Rocca, n.d.). While the small shifts to resist ableism within education and health may at times seem pointless, each action moves the dial some more.

In our everyday interactions and professional commitments, there lies a profound opportunity for change. By consciously adopting neurodiversity-affirming practices, we can create learning environments that honour and uplift every child, and embraces their differences. This isn't just about policy changes or curriculum adjustments; it's a cultural shift that requires empathy, understanding, and a willingness to challenge existing norms.

In doing so, we not only create more inclusive educational settings but also lay the groundwork for a society that values and respects diversity in all its forms. It's a journey that requires collective effort and unwavering dedication, but the rewards are immeasurable – a future where every child feels seen, heard, and valued for who they are.

ACTIVITY

GOAL

Not suitable: Key person will encourage sustained eye contact or provide appropriate gaze up to 30 seconds by holding a novel object near eyes during social interactions up to three times a day.

Why: Eye contact and gaze is influenced by a number of factors, for example, developmentally and culturally. There is a belief that eye contact is essential to successful interaction, but for some children, this can feel uncomfortable, and does not form part of their communication identity.

Alternative Goal: Encourage the child to look where feels comfortable during social interactions to support their personal communication style.

Not suitable: Will be able to answer what and how questions with 80% accuracy during play, for example, what colour, what shape, how many, where is it, etc.

Why: The more language you use, the more information a child has to process. Direct questions can feel too demanding on a child, and aiming for authentic interaction leads to more meaningful exchanges.

Alternative: A combination of declarative and direct questions will be used at appropriate intervals during a child's play along with commentary to identify which interactions encourage communication attempts.

Not suitable: To speak in an appropriate tone of voice (quiet) during circle time interactions three out of five times during the week.

Why: There may be a range of reasons why a child speaks in a particular tone or volume, and there are natural variations. While you may wish to support varied intonation in communication, to focus only on quiet could be discouraging to the child who is joining in and using language whether it is loud or quiet.

Alternative goal: Introduce a range of intonation games during circle time to support children's growing awareness of their voices and volume.

Not suitable: To increase tolerance to textures by incorporating into play experiences such as sensory play.

Why: Every individual has a unique sensory profile which includes things we can tolerate and things we cannot. For some children, the intolerance to sensory stimuli can be uncomfortable, overwhelming, and painful. Increasing tolerance teaches the child to override their needs for the comfort of others.

Alternative: To provide sensory experiences that are compatible with the child's preferences, and to provide ways for the child to communicate textures that they don't like with visual cards.

Not suitable: To accept the invitation to play with a different toy or game when initiated by another child.

Why: This goal does not take into account the child's autonomy. It assumes that all children should want to play alongside and with each other even when they do not. It might be that this child is not yet ready for this type of play, does not like the child in question, or is not interested in the play being offered. Children are entitled to turn down and decline invites to play.

Alternative: Support child to accept or decline offers to play from other children. Identify shared interests for the potential of parallel or associative play.

Not suitable: To use whole-body listening during circle time with a focus sitting still for 80% of circle time
Maintaining eyes looking forward for 80%
Keeping hands in lap when reminded of "quiet hands"

Why: Whole-body listening is a compliance method. No child should be expected to adhere to sedentary rules that do not influence attention, listening, or engagement.

Alternative: Introduce whole-body affirmations so that the child can communicate the way they attend, listen, and engage.

Not suitable: Encouraging use of appropriate language in various contexts over echolalia or familiar phrases. Ignore echolalia but respond to appropriate responses.

Why: Echolalia, in many cases, is an appropriate form of language and refers to natural language acquisition. Echolalia should never be ignored.

Alternative: Respond to and acknowledge echolalic language, identifying patterns and themes of potential meaning. Remember it is often non-literal.

Not suitable: Moves and walks like other children of the same age, understanding how to navigate space.

Why: This is a compliance-based goal that assumes all children should be normalised to think, behave, and act the same. It does not account for variations in physicality including physical disability.

Alternative: Moves and uses physicalities in a way that is suitable and comfortable to the child.

Not suitable: Greets peers by smiling, and providing eye contact.
Why: This goal is promoting neurotypical social skills which is not always the way a neurodivergent or disabled child will greet others.
Alternative: Help all children to understand each other's greeting styles and preferences. Provide options for greetings that the child may wish or wish not to choose from.

Not suitable: Engages in conversational turn-taking by waiting for a pause before responding.
Why: While some interactions may occur this way, often the way to learn about communication styles is to try out different ones. For example, some children may have a highly interactive conversation but may interrupt and speak over each other but the interaction is still successful.
Alternative: Help children to understand different ways of communicating.
Provide options for children to use during social interaction.

Unsuitable: Through prompting, the child asks for verbal permission to access a toy that has been intentionally placed out of reach (sabotage).
Why: Withholding items from a child to encourage language is inappropriate. It places pressure and unnecessary emotional distress on the child, and may force communication that does not feel comfortable.
Alternative: The child is given access to communication tools to be able to make requests, comments, or to express needs in their preferred communication mode.

Unsuitable: Child will use their words when upset to explain why they are upset rather than having a tantrum.
Why: When dysregulated or distressed, children cannot always find the words to express their feelings or what is happening. The pressure to use words when the child may be dealing with a stress response can exacerbate the situation.
Alternative: Language will be reduced when the child is distressed and the adult will provide whole-body co-regulation to support the child.

ACTIVITY - CHAPTER KEEPSAKES

Across this first chapter, think about what your keepsakes are, and note down the following:

- ✦ One thing you will start doing
- ✦ One thing you still stop doing
- ✦ One keepsake you will share with others
- ✦ One thinking knot that requires further exploration

REFERENCES

Early Education. 2022. The Ofsted early years curriculum review. [Online] Available at: https://early-education.org.uk/the-ofsted-early-years-curriculum-review/#:~:text=The%20Ofsted%20definition%20of%20curriculum&text=The%20review%20includes%20statements%20that,are%20most%20effective%20for%20teaching.%E2%80%9D

Department for Education (DfE). n.d. Best start in life: A research review for early years. [Online] Available at: https://www.gov.uk/government/publications/best-start-in-life-a-research-review-for-early-years

Early Intervention Foundation. n.d. Home. [Online] Available at: www.eif.org.uk/

Bloem, M.A. and Evans, K. 2024. What to make of developmental milestones. [Online] The Informed SLP. Available at: www.theinformedslp.com/review/what-to-make-of-developmental-milestones

Child Development Institute. n.d. The Power of Attunement. [Online] Available at: https://cdikids.org/autism/power-attunement/?utm_source=chatgpt.com.

Cowan, K. and Flewitt, R. 2023. Moving from paper-based to digital documentation in Early Childhood Education: Democratic potentials and challenges. *International Journal of Early Years Education*, 31(4), 888–906.

Department for Education (DfE). 2023. Early Years Foundation Stage (EYFS) Framework statutory requirements. [Online] Available at: www.gov.uk/government/publications/early-years-foundation-stage-framework–2.

Early Intervention Foundation. n.d. What is early intervention? [Online] Available at: www.eif.org.uk/what-is-early-intervention.

Education Ofsted. 2022. Education inspection framework: Overview of research. [Online] Available at: www.gov.uk/government/publications/education-inspection-framework-overview-of-research.

Hammond, E. 2023. S3 E29: The NeuroWild Shift for Neurodivergent Kids at School. NeuroWild. [Video online] Available at: www.youtube.com/watch?v=mKZkOsTdiO8

McGreevy, E., Quinn, A., Law, R., Botha, M., Evans, M., Rose, K., Moyse, R., Boyens, T., Matejko, M., and Pavlopoulou, G. 2024. An experience sensitive approach to care with and for autistic children and young people in clinical services. *Journal of Humanistic Psychology*, 0(0). https://doi.org/10.1177/00221678241232442.

Murphy, K. and Benham, F. 2023. *50 Fantastic Ideas for Supporting Neurodiversity.* London: Bloomsbury

McGreevy, E. and Price, E. 2022. Neurodivergent affirming report writing. Divergent perspectives. [Online] Available at: www.divergentperspectives.co.uk/post/neurodivergent-affirming-report-writing-2.

Reference websites

https://childdevelopmentinfo.com/

www.divergentperspectives.co.uk/post/neurodivergent-affirming-report-writing-2

www.pengreen.org/a-celebratory-approach-to-send-assessment-in-the-early-years/

www.gov.uk/government/publications/development-matters--2

www.gov.uk/government/publications/early-years-foundation-stage-framework--2

www.gov.uk/government/publications/send-code-of-practice-0-to-25

www.teacherspayteachers.com/store/emily-hammond-neurowild

www.zinnedproject.org/author-bios/ursula-wolfe-rocca/

PUT IT INTO PRACTICE

NEURODIVERSITY-AFFIRMING DOCUMENTATION

EXAMPLES OF NEURODIVERSITY-AFFIRMING GOALS

Providing educators with examples of neurodiversity-affirming goals can increase their awareness of ableist practices. The list below serves as a provocation to inspire thoughtful goal-setting. These examples are not intended as ready-made templates but rather as guidance for creating goals that focus on strengths rather than deficits.

Transition: To support child with using objects or transition and transitional objects to support with change and adaptation.
Transition: To provide consistency in key person handover where possible. For example, same person meeting child and family at the door, and following the same morning rituals.
Transition: Educator will offer low demand support during play and routines, ensuring that they are adjusted to match child's current social and emotional state. For example, parallel play in a quiet area.
Routine engagement: Declarative questioning will be used to support child to engage in routines and rhythms. For example, "I am about to have some snack, so I will need to wash my hands", which invites the child to do the same.
Early self-advocacy: Child will begin to use personal consent visuals for routines, rhythms, and interventions to say yes or no (or thumbs up/thumbs down).

DOI: 10.4324/9781003323211-11

Self-regulation: Child will know they can access different mood zones based on desired self-regulation through preferred communication method (visuals, sign, actions, words). For example, the calm den for relaxation, or outdoors for active physical play.

Self-regulation: The child will gain confidence in selecting different rest visuals and choosing a form of co and self-regulation.

Play patterns: Key person and child will engage in spontaneous bursts of parallel play. Key person to wait for child's initiations, and not to interfere in play.

Self-regulation: Child will be supported to match regulation state to the task through co-regulation and modelling. For example, deep breathing and movement when stressed.

Play: Children's interests and motivations will be incorporated into adult-led activities and experiences. For example, using familiar gestalts during group time.

Attention: Novel experiences will be used to create suspense or to support self-regulation. A child will not be subject to neuronormative attention expectations.

Communication: To respond to both immediate and delayed echolalia, with repeating back and positive acknowledgement. Intonation should be matched.

Communication: To document personal communication dictionary including familiar phrases, words and sounds.

Communication: To use first and then board to guide familiar routines and choices.

Communication: A communication passport will be used to support the understanding of the child's communication identity.

Play: Key people will consistently mirror child's communication and play to show connection and encourage shared experiences.

Communication: Total communication will be valued and respected. Key people will not pressure children to "use your words".

Communication: Direct questioning will be limited, instead the use of narration and declarative statements are utilised to support child.

Social preferences: Neuroinclusive stories to be used to support differences in social skills, for example, differences in eye contact, and social pragmatic skills which differ based on neurotype.

Communication: Child will be offered serve and return, and cause and effect experiences to support interactions.

Movement: Providing flexible seating for comfort and engagement during familiar routines. For example, wobble cushions at circle time.

Movement: To respect and affirm stimming preferences and to identify any associated needs. For example, stimming as regulation versus stimming as distress.

Movement: To respect and affirm whole-body movement preferences, and provide affirmation cards so that the child can select their preferences.

Movement: Whole-body preferred experiences will be provided to support self-regulation, engagement and wellbeing.

Executive function: Backwards chaining will be used to build confidence in self-care skills with clear praise and affirmation.

A LETTER TO A PARENT FOLLOWING DIAGNOSIS

Dear (insert parent x caregivers name),

I hope you are well!

Thank you for sharing with me your child's recent diagnosis of (insert diagnosis). I hope that this process was affirming and supportive and that knowing your child's neurotype and disability becomes a further gateway for both you and your child to understand their **strengths, traits, differences** and **needs**.

The way in which children and adults are currently diagnosed can feel quite confusing. We spend so much time talking about the importance of recognising strengths but then a diagnosis can feel like a focus on your child's difficulties or perceived negative aspects. I want to assure you that while diagnosis is necessary, it does not necessarily tell your child's whole story. I am writing this letter because I want to make sure that you know that as a key person, and as your child's setting, we want to tell the other parts of their story alongside you

I want to begin by talking a little about your child's strengths and what I appreciate about your child:

> *Strengths that are meaningful to your child*

We understand from your child's diagnosis that they may need support in particular areas, but we also know that the diagnosis includes the following traits. Your child might do things differently but these are equally valid and valued. I have noticed:

> *Here reframe differences that have been historically pathologised*

This transition over the next few months will likely have highs and lows as we all adjust to understanding your child better, but I want to assure you that we are by your side, and we are keen to learn about what is best for your child, and for you. Below are a few ways that we can support, but please feel free to add your own suggestions.

> *examples of supports and signposts to useful information*

Lots of solidarity,
Key Person's name.

LAST WORDS

Writing a book and feeling like you have done a topic justice is incredibly challenging. This book started as one thing and quickly evolved into many things. It is book where I have attempted to contexualise neurodiversity for early childhood education, aiming to show how nuanced this paradigm can be, while also trying to ensure it is practical and feels somewhat tangible. I wanted to give life to neurodiversity-affirming practice in early childhood.

I found in my writing that I frequently came up against unanswered questions or curiosities about certain aspects of neurodiversity-affirming practice, and knowing that humans like answers, or clear paths forward, it felt difficult to leave lots of provocations across this book but I think it is a really important aspect of the book, and it speaks to a number of points I raised in the book disclaimer. Let's revisit them:

LANGUAGE

At the start of this book, I stated that I would default to identity-first language (disabled person) as opposed to person-first language (person with a disability) to reflect that disability and neurodivergence is a part of a person's identity, not an add-on. You will have likely noticed that throughout this book, there was a frequent interrogation of the impact of language. To put it simply, the way we communicate with and about each other matters to our identity, wellbeing, self-esteem and how we show up in the world. We live in an increasingly divisive and polarising world where compassionately thinking about the impact of our words and actions is considered a weakness. However, our voices can easily become the internalised voices of the children we care for and educate, and we have to ask what we want that voice to say to a child.

DOI: 10.4324/9781003323211-12

LIVED EXPERIENCE

I believe in the importance of lived experiences to ensure people's views, perspectives, wants, ideas, and needs are understood and supported. Every author brings their own identity and characteristics to their writing, and I am no different. I have drawn on my own expertise while attempting to push beyond my comfort zones to understand experiences beyond my own. However, I recognise that this book cannot represent every single lived experience, and that is not the aim of neurodiversity-affirming practice. It is collective knowledge that leads to more compassionate practices. As stated at the beginning, this book is pulling at some threads, but there are so many other voices and views that also need attention. To clarify: this book should be seen as a contribution rather than a comprehensive guide.

HOLD YOUR KNOWLEDGE LIGHTLY

One of the most important pieces of advice I've received is to hold my knowledge lightly, so if things change for the better, I can adapt as well. The neurodiversity paradigm has a long way to go, and for many of us, this is legacy work. We might not see all the changes in our lifetime, but we can certainly stir things up to help progress happen faster and more sustainably. With this in mind, you might pick up this book in a year or two and think, "I can't believe she wrote that". That's okay for both of us. It's important to value what we believe now, even if we might resist it tomorrow. That's progress.

NOT ONE-SIZE-FITS-ALL

As I wrote this book, I flitted between casual and informal writing, and then writing more formally, and at times academically. This has been referred to as nomadic writing and is the recognition that writing often reflects the diverse and rhizomatic mind of the author. As an autistic person with ADHD, I have periods of hyperfocus, periods of procrastination and periods utterly chaotic and wild thinking. And so, in writing this book, I decided to unmask my writing and to resist the neuronormative expectation to pick a style and to stick to it. All kinds of writing are equal and valid, and I hope that somewhere in these pages, you found places of comfort, challenge, joy, anger, defensiveness, inquisitiveness, shock, awe, horror, hope, and a whole other heap of responses. Ultimately this book is not about stating anything is right or wrong but offering a provocation for much needed change.

INDEX

Note: For figure citations, page numbers appear in *italics*.

Printed in the United States
by Baker & Taylor Publisher Services